It's About TIME

Planning Interventions and Extensions
in Elementary School

Austin Buffum   Mike Mattos

Brian K. Butler | Paul Goldberg | Merrilou Harrison
Susan B. Huff | Lillie G. Jessie | Sharon V. Kramer
Maria Nielsen | Regina Stephens Owens | Will Remmert
Paula Rogers | Chris Weber | John Wink

Foreword by Rebecca DuFour and Richard DuFour

Solution Tree | Press
a division of
Solution Tree

555 North Morton Street
Bloomington, IN 47404
800.733.6786 (toll free) / 812.336.7700
FAX: 812.336.7790

email: info@solution-tree.com
solution-tree.com

Visit **go.solution-tree.com/rtiatwork** to download the reproducibles in this book.

Printed in the United States of America

FSC
www.fsc.org
MIX
Paper from
responsible sources
FSC® C011935

18 17 16 15 14   1 2 3 4 5

Library of Congress Cataloging-in-Publication Data

Buffum, Austin G.
  It's about time : planning interventions and extensions in elementary school / Austin Buffum and Mike Mattos, editors ; contributors, Brian K. Butler, Paul Goldberg, Merrilou Harrison, Susan B. Huff, Lillie G. Jessie, Sharon V. Kramer, Maria Nielsen, Regina Stephens Owens, Will Remmert, Paula Rogers, Chris Weber, John Wink.
      pages cm
  Includes bibliographical references and index.
  ISBN 978-1-936763-03-0 (perfect bound) 1. Remedial teaching. 2. Response to intervention (Learning disabled children) 3. Learning disabled children--Education. 4. Learning disabilities--Diagnosis. 5. Elementary school teaching. I. Mattos, Mike (Mike William) II. Title.
  LB1029.R4B783 2015
  371.102--dc23
                                        2014030951

Solution Tree
Jeffrey C. Jones, CEO
Edmund M. Ackerman, President

Solution Tree Press
President: Douglas M. Rife
Editorial Director: Lesley Bolton
Managing Production Editor: Caroline Weiss
Production Editor: Rachel Rosolina
Copy Editor: Sarah Payne-Mills
Proofreader: Elisabeth Abrams
Text and Cover Designer: Laura Kagemann
Compositor: Rachel Smith

I dedicate this book to the staff, students, and parents of Ole Hanson Elementary School, where I had the privilege of serving as principal. In particular, I want to thank Mr. Lee Watson, my daughter's sixth-grade teacher at Ole Hanson, for giving her the priceless gift of the love of reading and the wonder of the written word.

—Austin Buffum

I dedicate this book to the exceptional educators and support staff of Marjorie Veeh Elementary School in Tustin, California. They were most patient of their rookie principal, and tireless advocates for their students. Much of what I know about what it takes to become a great elementary school is due to what we learned together by doing the work. I am forever grateful for the privilege to serve as the principal of this outstanding school.

—Mike Mattos

Acknowledgments

Bringing this anthology from concept to completion was truly a collaborative effort, beginning with the outstanding professionals at Solution Tree. Guided by the leadership of CEO Jeffrey C. Jones and Solution Tree Press president Douglas M. Rife, Solution Tree has become the premier educational publishing and staff development company in the world. Specifically, we would like to thank Lesley Bolton for her efforts to coordinate this project and Kari Gillesse for her superb editing of this anthology. We hope that this book moves Solution Tree one step closer to achieving its vision of transforming education worldwide.

This book would not have been possible without the contributing authors: Brian K. Butler, Paul Goldberg, Merrilou Harrison, Susan B. Huff, Lillie G. Jessie, Sharon V. Kramer, Maria Nielsen, Regina Stephens Owens, Will Remmert, Paula Rogers, Chris Weber, and John Wink. These individuals do not make their living as writers—they are exceptional educators, working primarily as site-, district-, and county-level administrators. We have tremendous empathy and appreciation for their efforts, as we know what it's like to try to find time to write after working as an educator all day. Their prose has brought the journey of each school to life.

We thank the exceptional schools that are featured in this book: Anoka-Hennepin Schools, Cartwright School District, Washington Elementary School, Mason Crest Elementary School, Gilmer Elementary School, Spanish Oaks Elementary School, Elizabeth Vaughan Elementary School, Gilbert Elementary School, Millville Elementary School, John Muir Literacy Academy, Hallsville Independent School District, CICS West Belden Elementary School, and the Virtual School and Early College program. These schools did not wait for the perfect conditions to begin restructuring to better serve their students. Instead, they got started, made mistakes, tried again, stayed focused, and most importantly, achieved! The lessons they learned from doing the work have blazed a trail for others to follow. We applaud their collective courage and dedication to ensure that every student succeeds on their campuses.

We would also like to acknowledge and thank the outstanding educators of Adlai E. Stevenson High School, both past and present. While no chapter in this anthology focuses specifically on Stevenson, that school has directly and indirectly influenced almost every other school mentioned. Over twenty years ago, the Stevenson staff started the journey of becoming a professional learning community (PLC), causing them to rethink every traditional policy, procedure, and schedule. As a four-time National Blue Ribbon School, Stevenson continues to serve as a model of success for schools across the world.

Finally, while the schools described here represent a wide range of locations and demographics, they all share one underlying trait—each functions as a PLC. Richard DuFour, Robert Eaker, and Rebecca DuFour have dedicated their lives to developing, articulating, promoting, supporting, and living the Professional Learning Communities at Work™ process. Generously giving of their time and expertise, they have personally mentored almost every contributor to this anthology. We are forever grateful for their support, wisdom, and friendship.

Visit **go.solution-tree.com/rtiatwork** to download the reproducibles in this book.

Table of Contents

Chapter 2

Looking in the Mirror **31**

By Will Remmert

Chapter 3

Collaborating in the Core **51**

By Brian K. Butler

Chapter 4

Making Mid-Unit Interventions as Easy as 1-2-3 . . . . **81**

By John Wink

Chapter 5

By Susan B. Huff

Chapter 6

By Lillie G. Jessie

Chapter 7

By Merrilou Harrison

Chapter 8

Chapter 9

Chapter 10

Chapter 11

Chapter 12

Personalizing Learning Through Online Interventions **255**

By Regina Stephens Owens

About the Editors

Austin Buffum, EdD, has thirty-eight years of experience in public schools. His many roles include serving as former senior deputy superintendent of the Capistrano Unified School District in California. Austin has presented in over five hundred school districts throughout the United States and around the world. He delivers trainings and presentations on the Response to Intervention (RTI) at Work™ model. This tiered approach to RTI is centered on Professional Learning Communities (PLC) at Work™ concepts and strategies to ensure every student receives the time and support necessary to succeed. Austin also delivers workshops and presentations that provide the tools educators need to build and sustain PLCs.

In 2006, the Association of California School Administrators named Austin the Curriculum and Instruction Administrator of the Year. He attended the Principals' Center at the Harvard Graduate School of Education and was greatly inspired by its founder, Roland Barth, an early advocate of the collaborative culture that defines PLCs. Austin later led Capistrano's K–12 instructional program on an increasingly collaborative path toward operating as a PLC. During this process, thirty-seven of the district's schools were designated California Distinguished Schools, and eleven received National Blue Ribbon recognition. Austin is coauthor of *Generations at School: Building an Age-Friendly Learning Community, Pyramid Response to Intervention: RTI, Professional Learning Communities, and How to Respond When Kids Don't Learn, Simplifying Response to Intervention: Four Essential Guiding Principles,* and *Uniting Academic and Behavior Interventions: Solving the Skill or Will Dilemma.*

A graduate of the University of Southern California, Austin earned a bachelor of music and received a master of education with honors. He also holds a doctorate in education from Nova Southeastern University.

To learn more about Austin's work, visit www.abuffum.com or follow @agbuffum on Twitter.

Mike Mattos is an internationally recognized author, presenter, and practitioner who specializes in uniting teachers, administrators, and support staff to transform schools by implementing RTI and PLCs. Mike cocreated the RTI at Work™ model, which builds on the foundation of the PLC at Work™ process by using team structures and a focus on learning, collaboration, and results to drive successful outcomes.

He is former principal of Marjorie Veeh Elementary School and Pioneer Middle School in California. At both schools, Mike helped create powerful PLCs, improving learning for all students. In 2004, Marjorie Veeh, which has a large population of youth at risk, won the California Distinguished School and National Title I Achieving School awards.

A National Blue Ribbon School, Pioneer is among only thirteen U.S. schools the GE Foundation selected as a best-practice partner and is one of eight schools Richard DuFour chose to be featured in the video series *The Power of Professional Learning Communities at Work™: Bringing the Big Ideas to Life.*

Based on standardized test scores, Pioneer ranks among the top 1 percent of California's secondary schools and, in 2009 and 2011, was named Orange County's top middle school. The Association of California School Administrators named Mike the Orange County Middle School Administrator of the Year for his leadership.

To learn more about Mike's work, visit www.mattos.info or follow @mikemattos65 on Twitter.

To book Austin Buffum or Mike Mattos for professional development, contact pd@solution-tree.com.

Foreword

Rebecca DuFour and Richard DuFour

As former school principals, working with very dedicated faculties to implement the PLC at Work™ process, we recognize the significance of allocating resources to the priorities of the school. If the fundamental priority of school is to ensure high levels of learning for all—students and adults—then the precious resource of time must be aligned to that priority. If educators don't have time to collaborate with their colleagues about the critical questions of learning, time to deliver first-best instruction, time to monitor learning, and time to intervene for and extend each student's learning, then the mission of ensuring all students learn at high levels will never become a reality.

In *It's About Time: Planning Interventions and Extensions in Elementary School*, editors Austin Buffum and Mike Mattos insist that schools must first embrace the culture of a PLC before moving to the questions of intervention and extension. It is evident that the authors of each chapter in this book have taken their message to heart. Every school staff highlighted in this anthology went beyond writing mission statements about learning for all to addressing the four questions that bring that mission to life (DuFour, Eaker, & DuFour, 2008).

1. What knowledge, skills, and dispositions do we want students to learn?

2. How will we know when each student has learned?

3. How will we respond when some students don't learn?

4. How will we respond when some students are already proficient?

The editors and authors make the compelling case that a school with a mission to help all students learn must recognize that when students struggle, they should be entitled to extra time and support. They assert that the real test of a school's commitment to learning for all students is not the eloquence of its mission statement but rather what happens in the school when students don't learn.

More Than Time

The first key to supporting the learning of all students is to ensure that the schedule provides educators with access to the students who need them most during the school day in a way that never removes a student from essential new instruction. While addressing that key is absolutely critical, it is not sufficient. Educators must also ensure that they use the extra time for learning in the right way and for the right purpose. No one has provided greater clarity on the critical conditions for effective intervention and extension than editors Austin Buffum and Mike Mattos.

They have presented a clear and compelling picture of what effective systems of intervention and extension will look like in the real world of schools. We urge you to read carefully the section High Levels of Learning for All (page 5) in their introduction. Then, read the chapters to see how each school has used evidence to ensure that students who struggle receive additional time and support in a way that is timely, directive, diagnostic, tiered, and systematic. In these schools, what happens when students struggle is not left solely to the teacher to whom they are assigned, but rather to teams of teachers who take collective responsibility for students. Students are guaranteed additional time because the entire *school* responds in a way that provides assistance, again without removing the student from essential new direct instruction or lowering curriculum standards. Furthermore, accompanying the focus on intervention is a commitment to extend the learning for students who are highly proficient. In chapter after chapter, the authors describe how the commitment to help all students learn at high levels has increased the percentage of students moving from proficiency to advanced levels of learning.

Common Themes

The editors of this anthology showcase a variety of schools. Despite the differences among them, several common themes emerge as each school's story unfolds.

Linking Systematic Intervention and Enrichment to the PLC at Work Process

In every chapter, readers will hear consistent advice: systematic intervention and enrichment must occur in the larger context of a professional learning community (PLC). Unless the three big ideas of a PLC—(1) a commitment to help *all* students learn at high levels, (2) a collaborative and collective effort to foster that commitment, and (3) a focus on results to meet students' individual needs and to inform and improve individual and collective professional practice—are driving the school's work, time and structures to support intervention will have little impact. In fact, in the wrong school culture, teachers may view intervention as one more reason they are not responsible for student learning. If teachers assume, "I taught it, they didn't learn it, so let the intervention system deal with it," they will accomplish little.

We are certain that many people who purchase this book will be looking for an intervention and extension schedule to copy for their school. However, no schedule has the power to change the culture of a school. It is the thinking behind the schedule—the assumptions, beliefs, and expectations that led to its creation—that makes a schedule so powerful. Building an effective system of intervention and extension is a natural outgrowth of a faculty's recognition that its professed mission to help all students learn will never be more than words on paper until they take specific actions. Most importantly, staff must clarify what students are to learn in every unit of instruction; establish an ongoing process of gathering evidence of student learning; provide individual students with additional time and support for learning in a timely, directive, diagnostic, and systematic way; and use evidence of student learning to inform and improve instruction.

Engaging Staff in Dialogue Throughout the Implementation Process

Leaders must engage all staff in dialogue regarding their assumptions about the school, the rationale for creating systematic intervention, and ways to overcome the inevitable difficulties that occur throughout implementation. Shaping culture requires conversations rather than presentations and dialogue, not monologue. School leaders in these chapters didn't make a PowerPoint presentation on systematic intervention and extension before plunging ahead. They linked the idea to a larger purpose, stressed why the system was needed before delving into how it would operate, and encouraged feedback from the staff. These educators avoided the common tendency to regard systematic intervention and enrichment as a program to add to their existing structure and culture. They engaged their faculties in dialogue to shape the assumptions, beliefs, and expectations that constitute school culture. They built shared ownership to ensure that the system was not an administrative mandate but a collective decision all staff embraced.

Persevering in the Face of Setbacks

No chapters will describe how a school's initial implementation of systematic intervention and enrichment worked flawlessly and has continued without difficulty.

Initial efforts often led to new problems and unanticipated consequences. Rather than abandoning their efforts in the face of challenges, the educators began again more intelligently. When one approach failed to bring about the desired results, they tried another, and another, and another. Their commitment to continuous improvement led these educators to search constantly for better practice.

The best strategy to ensure that people sustain a collective effort over time is to remove obstacles to progress and provide the resources and support that enable them to feel successful in the work they are being asked to do (Amabile & Kramer, 2011). The school leaders featured in this book were constantly seeking feedback about problems that were occurring and then engaging the entire staff in finding solutions. They did not assume they had all the answers to every issue. They recognized, however, the importance of calling the attention of people throughout the organization to an obstacle to progress and then enlisting their help in seeking ways to remove the obstacle. They also created a sense of momentum by calling attention to small, incremental progress as soon as it occurred.

Focusing on Results

Each author demonstrates that the effectiveness of his or her school's systems of intervention and enrichment must be determined by concrete results rather than noble intentions. The authors appeal to the moral imperative of providing greater individual support to meet the needs of each student. Some authors provide anecdotal accounts of how individual students benefitted. Some share staff members' positive perceptions about their school's journey to develop effective interventions. In the final analysis, however, true to the PLC process, they recognize the need to answer the question, "How do we know our students are learning?" Each contributor then provides compelling evidence of the significant impact systematic intervention and extension had in his or her school on higher levels of learning for students.

How many elementary schools would you need to see to be convinced that educators can provide students with extra time and support for learning? Is it five; is it ten? Thanks to their tireless work in supporting educators, the editors of this book can point you to the website www.allthingsplc.info, where hundreds of educators have solved the riddle of time. It is imperative that educators acknowledge that they are not the victims but the masters of time. As the title of this wonderful volume makes clear, *it's about time* educators respond to the question, "Do you work in a school where students are guaranteed additional time and support for learning when they struggle?" If not, the time is right for *It's About Time: Planning Interventions and Extensions in Elementary School!*

References

Amabile, T., & Kramer, S. (2011). *The progress principle: Using small wins to ignite joy, engagement, and creativity at work.* Boston: Harvard Business School Press.

DuFour, R., Eaker, R., & DuFour, R. (2008). *Revisiting professional learning communities at work: New insights for improving schools.* Bloomington, IN: Solution Tree Press.

Introduction: Harnessing the Power of Time

Austin Buffum and Mike Mattos

Time. It waits for no one, flies when you are having fun, and heals all wounds. Just a stitch of it saves nine. It can be raced against, borrowed, wasted, and served. It may be ripe, due, on your hands, and on your side. You can have a whale of it, yet when you have much to do, have so little.

In the world of education, these common idioms about time hold true. In the United States, the average student spends thirteen years and approximately fifteen thousand hours of time at school from kindergarten through high school—a boat-load of time. Yet, with the staggering amount of required curriculum that must be taught each year, teachers are faced with a daunting reality: so much to teach, so little time.

At the elementary level, this time crunch is impacted by the fact that each grade-level teacher is responsible for not one area of the curriculum but as many as seven or eight, working his or her daily schedule like a juggler at the circus. Now add the developmental issues of primary students, the emerging social behaviors of up-per-grade students, playground duty, and rainy day lunch duty—suddenly you have a seemingly infinite number of demands expected in an undeniably finite amount of time. Because adequate time is an essential variable in the formula of learning, this dilemma has a profound impact on both students and educators.

The Importance of Time to Student Learning

It is commonly said that in this world, nothing can be certain except for death and taxes. In the education world, we have our own two universal truths.

1. **Every student does not learn the same way:** Every student has unique learning needs, based on his or her prior knowledge and experiences, cultural values, learning styles, and aptitudes. Due to these differences, no matter how well a teacher teaches a concept, we know some students won't get it the first time, because the best way to teach a concept to one student might fail miserably with another student in the same class.

2. **Every student does not develop at the same speed:** We know that there are spans of time in which students mature, both physically and intellectually. Some of these developmental spans, such as the period in which students start to show the physical changes of puberty, can be quite significant—it is not uncommon for a high school classroom to have a boy still waiting for his growth spurt sitting next to a fellow classmate who is a foot taller and already shaving. Less visible to the eye, but just as age-appropriate and extreme, are the differences in which adolescents develop intellectually and socially. Just as a group of boys won't develop the need to shave at the same speed or on the same day, secondary school students will not acquire the ability to solve abstract equations or display empathy at the same speed.

If we condense these two universal truths into a simple formula to ensure student learning, the equation would look like this (Bloom, 1968; Buffum, Mattos, & Weber, 2012; Guskey & Pigott, 1988):

$$\text{Targeted Instruction} + \text{Time} = \text{Learning}$$

If a school can make both teaching and time variables in this equation and target them to meet each student's individual learning and developmental needs, the school is more likely to achieve high levels of learning for every student.

For any school dedicated to ensuring that all students learn at high levels, making the time to meet each student's varying learning needs is a critical consideration. Achieving this goal would be much easier if the U.S. education system was purposely designed around this outcome. Unfortunately, our traditional elementary model of education is not only misaligned to this goal but is also jam-packed full of "things to do." The brutal reality is that only some students leave elementary schools reading with comprehension, able to capture their thinking in writing, and possessing a sense of and fluency with numbers.

The Original Purpose of Elementary Education

We should hardly be surprised that our traditional elementary school practices fail to make teaching and time variables, as the original purpose of elementary education in America was far different than high levels of learning for all. In the sixteenth and seventeenth centuries, primarily European settlers initially recreated the school systems of their homelands. They established a two-track school system in which the lower socioeconomic classes attended primary vernacular schools and upper-class males attended separate preparatory schools and colleges. These primary schools—elementary institutions under church control—offered a basic curriculum of reading, writing, arithmetic, and religion.

During the first half of the nineteenth century, Thomas Jefferson argued that the United States needed to develop republican schools that were different from those found in the European monarchies. Jefferson's Bill for the More General Diffusion of Knowledge introduced in the 1779 Virginia legislature would have (if passed) made the state responsible for providing both girls and boys with a basic elementary education, in a local ward school, at public expense.

In the 1830s and 1840s, this thinking led to the formalization of common or public schooling throughout the United States. It should be noted, however, that with our historic tradition of local and state control, the movement to establish public elementary schools was not national but instead determined state to state. The common school sought to develop the literacy and numeracy needed for everyday life and work, which was predominately agricultural in nature. Its basic curriculum stressed reading, writing, spelling, arithmetic, history, and geography. Emphasizing American patriotism and Christian piety, the common school was regarded as the educational agency that would help assimilate the children of immigrants but certainly not ensure that all students would learn at high levels.

Frank M. Leavitt from the University of Chicago provides a great glimpse into the purpose of elementary education at the beginning of the 20th century in his article in the October 1912 issue of the *Elementary School Teacher*:

> A generation ago the expression "a common school education" meant the training given to that large majority of school children who never had any intention of going to a "high" school. No one thought of criticizing the common or grammar school because only a small percentage of its graduates went to the high school. Preparation for high school was not the primary purpose of such schools. (p. 80)

According to Leavitt (1912), in the common or grammar school:

> There was little doubt that somewhere the boy would be taught to be a shoemaker, a machinist, a salesman, a bookkeeper, or what not, but it was believed that he would be more intelligent, both in his business and outside of it, because of the sharpening and the habitual drill which he was to receive in school. (p. 81)

John Stuart Mill from the University of St. Andrews also clearly states the purpose of the common school in his 1867 inaugural address:

> Education makes a man a more intelligent shoemaker, if that be his occupation, but not by teaching him how to make shoes; it does so by the mental exercise it gives and the habits it impresses. (p. 7)

Only the lucky few went on to complete a high school education, with virtually no thought of college or beyond.

The Brutal Facts

Drastic economic changes driven by global competition and technological advances require us to rethink and revise our fundamental purpose and practices in elementary education. Consider the following characteristics of the 21st century U.S. economy.

- Less than 1 percent of the population directly farms for a living, and less than 10 percent work in factories (Hagenbaugh, 2002; U.S. Department of Agriculture, Utah State University Extension, & LetterPress Software, n.d.).

- According to the U.S. Department of Labor, nearly two-thirds of the new jobs created between 2006 and 2016 will be in occupations that require postsecondary education or considerable on-the-job training, while jobs requiring routine manual tasks will continue to decrease (Chao, 2008).

- Among traditional blue-collar trades, higher levels of academic preparation will be a prerequisite for employment. For example, the nonprofit organization ACT (2006) examines mathematics and reading skills required for electricians, construction workers, upholsterers, and plumbers and concludes they match what's necessary to do well in a first-year college course.

- Wages for careers that require higher levels of education and training will outpace non-degreed jobs, with the average college graduate earning 77 percent more than the typical high school graduate (Bureau of Labor Statistics, 2008).

Educators commonly say that it is our job to prepare students for the real world. Well, the stats we've just listed are the real world. In our current global economy, there is virtually no pathway to the middle class that does not require a postsecondary education—anything less is a one-way ticket to poverty. As the American Diploma Project (2004) states:

Successful preparation for both postsecondary education and employment requires learning the same rigorous English and mathematics content and skills.
No longer do students planning to work after high school need a different and
less rigorous curriculum than those planning to go to college. In fact, nearly
all students will require some postsecondary education, including on-the-job
training, after completing high school. Therefore, a college and workplace readiness curriculum should be a graduation requirement, not an option, for all high
school students. (pp. 8–9)

Restructuring education to meet 21st century needs has been the driving force behind many educational reform initiatives. From using whole language to implementing new mathematics, from lengthening the school day to tinkering with class size,
and from overemphasizing high-stakes testing to focusing on world-class standards,
a majority of these reforms has focused primarily on structural changes while mostly
ignoring the underlying cultural change so necessary to true educational reform.

High Levels of Learning for All

To achieve high levels of learning for every student, schools must restructure their
assumptions and practices around the following essential outcomes.

- All students must leave high school with the skills, knowledge,
  and dispositions necessary to succeed in postsecondary education,
  so all students must have access to college-readiness coursework.
  Schools must remove tracks of core instruction focused exclusively
  on below-grade-level expectations.

- Because all students do not learn the same way, develop at the
  same speed, enter school with the same prior knowledge, or have
  the same academic supports at home, students will be provided
  additional time and support to achieve these rigorous expectations.

- Because a single teacher could not possibly meet the diverse
  needs of all his or her students, schools will create a systematic
  intervention process to ensure that struggling students are
  guaranteed to receive additional time and support for learning
  that go beyond what an individual classroom teacher can
  provide. Achieving this goal will require staff members to work
  collaboratively and take collective responsibility for each student's
  success.

- Some students will need a little extra support from time to
  time, while others will enter school with profound gaps in their
  foundational skills. To meet this diverse range of needs, schools

will provide both supplemental (Tier 2) and intensive (Tier 3) interventions.

- Teachers will provide interventions in addition to core instruction, not in place of it. Students will not miss new essential core instruction to get extra help.

- Extra support will be available to all students who demonstrate the need. Because some students cannot come to school early or stay late, schools will embed this help during the school day, when students are required to be at school and all staff members are available to assist.

- Some students will not choose to voluntarily take advantage of this additional support. This should be expected, as some will lack the maturity, self-motivation, parental support, or vision of what is necessary to succeed as an adult. Because success or failure in school is life altering, students will not be given the option of failing. Interventions, when necessary, will be directive.

- Some students will enter school already meeting grade-level expectations. Additional time and support should not come at the expense of these students. Just as schools establish extra assistance to help at-risk students reach grade-level expectations, they will also provide all students with additional time and support to help them succeed in the most rigorous coursework.

Achieving these outcomes for every student will require more than a new bell schedule. To use an analogy, if reforming elementary education were likened to remodeling a house, we need more than new flooring and some fresh paint; we need to take the house down to the foundation and rebuild. This level of change is difficult, messy, and full of unexpected obstacles. If you have ever taken on the task of a major home remodel, you quickly learn that the devil is in the details.

The Real Problem

Creating a systematic process to provide students with additional support, offered in addition to grade-level core instruction, will undoubtedly require significant revisions to a school's schedule. Most schools assume that the biggest obstacle to this goal is determining how to manipulate the minutes within the school's current bell schedule to make interventions possible during the school day. In reality, this is often the easiest part of the process. There is not an elementary school in the United States that does not create special schedules throughout the year—for assemblies, fine arts events, testing, and so on. Creating these unique schedules comes down to basic mathematics. For example, if a school wants thirty minutes for a pep rally, the administrative team shaves minutes off of periods and transition times throughout the day to total thirty and then adds these borrowed minutes together and inserts them back into the schedule. Completing this task does not require a task force to study the problem. Creating the time needed for elementary supplemental intervention periods would follow the same process.

The real obstacles begin when a school considers the logistics of having potentially hundreds of students transitioning to specific interventions. Critical questions arise, such as:

- How do we successfully use this time to support student learning?

- How do we determine what interventions to offer?

- How do we assign staff?

- How do we transition students to the correct help sessions?

- How do we hold students accountable to attend?

- How do we move beyond a study hall approach and actually provide targeted instruction?

- How do we efficiently monitor student progress?

- What do we do with students who don't need extra help?

- How do we provide intensive interventions to students who lack the foundational skills of reading, writing, number sense, or the English language and still give them access to grade-level curriculum?

- What if students need help in multiple academic areas?

- What if a student's needs are not academic, but instead the student lacks the motivation to try?

- How do we keep the process from becoming a paperwork nightmare?

- If we shave minutes off regular classes, how will teachers be able to cover the required curriculum?

- How can we achieve these outcomes within our current resources and without asking teachers to work beyond their contractual obligations?

- Where does special education fit into this process?

These are all legitimate and difficult logistical questions that can stall a school's efforts to provide students additional time for learning. Fortunately, there are elementary schools across North America and beyond that have grappled with these questions, overcome the obstacles, and seen significant and sustained improvement in student achievement. Having some of these schools share specific, proven solutions is the purpose of this anthology.

Proven Solutions From Real-Life Schools

There is an old Chinese proverb that says, "To understand the road ahead, ask those coming back." The contributors to this anthology work on the frontlines of education. They have rolled up their sleeves, worked collaboratively with their colleagues, and addressed the obstacles that hinder a school's ability to provide students with systematic, timely, targeted, and directive interventions during the school day.

We have purposely selected a wide variety of schools for this anthology, including:

- K–5 schools, K–6 schools, a K–8 school, and a district perspective
- Suburban schools and urban schools
- Smaller schools and larger schools—even a virtual school
- Demographics that range from majority at-risk to extremely affluent
- Locations that range from Minnesota to Texas and from Arizona to Virginia
- Schools that grew from good to great, as well as schools that moved from the brink of state takeover to state awards

While the specific demographics and schedules vary from school to school, the essential outcomes are the same: each of these schools created the time and processes necessary to ensure that all students had access to both rigorous core instruction *and* the extra individualized support needed to achieve these outcomes.

Equally important, educators at each of the contributing schools realized that a new schedule alone would not be enough. Success with this goal requires creating a school culture focused on student learning and collaborative structures. To this end, these schools implemented Professional Learning Community (PLC) at Work™ practices. The solutions we offer in each of the following chapters are by-products of the collective efforts of all staff members working together to answer the four critical questions of a PLC (DuFour, DuFour, Eaker, & Many, 2010).

1. What do we expect students to learn?
2. How do we know they are learning it?

3. How do we respond when they do not learn?

4. How do we respond when they have already learned?

Finally, we specifically selected model schools that created time and effective interventions without receiving additional funding, staffing, or concessions to lengthen their school day. It would hardly be replicable if one of our contributing schools started its story with the narrative, "We received a two-million-dollar school-improvement grant, which funded paying our staff a stipend to lengthen the school day." Almost every example in this book was achieved within the school's existing resources, in accordance with teacher contractual agreements, and in compliance with district, state, and federal regulations. In fact, many were achieved during a time of diminishing resources.

An Overview of This Anthology

The goal of each chapter is to provide more than a broad explanation of how a particular school created time for interventions; instead, the text digs deeper into exactly how the school used time for interventions and extensions and provides the reader with actual schedules, tools, and examples. At the beginning of each chapter, we provide a short commentary to emphasize the critical considerations that led to the school's success. The chapters themselves address the unexpected obstacles that came up during implementation, showing how the school successfully overcame these hurdles and providing evidence that the school's efforts significantly improved student learning.

It is not necessary to read each chapter in order; in fact, depending on the current needs of your school or district, some chapters might be more relevant and helpful to your journey. However, while each chapter can be read independently, the chapter order represents a continuum of intensity, starting with interventions that will best support student success in Tier 1 core instruction and ending with interventions more directly focused on students who need intensive remediation in foundational skills and behavior.

To assist, following is a brief overview of each chapter.

In chapter 1, Sharon V. Kramer shares how elementary schools in Minnesota and Arizona have learned to collaboratively differentiate during Tier 1 instruction to make certain all students are successful. She shares specific tools and processes that demonstrate how collaborative planning and instruction help ensure solid core instruction every day in every classroom.

In chapter 2, Will Remmert describes the journey of an elementary school in Mankato, Minnesota, from three years of not making adequate yearly progress (AYP) to being designated a Reward School by the Minnesota Department of Education and a Title I School of Distinction. Through the development of What I Need (WIN) time and a focused effort to address cultural changes, the school overcame initial obstacles and continues to improve.

In chapter 3, Brian K. Butler demonstrates how an elementary school of approximately five hundred students in Annandale, Virginia, helped ensure high-quality Tier 1 instruction for all students through job-embedded professional development. This chapter gives very detailed, specific information about how the capacity of individual teachers, as well as collaborative teacher teams, was enhanced through multiple learning activities and highly targeted professional development.

In chapter 4, John Wink explains how interventions in a rural Texas elementary school have become as easy as 1-2-3. Teacher teams employ this focused process to help them collaborate around the most important topics that impact learning. While the school's PLC process serves as a vehicle to design high-quality instruction and assessments, the 1-2-3 process serves as the litmus test to ensure that the beginning of the response to intervention (RTI) process is implemented with fidelity.

In chapter 5, Susan B. Huff describes the good-to-great journey of Spanish Oaks, a suburban Utah elementary school with 35 percent of its students receiving free or reduced lunch. She explains how first building a strong PLC foundation helped the school create a system of timely interventions for students at the same time that budgets were cut to the bone.

In chapter 6, Lillie G. Jessie speaks to the incredibly important role of the principal in ensuring high levels of learning for all students. In doing so, she describes the journey of Elizabeth Vaughan Elementary School, a high-minority, highly diverse, Title I school in Woodbridge, Virginia, and how she, as principal, helped provide the structural and emotional support to her teachers and students that led to the development of a schoolwide system of tiered interventions.

In chapter 7, Merrilou Harrison explains how she, as principal of Gilbert Elementary in Yakima, Washington, faced significant challenges. This low-performing urban school enrolled 525 students, which included a high percentage of at-risk youth. This urban school was 61 percent minority students, 75 percent students of poverty, 22 percent special education students, and 25 percent English learners (ELs). Merrilou led her staff in building a PLC to ensure all students received the time and support necessary to succeed. The school is featured on the All Things PLC website (www.allthingsplc.info) as an exemplary PLC school.

In chapter 8, Maria Nielsen gives specific tools and tips on how she helped build a system of powerful Tier 2 interventions at Millville Elementary School in Utah. The school has garnered numerous awards, including Reward School status from the

Utah State Department of Education. This was accomplished through developing a guaranteed and viable curriculum, common assessments, common pacing guides, and common interventions and extensions and taking collective ownership of all students across a grade level. As a result, the school's end-of-level scores have soared above 90 percent in all curriculum areas.

In chapter 9, Paul Goldberg details the journey of John Muir Literacy Academy in Schaumburg School District 54 in Illinois, a Title I school with a minority student population of over 80 percent. This suburban school, with more than five hundred students in preK through sixth grade, was on the state watch-list for not making AYP and had only 69 percent of students meeting state standards in 2005. By 2012, through its curriculum-aligned acceleration model, approximately 90 percent of its students were proficient on state assessments in reading and mathematics. Muir has achieved some of the highest student learning growth in the United States in both mathematics and reading, performing near the 99th percentile.

In chapter 10, Paula Rogers delves into the all-important topic of positive behavioral support for individual students. As deputy superintendent of the Hallsville Independent School District in Hallsville, Texas, she made it her goal to design a behavior support program that met the wide spectrum of students' needs while maintaining their placement in their academic setting. Her chapter provides examples of behavioral interventions at all three tiers and discusses how behavioral and academic interventions intertwine.

In chapter 11, Chris Weber discusses how student behaviors were improved at Bucktown Elementary School, a K–8 school in Chicago serving 750 students. The student population is diverse, reflecting the neighborhood and city in which it is located, with over 65 percent of students qualifying for free and reduced price lunch and over 53 percent of students designated as ELs. Through collective commitments and the consistent application of research-based practices, the Bucktown staff have implemented a system of positive behavioral supports that ensures all students learn at high levels.

In chapter 12, Regina Stephens Owens describes how Spring Independent School District in Spring, Texas, used technology tools and social media to provide students with additional time and support. Her chapter encourages us all to move from paralyzing programs to personalized learning, demonstrating this primarily through the use of technology tools.

In closing, here's a point of caution: Richard DuFour often says, "Embrace the forest; don't fall in love with a tree." While the goal of this book is to provide educators with detailed examples of exactly how real-life schools created time to implement specific interventions, there will undoubtedly be aspects in every example that do not perfectly match your school's current resources and reality. Our bigger goal is not only to show you detailed examples of specific interventions, but more importantly the larger guiding priorities and collaborative processes that created them.

The model schools in this anthology did not look to buy an intervention "program" to improve their school; rather, they focused on an ongoing, collaborative process of improvement. While you may not be able to re-create the exact interventions described in each chapter, you can re-create the process, tailoring these examples to your students' unique needs and building on the specific talents and resources available at your school and within your own local, state, or provincial guidelines.

Keeping this important point of caution in mind, a forest awaits!

References and Resources

ACT. (2006). *Ready for college and ready for work: Same or different?* Iowa City, IA: Author.

American Diploma Project. (2004). *Ready or not: Creating a high school diploma that counts.* Washington, DC: Achieve. Accessed at www.achieve.org/files/ReadyorNot.pdf on March 5, 2014.

Bloom, B. S. (1968). Learning for mastery. *Evaluation Comment, 1*(2), 1–12. (ERIC Document Reproduction Service No. ED053419)

Buffum, A., Mattos, M., & Weber, C. (2012). *Simplifying response to intervention: Four essential guiding principles.* Bloomington, IN: Solution Tree Press.

Bureau of Labor Statistics. (2008, February). *Occupational projections and training data: 2008–9 edition.* Washington, DC: U.S. Department of Labor.

Chao, E. L. (2008, June 23). *Remarks prepared for delivery by U.S. secretary of labor Elaine L. Chao to the Greater Louisville Inc. Metro Chamber of Commerce.* Washington, DC: U.S. Department of Labor. Accessed at www.dol.gov/_sec/media/speeches/20080623_COC.htm on March 5, 2014.

Dorn, S. (1996). *Creating the dropout: An institutional and social history of school failure.* Westport, CT: Praeger.

DuFour, R., DuFour, R., Eaker, R., & Many, T. W. (2010). *Learning by doing: A handbook for professional learning communities at work* (2nd ed.). Bloomington, IN: Solution Tree Press.

Guskey, T. R., & Pigott, T. D. (1988). Research on group-based mastery learning programs: A meta-analysis. *Journal of Educational Research, 81*(4), 197–216.

Hagenbaugh, B. (2002, December 12). U.S. manufacturing jobs fading away fast. *USA Today.* Accessed at www.usatoday.com/money/economy/2002–12–12-manufacture_x.htm on July 8, 2011.

Leavitt, F. M. (1912, October). The need, purpose and possibilities of industrial education in the elementary school. *Elementary School Teacher, 13*, 80–90.

Mill, J. S. (1867). *Inaugural address, delivered to the University of St. Andrews, February 1, 1867.* Accessed at https://archive.org/details/inauguraladdres00millgoog on June 30, 2014.

Oakes, J. (2005). *Keeping track: How schools structure inequality* (2nd ed.). New Haven, CT: Yale University Press.

U.S. Department of Agriculture, Utah State University Extension, & LetterPress Software. (n.d.). *Growing a nation: The story of American agriculture.* Accessed at www.agclassroom .org/gan/classroom/pdf/embed1_seeds.pdf on July 8, 2011.

Sharon V. Kramer, PhD, knows firsthand the demands and rewards of working in a professional learning community. As a leader in the field, she emphasizes the importance of creating and using quality assessments as a continual part of the learning process. Sharon served as assistant superintendent for curriculum and instruction of Kildeer Countryside School District 96 in Buffalo Grove, Illinois. In this position, she ensured all students were prepared to enter Adlai E. Stevenson High School, a model PLC. A seasoned educator, Sharon has taught in elementary and middle school classrooms and served as a principal, a director of elementary education, and a university professor.

Sharon earned a doctorate in educational leadership and policy studies from Loyola University Chicago.

To learn more about Sharon's work, follow @DrKramer1 on Twitter.

To book Sharon V. Kramer for professional development, contact pd@solution-tree.com.

Choosing Prevention Before Intervention

Sharon V. Kramer

Editors' Note

This chapter is presented first because it explicitly states one of the core ideas behind this book: prevention and intervention are not so much a set of strategies or activities, or even schedules; they should represent a way of thinking about teaching a learning process. As you progress through the chapters in this book, keep this in mind!

In addition to providing several illustrative and useful templates for teams to use, this chapter makes the important point that the only way to effectively differentiate learning for students is through a team process. The author reminds us that respectful differentiation builds on what students know and are able to do and does not mean "louder and slower." Similarly, differentiation for students who have already learned it should not mean more work of the same nature. It is important to note that this chapter gives equal emphasis to both those who have not yet learned and those who have already learned.

Finally, an important theme throughout the chapter is to be proactive rather than reactive. The author makes an important point in reminding us that the most effective kinds of differentiation are those that are preplanned rather than reactive and ad lib. Of course, this leads us back to the understanding that the best differentiation is a team activity.

The primary purpose of every school is to ensure high levels of learning for each student. To achieve this goal, a school must create a systematic process that ensures every student receives the time and support needed to learn at high levels. This means that to reach high levels of learning for *all*, we must focus on what *each* student needs.

Response to intervention is our best hope to provide this additional time and support. RTI's underlying premise is that schools should not delay in providing help for struggling learners until they fall so far behind that it is impossible to catch up. Instead, the RTI model is dependent on strong core instruction in every classroom every day that effectively responds to student learning; the core program must include support and interventions when students do not learn and extensions for students who have already learned. No amount of intervention can replace a solid Tier 1 core program. After all, the best intervention is prevention, and Tier 1 is that prevention.

One of the greatest challenges that teachers face daily is responding to the academic diversity in their classrooms. The question teachers across the United States most frequently ask is, "How does one teacher support the needs of all learners?" This question is usually followed by: "What new and comprehensive strategies will I use to re-engage students and extend learning, since I used my best strategy the first time I taught this? How do I find the time to do interventions and also keep up with the pacing of the curriculum? How will I extend learning for some students while I respectfully re-engage others?" These are practicalities teachers deal with on a daily basis. This chapter answers these questions and describes and highlights the real work of teachers in Arizona and Minnesota as they plan and deliver proactive instruction in Tier 1.

Supporting the Needs of All Learners

Many schools and districts believe that Tier 1, first-best instruction, or daily classroom instruction, is a solo activity; thus, they concentrate their efforts on improving what individual teachers do. The focus is on providing teachers with greater content knowledge, clustered ability grouping, improved teaching strategies, and a lockstep approach to instruction and pacing. But is this the best approach? What is the most effective way to improve teaching? According to John Hattie (2009) in his book *Visible Learning*, teachers must work together rather than in isolation. This means schools need to focus on building and sustaining highly effective and efficient collaborative teams. As Richard DuFour and Mike Mattos (2013) write, "The key to improved student learning is to ensure more good teaching in more classrooms more of the time" (p. 34). Teachers need to support each other in designing and delivering quality instruction that results in learning for all. In a PLC, collaborative teams do this by focusing on four critical questions (DuFour, DuFour, Eaker, & Many, 2010).

1. What do we expect students to learn?
2. How do we know they are learning it?
3. How do we respond when they do not learn?
4. How do we respond when they have already learned?

As teams answer these questions in recurring cycles on a unit-by-unit basis, they determine essential learning outcomes, create common formative and summative assessments, and plan and implement interventions and extensions for student learning. This means they plan for differentiation to ensure learning for all.

Differentiating instruction involves creating multiple paths of learning so that students of different abilities, interests, or learning needs experience equally appropriate ways to absorb, use, develop, and present concepts as a part of the daily learning process. The only way to truly differentiate to meet the needs of all learners in a classroom is through a collaborative team effort. Differentiation is too difficult for one teacher. In an elementary classroom, there are too many content areas, standards, and learning targets to expect one teacher to go it alone.

This process of responding to student learning is embedded in Tier 1 instruction. (See figure 1.1.) It is important to note that in this sense, differentiation is not a set of strategies but is instead a way of thinking about the teaching and learning process. Differentiation is not about who will learn what but rather how you will teach so that all students have access to, and support and guidance in, mastering the district and state curriculum.

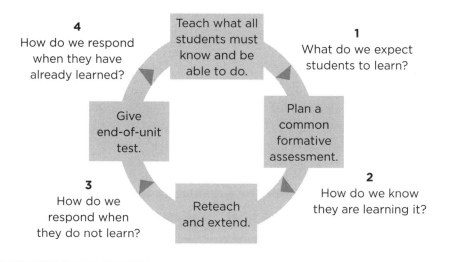

Figure 1.1: Tier 1 instruction.

Teams plan for differentiated instruction by following these six steps.

1. Determine the major standards for a unit or chapter; these are the must-knows (power or priority standards).

2. Unwrap the standards to build shared understanding of their meaning and to determine the depth of knowledge each standard requires.

3. Determine the learning progression, target, and key concepts.

4. Plan pre- and postassessments.

5. Plan differentiated teaching and learning strategies and activities.

6. Plan formative assessments.

Anoka-Hennepin Schools in Minnesota accomplish this level of differentiation by utilizing a collaborative team unit plan. (See figure 1.2.) Each school's content team answers all four critical PLC questions as it develops learning plans on a unit-by-unit basis. During this process teachers share strategies and materials for the diversity of learners in their classrooms.

Collaborative Team Unit Plan
Sample: Grade 3

Unit: Distinguish Among Stories, Dramas, and Poems

Time Frame: Three to four class periods

Collaborative Team Members:

1. **What do we expect our students to learn?**

    Common Core Standard: RL.3.5—Refer to parts of stories, dramas, and poems when writing or speaking about a text, using terms such as chapter, scene, and stanza; describe how each successive part builds on earlier sections.

    Common Core Standard: SL.3.1—Engage effectively in a range of collaborative discussions . . . with diverse partners on grade 3 topics and texts, building on others' ideas and expressing their own clearly.

    Common Core Standard: SL.3.4—Report on a topic or text, tell a story, or recount an experience with appropriate facts and relevant, descriptive details, speaking clearly at an understandable pace.

    Common Core Standard: L.3.6—Acquire and use accurately grade-appropriate conversational, general academic, and domain-specific words and phrases, including those that signal spatial and temporal relationships. (National Governors Association Center for Best Practices [NGA] & Council of Chief State School Officers [CCSSO], 2010a, pp. 24, 27)

    Identify essential unit learning targets (student-friendly language; post in classroom).

    a. I can examine an excerpt from a story, using academic vocabulary to describe elements of a story (chapter, paragraph, and so on).

    b. I can examine a play, using academic vocabulary to describe elements of drama (actor, scene, and so on).

    c. I can examine a poem, using academic vocabulary to describe elements of poetry (line, stanza, and so on).

    d. I can participate in reader's theater, reading lines of a play aloud.

    e. I can work with peers to prepare and deliver a shared oral report that identifies elements of stories, plays, and poems.

2. **How do we know if they are learning it?**

    Unit Assessment Plan

    a. Formative assessments (preassessment, formative assessments)
        (circle: CA—common assessments; FA—formative assessment)

        i. (CA)**FA** Preassessment: Types of Literature (Activity Sheet)

        ii. **CA**(FA) Discussion: Identify key elements of a story, drama, and
            poem.

        iii. **CA**(FA) Read lines of a play aloud.

    b. Preassessment: CA Types of Literature (Activity Sheet)

    c. End of unit: CA Have students work in groups of three to create
        shared oral reports that explain three types of literature: stories, plays,
        and poems. Each group member should prepare and deliver one part of
        the group's report. In their reports, students should use key academic
        vocabulary. Grades are based on points earned from a four-point rubric.

3. **How do we respond when they do not learn?**

    In small groups, use a short segment of the story and drama to teach the
    concepts, focusing on explaining keywords and their pronunciations and
    examining the formats of the genres.

4. **How do we respond when they have already learned?**

    Have students create genre-based reader's logs, labeling pages stories,
    dramas, and poems. Students keep the logs throughout the school year to
    affirm reading and building of academic language.

Source: Adapted from Anoka-Hennepin ISD #11, 2012. Used with permission.

Figure 1.2: Sample grade 3 collaborative team unit plan.

*Visit **go.solution-tree.com/rtiatwork** for a reproducible version of this figure.*

These overall unit strategies offer each teacher a variety of ways to meet all learners' needs. They are specific to the standards and learning targets that students are expected to know and be able to do and are guided by a defined set of formative and end-of-unit assessments. Each plan includes ways to differentiate instruction, as teams provide answers to the third and fourth critical questions.

The Cartwright School District in Arizona created a similar learning plan that teams use to map what they call *first-best-next instruction.* This type of instruction follows the four critical questions of a PLC through a lesson and includes implementation strategies and discourse or questioning strategies as a part of the first critical question. The *first-best* portion consists of a specific method to check for understanding, while the *next* portion helps teachers plan for when students do not learn or have already learned. Figure 1.3 (pages 20–21) is an example of the first-best-next instruction plan.

Date: October 24	Time: 10:00	Content: English Language Arts	Grade: 3	Teacher: S. Brandt

1. What do we expect students to learn?

Common Core Standard	**RL.3.5:** Refer to parts of stories, dramas, and poems when writing or speaking about a text, using terms such as chapter, scene, and stanza; describe how each successive part builds on earlier sections.	
Essential Unit Learning Target	I can examine an excerpt from a story, using academic vocabulary to describe elements of a story (chapter, paragraph). I can examine a play, using academic vocabulary to describe elements of drama (actor, scene). I can examine a poem using academic vocabulary to describe elements of poetry (line, stanza). I can work with peers to prepare and deliver a shared oral report that identifies elements of stories, plays, and poems.	
Language Objective	I can use grade-appropriate conversational, general academic, and domain-specific words and phrases.	
Anticipatory Set and Building Background	Students should know how to recognize stories and poems as separate genres or types of literature.	
Lesson Implementation	I Do: Story (*Herbie Jones and the Class Gift* [Kline, 2002]): The teacher will introduce Herbie Jones and read aloud chapter 1. Drama (*Herbie Jones and the Class Gift*): The teacher will explain key elements of a drama, creating a list on the board. Poem: The teacher will introduce the poem and point out key elements of a poem.	Discourse and Questioning Strategies: Knowledge: What are the key elements of a story, a drama, and a poem? Comprehension: What is the difference between stories and drama, stories and poems, and drama and poems? Analysis: Discriminate among key elements of a story, drama, and poem.

First-Best Instruction

First-Best Instruction		
	We Do: Story: Class discusses key elements of a story. Drama: Students perform a play. Poem: Students recite the poem.	
	You Do: Students will discriminate among key elements of a story, drama, and poem.	

2. How do we know they are learning it?

Assessment (formative and summative of the objective taught)	Students work in small groups to prepare an oral report to explain three types of literature: stories, dramas, and poems.	

Next Instruction

3. How do we respond when they do not learn?

Tier 1 Intervention (in class)	In a small group, use a short section of the story, drama, and poem, focusing on key words and the formats of genres.	

4. How do we respond when they have already learned?

Tier 1 Extension (in class)	Assign advanced students the longer role and sections of text. Advanced students can also research and present other examples of each genre.	

Every lesson must have a standard, language objective, essential unit learning target, and an assessment. The teacher must plan activities to support the learning target and employ best practices for student learning. Teachers will select the instructional elements relevant to each lesson and will include those in each lesson.

Source: Adapted from Estrella Middle School, Cartwright School District, Phoenix, Arizona, 2012. Adapted from NGA & CCSSO, 2010, p. 12.

Figure 1.3: Sample first-best-next instruction lesson plan.

Using Respectful Strategies to Differentiate

The goal is to plan respectful tasks—which include high expectations for all students with activities that equally engage each learner—so that every student puts forth effort to learn. Respectful tasks honor student learning and build on what a student knows at all levels. When students struggle, it is not respectful to ask them to do the same activity over while the teacher says it louder and slower. Re-engagement rather than mere reteaching is what students need. While reteaching involves teaching the unit lessons over again, re-engaging analyzes student errors and missteps and asks students to revisit their thinking. It is also not respectful to ask students who have demonstrated proficiency to do even more of the same work. Therefore, respectful re-engaging is high-interest, engaging, and appropriately challenging for all students.

One way to be proactive about re-engaging some students and extending learning for others with appropriate strategies is to develop leveled activities in every lesson. This is a part of the planning process for first-best-next instruction. In the flexible instruction model, the teacher addresses the overall standard and targets at three levels: (1) scaffolded learning, (2) core learning, and (3) extensions of learning. Teams, rather than individual teachers, work together to design specific activities that ensure all students will learn the standards, while students who demonstrate they already know the standards engage with extension opportunities. The scaffolded-learning level is designed to meet the needs of the students who have limited or no understanding of the standards. The core-learning level matches the proficiency expected on the standard and offers practice opportunities for students who still do not own the learning. The extensions-of-learning level applies the core learning and asks students to demonstrate learning that was not part of direct instruction.

To develop these activities, teams begin by describing their expectations for proficiency of the standard. In other words, they describe what it would look like if students met the standard. This becomes the core activity. Next, they determine scaffolded learning, as teams review the preassessment data and compare them to the proficiency expectations. They ask themselves, "What will our students need in order to reach proficiency on this standard? What are the steps or learning progressions necessary to meet this expectation?" Finally, teams develop the extensions of learning, as they discuss respectful tasks that require students to think beyond what was taught and apply their thinking to new and different situations. When developing these levels, teams consider a variety of ways to adjust the instruction and activities, including by task complexity, amount of structure, number of steps, pacing, materials, concrete to abstract thinking, or student interests. Tasks are also leveled by the degree of independence or the gradual release of responsibility. This process requires teachers to use flexible grouping with such strategies as the flexible instruction model, What I Need time, or the to-with-by model.

Flexible Instruction Model

Flexible grouping refers to consistently fluid work arrangements based on student readiness levels. Flexible grouping ensures that all students learn to work independently, cooperatively, and collaboratively in a variety of settings and with a variety of peers. It increases the chance that learning activities match more students' needs more of the time, leading to faster, better, deeper learning without tracking. Flexible grouping is most effective and efficient when collaborative teams create the learning plan for each group and take collective responsibility for learning by sharing students with like learning needs. This is an opportunity for teachers to work smarter, not harder. Figure 1.4 (page 24) provides an example of the flexible instruction model.

What I Need Time

Adams Elementary in Minnesota uses a similar proactive approach to differentiation. The teachers schedule a time during the day that they call What I Need (WIN) time. During this time, all students at a grade level are flexibly grouped for instruction on specific learning targets that are scaffolded learning, core learning, or extensions of learning. Teams also share the students and the work of gathering materials. WIN time operates on a ten-day cycle. For nine days, students receive instruction in their respective groups. The tenth day is a planning day for the next cycle. During WIN time, teachers work with their groups and use a short checklist to keep track of student progress on the learning target. They use these checklists, along with formative assessments they administer during regular instruction, to regroup students for the next learning cycle. To ensure that group sizes are small, all support staff (EL, special education teachers, teacher assistants, instructional coaches, reading and mathematics support) assist the grade levels during each planning cycle as well as during WIN time.

Adams Elementary has made extensive gains in student achievement since 2012. In fact, they are a Title I Minnesota Reward School. The principal and staff attribute the school's success to this relentless focus on what *each* student needs.

To-With-By Model

But what if you do not have additional support staff? How will one teacher support all three flexible groups? Individual teachers can use the to-with-by model to manage instruction during grouping. In this model, the teacher is able to vary the support each group receives by using the gradual release of responsibility approach. This means the teacher provides direct instruction and modeling *to* students in the scaffolded group, the teacher provides an opportunity to practice the skill or concept *with* support in the core group, and the students in the extension group deepen their

English Language Arts and Science
Boy, Were We Wrong About Dinosaurs!
by Kathleen V. Kudlinski (2008)
Grade 3

Standards	Preassessments of Prerequisite Skills and Knowledge
RI.3.2: Determine the main idea of a text; recount the key details and explain how they support the main idea. **RI.3.3:** Describe the relationship between a series of historical events, scientific ideas or concepts, or steps in technical procedures in a text, using language that pertains to time, sequence, and cause/effect. **RI.3.8:** Describe the logical connection between particular sentences and paragraphs in a text (e.g., comparison, cause/effect, first/second/third in a sequence).	Discuss as a class, What do we know about dinosaurs? Brainstorm—make a chart of all ideas. Discuss scientific method: Find clues, develop a hypothesis, and confirm hypothesis. Discuss cause and effect in everyday events. Model the use of diagrams to explain the event. Students are given versions of the assignment based on their preassessment work.

Introduction

Discuss with students that scientists find clues, develop a hypothesis from the clues, and as more information comes in, either confirm the earlier view or change it to account for new information. Read the book, *Boy, Were We Wrong About Dinosaurs!* by Kathleen V. Kudlinski.

Scaffolded	Core	Extension
A small group of students may need to reread the text—stopping often to discuss key ideas.	Students will pull key ideas from the text. Using the brainstorming chart, they will categorize ideas into two categories: (1) Boy, Were We Wrong and (2) This Is What We Now Know. Students will do a matching activity, pairing the cause-and-effect statements. Students will verbally share their choices and explain why they made their decisions.	Students visit www.watchknowlearn.org and view seven video clips on dinosaurs. Students create a presentation for the class on new information they were able to find on dinosaurs.

Closure

Lead a class discussion about the causes and effects the students found in the assignment. Use the time line at the end of the book to talk about why scientists believed what they did at certain times in history.

Source: Adapted from NGA & CCSSO, 2010, p. 14.

Figure 1.4: Sample flexible instruction model lesson plan.

learning through individual application *by* working on their own or in teams. In this way, students are engaged in appropriate activities, and the teacher is able to manage their learning.

Extending Learning

A teacher in Minnesota once said to me that she was most concerned about the students in her classroom who spend most of their day watching others learn. She was referring to those students who either know the learning targets before they are taught or learn them quickly. Because some students need additional teaching, others are given more work to keep them busy, asked to tutor peers, or left to fend for themselves. Collaborative teams must be intentional in answering the fourth PLC question: How will we respond when students have already learned?

Most of us think of differentiation as a reactive process that we implement after a lesson. During the usual instructional cycle, teachers deliver a lesson and assume all students will learn. The intent is to keep all students together. Obviously, this rarely occurs, since all students learn at different rates using a variety of methods. With the best of intentions, most teachers find themselves reacting to student learning by improvising in the moment. The typical scenario includes a whole-group lesson followed by guided practice. As students practice, it becomes obvious that some students did not understand and are struggling to complete the activity. Teachers begin to assist these students and may even call them up to a table or gather their desks together to re-engage with the lesson. But what will the others do? Often, these students are directed to take out a book to read, complete homework, or do more of the same work that they just completed.

According to Sylvia Rimm (2008), psychologist and director of the Family Achievement Clinic in Cleveland, Ohio, students who know the standards or learn quickly often do not understand the correlation between effort and learning. Sometimes the most capable learners give up when they do not know the answer or cannot solve the problem. This is because most of them have never had to put forth effort to learn. They do not have a set of strategies to help them persevere to the answer or solution. So they give up. Rimm (1986) states:

> The surest path to positive self-esteem is to succeed at something which one perceived would be difficult. Each time we steal a student's struggle, we steal the opportunity for them to build self-confidence. They must learn to do hard things to feel good about themselves.

The overall goal, after all, is to make sure that the curriculum appropriately challenges all students to put forth effort to learn.

Carol Ann Tomlinson describes differentiation as a way of planning for the unpredictable in the classroom (QEP Video Courses for Teachers, 2011). This is a proactive rather than a reactive approach to meeting the needs of all learners—including those who have already learned the content. It means that, from the beginning, the Tier 1 lesson includes more than one avenue for success—as described in the strategies listed in the previous section. Thus, teachers must purposefully plan to include multiple entry points for learners. The best comparison is a staggered start in a foot race. Runners may start in different places, but all of them cross the same finish line. The staggered start is the entry point or readiness of each learner, and the finish line is made up of the standards and learning targets that we expect all students to learn. This proactive approach to differentiation best occurs through team collaboration.

Finding Time for Interventions

Teachers have too much to teach and often feel that they cannot interrupt instruction to do all of these interventions and extensions of learning. Frequently, teachers are expected to follow rigid pacing guides with prescribed activities and detailed lesson plans. Unfortunately, these documents do not allow for the possibility that students may need preteaching of prerequisite skills before they can move on to the learning target for that day. Teachers need to teach the students they have in their class, not the ones the pacing guide was written to address.

The reality is that the currency of education is time. So how does a teacher find the time to do it all? Often, teachers will say, "I do not have time to intervene or extend the learning. I have to teach and move on." However, interventions and extensions are a part of the teaching and learning process—not separate. So, how do we manage it all?

One of the most effective ways to gain time in the curriculum is to administer short preassessments of prerequisite skills to determine what students already know and what may be a problem for them. This serves two purposes: (1) it allows you to treat the curriculum unequally, and (2) it provides information necessary to differentiate for individual students and small groups. Without the information from a short preassessment, teachers typically approach each unit in the same manner, teaching all of the standards and targets as if the students have no prior knowledge. When a teacher administers a preassessment, however, he or she is able to make critical decisions about what to spend more or less time on in the unit. It also allows for preteaching of short mini-lessons to specific students before whole-group instruction so that all students are actually able to keep up during the whole-group lesson. These students often need vocabulary instruction or other prerequisite skills to learn the expected content.

Preassessments provide information for small-group work as well. As teachers focus on learning targets, students can form flexible groups based on who was proficient or not proficient on a target-by-target basis. This process focuses instruction and saves time.

Beyond preassessments, assessment research is clear that the checks for understanding on a minute-by-minute basis are the most effective ways to respond to student learning (Hattie, 2012). These in-the-moment data allow teachers to meet learners' needs before they become problems. Checking for understanding saves time by minimizing the need for remediation later.

One thing all teachers can agree on is that time is a limited commodity, especially given the depth and breadth of the standards. A careful analysis of how teams use time is required to meet all of these demands. Consider these team questions.

- How do we spend the limited time we are given?

- Is this the right lesson for these students right now?

- Given the school year time frame, is this learning experience worthy of the time it will cost?

- Is there another way to approach this learning that might work better for these learners or be more efficient in moving them along?

As teams answer these questions, they are critically analyzing how they allocate their limited instructional minutes. Some activities and lessons are retained while others may need to be dropped or replaced with more targeted instruction. This ensures closer alignment to the essential or priority outcomes.

A Final Note

Why do we need to differentiate? Because the students we serve require differentiation to learn. The question is not whether we should differentiate but how we do this given the academic diversity in classrooms, the time restraints, and the overwhelming amount of standards and content required. Collaboration is the key to meeting all learners' needs. No matter how excellent a teacher is, the students in the class are still limited by what he or she brings to the learning process. When teachers work in teams, the options and opportunities grow exponentially for the students that they serve. Tier 1, first-best instruction, requires a team effort. Collaborative, proactive planning ensures solid core instruction every day in every classroom. The power is in the team!

Rick Wormeli (2006) says it this way:

> Differentiating teachers do not teach in isolation. They are ceaselessly collaborative, welcoming the scrutiny of colleagues and the chance to learn more about the ways students learn best. They are not threatened by the observations or advice of others, and they take frequent risks in the classroom—teaching in ways that students learn best, not the way they teach best. They shift their thinking from their own state of affairs to empathy for students. (pp. 197–198)

To truly be proficient at differentiation and most everything in life, it always comes down to learning by doing. As you reflect on the examples in this chapter, consider the following questions.

- What is one quick, easy strategy we can do right now?

- What is possible in the next unit of study?

- What does my team need to do to be more proactive in our approach to student learning and answering the third and fourth critical PLC questions?

As Tomlinson writes, "Excellence in education is when we do everything that we can to make sure they become everything that they can" (as cited in Slade, 2012).

References and Resources

Buffum, A., Mattos, M., & Weber, C. (2012). *Simplifying response to intervention: Four essential guiding principles.* Bloomington, IN: Solution Tree Press.

DuFour, R., DuFour, R., Eaker, R., & Many, T. W. (2010). *Learning by doing: A handbook for professional learning communities at work* (2nd ed.). Bloomington, IN: Solution Tree Press.

DuFour, R., & Mattos, M. (2013). How do principals really improve schools? *Educational Leadership, 70*(7), 34–40.

Eidson, C. C., & Tomlinson, C. A. (2003). *Differentiation in practice: A resource guide for differentiating curriculum, grades K–5.* Alexandria, VA: Association for Supervision and Curriculum Development.

Hattie, J. A. C. (2009). *Visible learning: A synthesis of over 800 meta-analyses relating to achievement.* New York: Routledge.

Hattie, J. A. C. (2012). *Visible learning for teachers.* New York: Routledge.

Kingore, B. (2004). *Differentiation: Simplified, realistic, and effective—How to challenge advanced potentials in mixed-ability classrooms.* Austin, TX: Professional Associates.

Kline, S. (2002). *Herbie Jones and the class gift.* New York: Puffin Books.

Kudlinski, K. V. (2008). *Boy, were we wrong about dinosaurs!* New York: Puffin Books.

Marzano, R. J. (2007). *The art and science of teaching: A comprehensive framework for effective instruction.* Alexandria, VA: Association for Supervision and Curriculum Development.

Moon, T. R., & Tomlinson, C. A. (2013). *Assessment and student success in a differentiated classroom.* Alexandria, VA: Association for Supervision and Curriculum Development.

National Governors Association Center for Best Practices & Council of Chief State School Officers. (2010). *Common Core State Standards for English language arts and literacy in history/social studies, science, and technical subjects.* Washington, DC: Authors. Accessed at www.corestandards.org/assets/CCSSI_ELA%20Standards.pdf on May 27, 2014.

Pfeiffer, S. I. (2008). *Handbook of giftedness in children: Psychoeducational theory, research, and best practices.* New York: Springer.

QEP Video Courses for Teachers. (2011). *Carol Tomlinson on differentiation: Responsive teaching* [Video file]. Accessed at www.youtube.com/watch?v=01798frimeQ on July 21, 2014.

Rimm, S. B. (1986). *Underachievement syndrome: Causes and cures.* Watertown, WI: Apple Publishing.

Rimm, S. B. (2008). *Why bright kids get poor grades and what you can do about it: A six-step program for parents and teachers* (3rd ed.). Tucson, AZ: Great Potential Press.

Slade, S. (2012). *In support of the whole child.* Accessed at www.huffingtonpost.com/sean-slade/in-support-of-the-whole-c_b_1643487.html on July 21, 2014.

Wiliam, D. (2011). *Embedded formative assessment.* Bloomington, IN: Solution Tree Press.

Wormeli, R. (2006). *Fair isn't always equal: Assessing & grading in the differentiated classroom.* Portland, ME: Stenhouse.

 **Will Remmert** is the principal of Eagle View Elementary in Elko New Market, Minnesota. He has nearly twenty years of experience as a teacher and administrator at both the elementary and secondary levels. He led Washington Elementary in Mankato, Minnesota, from not making AYP for three consecutive years to the Minnesota Department of Education naming it a Reward School. The honor that Washington earned gave it the recognition of being in the top 15 percent of all Title I schools in the state, and it received this honor for two consecutive years.

Will consults with schools and districts in the areas of professional learning communities, response to intervention, and instructional strategies to ensure student learning for all. He also teams with Solution Tree and All Things PLC (www.all thingsplc.info) to lead the #atplc weekly Twitter chat on Thursdays at 8:00 p.m. central time.

To learn more about Will's work, follow @willremmert on Twitter.

To book Will Remmert for professional development, contact pd@solution-tree .com.

Looking in the Mirror

Will Remmert

Editors' Note

This chapter tells the story of a school that stopped looking out the window and making excuses and developed a sense of collective responsibility for all students. The school realized that Tier 1 instruction needed to be its focus rather than waiting for students to fail, assigning them a label (such as *special education*), and then making someone else primarily responsible for fixing them.

The thinking that Washington Elementary used could benefit many schools.

• Stop blaming others, and take responsibility for the students we have.

• Shift more focus on Tier 1 instruction and prevention.

• Make certain that all students receive core instruction, while some will receive the core and more (Tiers 2 and 3).

• Provide professional development to add tools to teachers' Tier 1 toolboxes.

• Create a greater focus by prioritizing the curriculum.

• Keep track of learning by student, by standard, and by target.

It should also be noted that the principal met two to three times per year with each teacher to review the progress of individual students toward mastery of essential learnings. The purpose of these meetings was to allow the principal to provide support rather than to evaluate the teacher. We have noted a strong correlation between a principal's involvement in the intervention program and the efficacy and results of that program. The impact of this involvement cannot be overemphasized.

Washington Elementary, in Mankato, Minnesota, is about ninety miles south of the Twin Cities; nearly 45 percent of its students receive free or reduced-price lunch, and 10 percent of the student population speaks English as a second language. As one of the more demographically diverse schools in its district, Washington was underperforming academically in 2007. After we provided every intervention we had available, we were still failing to meet the needs of nearly one-third of our students. To compound this glaring statistic, we were also designated a School in Need of Improvement by the State of Minnesota under the No Child Left Behind Act. The support structure at Washington was one with very little alignment. The school culture consisted of a *me* rather than *we* mentality. If a non-English-speaking student needed additional support, it was generally the responsibility of the EL teacher to intervene. If a student was being served through special education, the classroom teacher often relied on the special education teacher to deliver the core instruction. We had paraprofessionals serving our underperforming students, while our most highly trained teachers were working with students who didn't necessarily need a high level of support.

We also had a significant climate issue. We frequently made excuses about not having enough time to get everything done or enough support from the district and parents, and the general feeling was that our students were unmotivated to learn. As Richard DuFour and Michael Fullan (2013) state in *Cultures Built to Last*, "People must be willing to look in the mirror for solutions, rather than out of the window while waiting for others in the system to save them" (p. 11). So, we began looking at what we could control and what we couldn't. We needed to acknowledge that we couldn't choose the students that the parents were sending us and that we were not in the business of deciding which students we serve. We began to understand that placing the blame of student achievement on factors beyond our control wasn't improving student learning, and our students' parents were giving us the very best they had rather than keeping their proficient or exceeding children at home. The hard truth was, it was our responsibility to do everything we could to meet the needs of our students, because the only thing we could change was how we responded within the hours of the school day.

As Ronald Edmonds (1979) states in an article from *Educational Leadership*, "We can, whenever and wherever we choose, successfully teach all children whose schooling is of interest to us" (p. 23). We started carefully analyzing our behaviors as professionals as well as the instructional minutes allotted throughout our day. We needed to ensure we were utilizing our time with students to the best of our ability because all of our students need to be of interest to us. It became apparent that we could, and needed to, create more time within the school day to intervene and enhance learning. This block of time was named What I Need (WIN) time and was used to structure and strengthen the way we responded to our students' needs. We realized we needed the right people, working with the right students, on the right things.

Through the implementation of professional learning communities, which provided a systematic approach to responding to students' needs and creating a culture in which all staff members understood they played a critical role in ensuring high levels of learning for all students, Washington had a dramatic increase in student proficiency on the required state assessments. The results of the Minnesota Comprehensive Assessments from 2007 to 2012 show student proficiency increased by 17 percent in reading and 11 percent in mathematics. There were also tremendous increases in Washington's percentage above the state average. Reading scores grew from 5.9 percent above the state average in 2007 to 15 percent in 2012, while mathematics scores increased from 2.8 percent in 2007 to 13 percent in 2012.

Before, our students were living up to the marginal expectations we had for them and certainly were not learning at high levels. So, we stopped making excuses, shifted the focus to how we could improve our Tier 1 instruction, created structures to intervene, and became transparent with our data and instructional strategies to ensure learning for all students.

Our Process

Washington invested in functioning as a professional learning community by acknowledging the brutal facts of our reality, moving the focus of our work from teaching to learning, and having collaborative teams meet interdependently. We began using data to analyze our strengths and areas for growth as professionals, as well as to determine how our students performed academically. This focus helped us diagnose student needs and led us to begin sharing instructional strategies, with the goal of ensuring high levels of learning for all students.

We defined the shift in focus from teaching to learning as moving away from the traditional structure of the classroom, where the role of the teacher was to dispense knowledge and the role of the student was to act as a sponge and soak it all in. We worked toward becoming a school that valued engaging students in significant learning.

We met collaboratively at a minimum of every other week to compare assessment results. Through these collaborative meetings, teachers analyzed formative assessment data and discovered which areas students were proficient in, where they had additional needs, and where we needed to re-engage. Transforming our school into a PLC helped blur the four walls of the classrooms, making a seismic cultural shift from *my students* to *our students*.

Understanding that our students frequently needed immediate support and that the days of waiting for students to fail were over, we began transforming belief systems and implementing structures designed to become more responsive. For example, instead of placing students in afterschool programs or summer school, where there is little evidence of increased student learning (Hattie, 2009), we created a structure within the school day that responded to what students needed when they needed it.

We kept the formula for learning (Buffum, Mattos, & Weber, 2012) as a focus:

$$\text{Targeted Instruction} + \text{Time} = \text{Learning}$$

It was critical that we create a mandatory time within the school day to intervene and extend learning, so we used WIN time to respond to students in a timely manner to meet their individual needs. Understanding that we communicate our priorities by how we utilize our resources, we redesigned our master schedule around two key structures.

1. Time for teams to collaborate to improve student learning

2. Thirty-minute WIN time for intervention or extension

The creation of the master schedule is absolutely critical to a successful support structure for students. Because it is critical to maximize the instructional minutes throughout the day, the master schedule is in five-minute intervals, and teachers hold firm to these times. In order to align support structures to ensure student learning, the core subjects of mathematics and reading were scheduled for each grade level, as were the times students attend specials (art, music, physical education, and so on), lunch, and recess.

We found that we needed to proactively schedule the specials *and* the core subjects of reading and mathematics in advance in order to maximize support and keep the focus on student learning. Each grade level had, with few exceptions, a sixty-minute block of time for both core reading and mathematics. As part of our structure to intervene and extend students within the school day, each grade level also had, at a minimum, a twenty-five-minute block of WIN time, during which the classroom, intervention, and Title I teachers intervene or extend learning for students, as data indicate. WIN time allows teachers and support staff to collaborate and flexibly group students on a skill-by-skill basis.

Through the creation of WIN time, we adopted and developed a *Pyramid Response to Intervention* (Buffum, Mattos, & Weber, 2009) philosophy and structure, which means we no longer waited for students to fall behind. In addition, after trying to cover all the standards throughout the school year, we adopted Robert Marzano's recommendation that we need to select a few standards to teach in depth rather than teaching everything with the breadth we traditionally had (Scherer, 2001). With this clarity, we began working with the standards as indicated in *Power Standards* (Ainsworth, 2003) to make sure we were focusing on the right work. Careful analysis allowed our collaborative teams to pick a manageable number of standards—eight to ten essential standards in both mathematics and reading. Once we ensured that the standards we were working with had endurance (value beyond a single test date), had leverage (knowledge across multiple disciplines), and provided readiness (student success in the next level), we began teaching a smaller number of standards to mastery, while still exposing students to the other required standards.

The entire process afforded our professionals the opportunity to become more effective with core instruction and gave us the clear understanding of the first critical PLC question (DuFour, DuFour, Eaker, & Many, 2010), What do we expect students to learn? As our teachers became students of the standards, they were able to clarify what students need to know versus what pieces of the standards were simply nice to know. This process allowed us to refine our assessment work to align with our essential standards and became our formative mode for monitoring student learning.

Transparency was critical to our professional work, and we established data walls to allow for this transparency. Lyn Sharratt and Michael Fullan (2012) state that "data walls create visuals of all students' progress and provide a forum for rich conversation among teachers" (p. 78), which is what defines the work of a PLC. Our data walls were in a secure location, renamed the Leadership Room, where the names and pictures of students remained confidential from parents and students. Washington had two separate data walls, one for mathematics and the other for reading.

For mathematics (figure 2.1, page 36), at Washington we placed a photograph of every student on the wall, with a different background color representing each classroom. Each collaborative team determined what mastery looked like after going through the process of analyzing and prioritizing the essential standards and collaboratively establishing common formative assessments. As students achieved mastery in one of these essential standards, the teachers worked together to shift the student pictures vertically up the wall while discussing instructional strategies to ensure all students were learning. This visual representation of student learning was very powerful in that it clearly showed which students were falling behind and which students were meeting or exceeding the standards; this approach helped create a sense of urgency for a timely response.

Figure 2.2 (page 36) shows the reading data wall. Teachers developed a note card for each student currently reading below grade level. Teams coded each card by classroom and placed it on the wall in correlation to the student's level of reading; in addition, each card indicated the current interventions in place, the person responsible for delivering the intervention, and the beginning and ending dates of the intervention. When students progressed to a new reading level, the collaborative team updated and moved the card horizontally along the wall to the appropriate level. When students met grade-level standards, they became data wall graduates, and

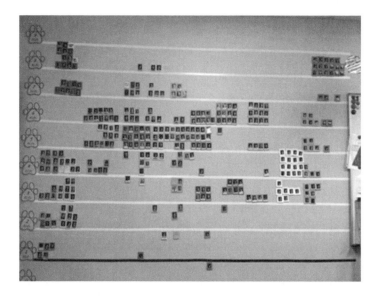

Figure 2.1: Washington mathematics data wall.

Figure 2.2: Washington reading data wall.

we moved their note cards to the wall on the right side of the photograph, but they could be moved back onto the wall if they did not maintain their current trajectory.

The process of physically maneuvering students' cards or pictures on the data walls is an amazing opportunity for teams to celebrate. This type of visual representation also provides the transparency needed for the school community to come together and respond to students who are in dire need of immediate support.

Our Obstacles

As a school, the biggest obstacles we needed to address at Washington were our belief system and our need for additional professional development to better meet our students' needs through core instruction. Our belief system focused on the traditional method of sorting students and acknowledging that certain students just couldn't learn at high levels. While we were frustrated that we weren't able to meet their needs, we tended to accept this as fact and move on to cover the overwhelming amount of content. Historically, as noted, our default setting when meeting a barrier of this nature was to delegate the duty to a paraprofessional, because we believed we weren't skilled enough to meet the student's needs. We also thought the student needed to be tested for a learning disability and hoped he or she would qualify for special education. At the time, Washington was performing below 75 percent proficiency in both reading and mathematics, and we were trying to push students into interventions often taught by an adult less skilled than the classroom teacher. As a staff we began to understand that our students needed additional support and that we didn't believe we knew how to meet their individual needs; we needed to develop a toolbox of instructional strategies to ensure student learning. Austin Buffum, Mike Mattos, and Chris Weber (2009) state, "A school that has significantly less than 75 percent of its students at or above grade-level proficiency has a core program problem, not an intervention problem" (p. 74). As we continued to analyze and question our work, we realized we didn't actually feel like we had the capacity to do the right work up front, that we didn't have the right tools in the toolbox, and that we needed more professional development focused on quality core instruction.

The hard truth is, we generally taught students the same way we were taught as children, and we lived under the assumption that if it was good enough for us, it would be good enough for our students. We soon became aware that the current system and structure of education were developed long ago to sort students and that this archaic system is no longer feasible, and it was our moral obligation to ensure high levels of learning for all.

While our students were achieving at levels approaching 75 percent, this also meant that we were leaving, at a minimum, 25 percent of our students behind. The traditional methods for instruction weren't effective for all of our students, and while not everyone agreed how, we knew we needed to change. We also had to make this dilemma personal. We began having very belief-challenging conversations with prompts such as, "If your child were in that 20–30 percent not making grade-level proficiency, would that be good enough for you as a parent? If that type of instruction and performance isn't acceptable to you as a parent, why would it be acceptable to you as an educator for someone else's child?" Making the conversations real shifted the thinking and made everyone see we needed to improve what we did on a daily basis.

As a faculty, we started investing in ourselves professionally to improve student learning. After participating in a book study of Carol Dweck's (2006) work *Mindset*, teachers began viewing their interactions with students in a different manner. One quote from the book that stuck with a particular teacher was:

> So what should we say when children complete a task—say, math problems— quickly and perfectly? Should we deny them the praise they have earned? Yes. When this happens, I say, "Whoops. I guess that was too easy. I apologize for wasting your time. Let's do something you can really learn from!" (Dweck, 2006, p. 179)

The idea that we were raising our expectations of our students through the interactions we had with them made a significant impact at Washington. This same teacher frequently stated to students in her classroom, "I know you can do it, and I'm going to stick with you until you do." This was a definite shift in mindset, and students responded positively, knowing that our staff wouldn't give up on them.

The staff also became immersed in efforts for improving Tier 1 instructional strategies, primarily through the following collaborative efforts and resources.

- *The Highly Engaged Classroom* **(Marzano & Pickering, 2011):** Teachers participated in a book study focusing on strategies to improve student engagement across all disciplines.

- *Reciprocal Teaching at Work* **(Oczkus, 2010):** Teachers participated in a book study, and staff meetings focused on sharing information and strategies, viewing video of colleagues' instruction, and sharing materials staff members found beneficial to increase student comprehension.

- *Instructional Rounds in Education* **(City, Elmore, Fiarman, & Teitel, 2009):** We developed a process based on the book for teachers to have the opportunity to observe their colleagues practicing their craft. With substitute teachers to cover classrooms, groups of teachers began visiting their colleagues' classrooms for short snippets of time, gathering observations and then moving to additional rooms for more learning opportunities. Following each visit to the classrooms within their own building, the group of teachers would discuss the strategies they found applicable and how that would translate to their own practices. This also became a forum for exchanging ideas and becoming professionally transparent for the benefit of student learning.

- *Enhancing RTI* **(Fisher & Frey, 2010):** Our professional development focused on enhancing the core instruction as an essential component of what we do on a daily basis. The conversations within their collaborative teams focused on the gradual release of responsibility model and the understanding that to be responsive to what students need is at the heart of good instruction.

- *Conferring With Readers* **(Serravallo & Goldberg, 2007):** Instructional staff engaged in professional development on the gradual release of responsibility model and conferring with students. Staff members deepened their understanding of instruction and how to respond to struggling learners in a formative way. This professional development was particularly successful in the area of reading, for which there was an overreliance on packaged intervention programs to "fix" a reading issue. The ability for teachers to handle reading concerns immediately and in real time strengthened their abilities to meet the needs of students and created additional support for students who truly struggle.

Until this point, we were viewing our professional shortcomings through the wrong lens; we had a systematic issue with instruction, and we were trying to fix it through Tier 2 and Tier 3 interventions. Through our learning, it became evident that we didn't have an intervention issue; rather, we had a core instruction or Tier 1 issue. We were trying to intervene for nearly one-third of our student population and were overwhelming our intervention system because of our marginally successful core instruction. Our new focus on raising expectations for our students and ourselves, as well as delivering great Tier 1 instruction from the very beginning, shifted our school from a place of isolation and excuses to a community of professionals ensuring learning for all.

Our Schedule

Anthony Muhammad stressed in his 2009 book *Transforming School Culture* that before we begin making technical changes in our schools, such as altering the schedule, we need to address the school culture (practices, procedures, traditions, and beliefs). As an entire school staff, we had difficult conversations about why our school exists. It can make adults uneasy to hear and accept the brutal and honest truth that the school was not constructed for their employment but was instead established to educate students. Once we were able to agree on the purpose of our school, we were able to move to evaluating our schedules with the intention of ensuring student learning.

The creation of WIN time allowed the staff opportunities to intervene and extend learning. There were three main challenges in carving out this time.

1. Believing all students can learn through our instruction

2. Finding time within the school day

3. Supporting students during this additional time

Finding time within the school day certainly can be a struggle because of the increasing responsibilities placed on schools, which we must acknowledge; but we also have unnecessary practices, procedures, and traditions engrained in the way we operate our schools. Particularly in the primary grades, classrooms use up instructional minutes working on nonacademic items such as learning how to sit properly, lining up in the hallways, and learning how to appropriately use the bathroom facilities and wash hands, to name a few. We recognize these are much-needed practices, but we had to raise our expectations of what students are capable of, continue to work on these pieces throughout the year, and stop using them as excuses for wasting instructional time. We needed to be reflective and ask questions such as the following.

- Are we using our minutes wisely or taking extra minutes to line up?

- Are we picking up our students on time or arriving for the transition late?

- When the bell rings at the beginning of the day, are our students in their seats ready to learn, or do we lose five to ten minutes moving about the room before taking attendance?

- How soon do we finish teaching for the day, or do we utilize every possible minute we have allocated before packing up?

We had to become strategic and intentional about everything we did in order to maximize our learning environment for our students.

Creating a master schedule that would support student learning and teacher collaboration was not a job for the principal alone but instead one for distributed leadership (Abbott & McKnight, 2010). Building the leadership capacity of the school community not only helped staff understand the purpose for the shifts in structure but also began to change the belief systems we once operated under. The development of WIN time, for instance, came with significant hurdles. The Washington leadership team—representing a member from each grade level, a special education teacher, an intervention teacher, and a specialist—determined this was the direction the school needed to go to ensure learning for all. Breaking tradition is a challenging conversation, but through analyzing our current practice, acknowledging our traditions, and questioning our long-established habits, we were able to allocate thirty minutes for WIN time. While this was a great start, the real challenge came with knowing how to support and extend for our students.

During WIN time, we utilized an all-hands-on-deck approach, flooding the grade level with every support person we had at our disposal. We utilized a push-in model as much as possible to take advantage of the precious instructional minutes available. All Title I paraprofessionals, EL teachers, and special education teachers, as well as our interventionists, reported to the classrooms and worked with specific students or groups of students needing support, leading to a true team approach.

When I became principal of Eagle View Elementary in Elko New Market, Minnesota, we used a master schedule to create intervention and extension time similar to the WIN time we implemented at Washington (visit **go.solution-tree.com /rtiatwork** to see a sample schedule). The left side of the master schedule shows each grade level's reading and mathematics blocks, specials, lunch, and WIN time (labeled as reading intervention). Each grade level has a minimum of twenty-five minutes of intervention or extension support except for kindergarten. The reason for the shortened time is twofold. First is the pure challenge of creating a schedule that works for each grade level with the support staff we are afforded. The second reason for a shorter block of time in kindergarten is one of philosophy; we believe kindergarten students should be given the opportunity to be exposed to classroom instruction before intervening, since, for many students, this is their first experience in school.

The right side of the master schedule identifies the schedule of each support person. When compared to the left side of the schedule, it aligns directly with WIN time. This type of alignment allows us to inundate the grade level with support and minimize the amount of time students are removed from their regular classroom for additional support throughout the day, ultimately keeping students from missing other subjects. The schedule does not list special education because it is on more specific individual education plans (IEPs), but most students receive their special education support during WIN time.

WIN time became as important a structure in our schedule as the creation of collaborative team time. It is safe to say that if we hadn't established the belief system and structure of a PLC, WIN time would not have been successful, and we would not have been able to meet the needs of our students to the same degree of success.

Our Identification Process

When identifying student strengths and areas for improvement at Washington, teachers became excellent at analyzing data and understanding that one datum doesn't tell the complete story of what a student can and can't do. We screened all students three times a year in Dynamic Indicators of Basic Early Literacy Skills (DIBELS) and the Northwest Evaluation Association (NWEA) Measures of Academic Progress (MAP) test to identify areas for growth; we then used this information to begin the conversation of student needs. As we grew more sophisticated with our use of common formative assessments (Bailey & Jakicic, 2012), which we developed through establishing learning targets aligned to the state standards, we were able to begin meeting students at their level on a week-to-week, day-to-day, and skill-by-skill basis.

Identifying students who needed additional time and support became a critical piece of our school culture; those students not performing at grade level became known as our WIN kids. To ensure accuracy, it was extremely important for us to use as many data points as possible to determine which students were struggling. This process also helped us flexibly group students for WIN time across the grade level with the support staff available.

Two to three times a year, each classroom teacher met with me, as the principal, about their WIN kids and any other students they were concerned about, whether it was academically, socially, or emotionally. During these meetings, we discussed the support system in place for each student, what his or her daily schedule looked like, and maybe most importantly, how the teacher's collaborative team was working to meet the needs of the student before seeking support outside of their team. Working interdependently to ensure student learning was a critical component to bringing the focus back to great Tier 1 instruction and for us to function as a PLC. If teachers were relying on the intervention system to fix the students before their collaborative team had worked to meet the needs, it was time to refocus and rethink options.

PLCs create opportunities for grade levels to collaborate and respond to all students' needs through instruction. When students struggled to master a learning target within an essential standard, the collaborative team determined who needed additional support and how the collaborative team could respond to meet those needs. The teams worked together to analyze data from their common formative assessments and determined two things.

1. Which students needed interventions because they didn't master the learning target

2. Which teacher was most successful teaching a particular skill identified by the learning target in question, or which staff member was most qualified to support the struggling student

Thus, during WIN time, we flexibly grouped students and matched them with the most highly skilled professional in that particular discipline. If, during WIN time, the students did not master the skill, the team continued to analyze the data to find the best person or strategy to assist the student.

Determining which skills particular students need to learn and who should work with the students isn't something that should be done independently. It is critical for teams to rely on the strengths of one another to best meet students' needs. No single person has all the answers, so to ensure student learning, professionals must engage in meaningful dialogue, rather than monologue. Therefore, the analysis of the common formative assessments drove our dialogue.

Our Monitoring Process

Once collaborative teams established their learning targets and common formative assessments, they created a consistent, aligned method to monitor the learning of all students. Utilizing the MAP and DIBELS testing as benchmark progress checks throughout the year, as well as the team-developed common formative assessments, collaborative teams were able to monitor the progress of their students, determine whether the information was accurate, and then respond accordingly. We understood that the DIBELS assessment, as well as the MAP, would give us an idea of areas to intervene with students, but the development, delivery, and analysis of our common formative assessments between benchmarking periods would be the best diagnostic tool. Through timely formative assessments (at least weekly), we were able to monitor students' mastery of the learning targets and then use the DIBELS and MAP tests to verify if we were meeting our students' needs as compared to national norms.

For instance, second-grade teachers utilize DIBELS data from the initial screening at the beginning of the year to form small groups for their Tier 1 reading block. During instruction, teachers carefully monitored learning and formatively assessed their students to determine what skills students needed additional time and support on. This information would do two things.

1. Help teachers determine how they could flexibly group students for future instruction within the classroom

2. Help teacher teams determine which students needed additional support during WIN time and how they could interdependently support one another as a team and their students

Typically, the second round of DIBELS and MAP testing occurred midyear, which was a wonderful way to either validate our work or let us know we weren't focused on the right things. Because of our proactive stance in developing the learning targets and monitoring the progress of all students on a weekly basis, rarely did we have a surprise during the benchmark-testing window.

The data walls (figures 2.1 and 2.2, page 36) became one way for us to visualize how students were progressing academically, monitor the learning of individual students, view the growth of students in a vertical or horizontal manner, and provide amazing opportunities for collaboration across teams, as well as celebrate as a school. This type of transparency truly removed the barriers of individual classrooms and teams and opened the door to Washington functioning as a PLC focused on ensuring high levels of learning for all students.

Our Revision Process

The development of a problem-solving team (PST) at Washington helped when students weren't progressing at an appropriate rate. It was developed for collaborative teams to turn to for additional support when needed, and it consisted of the principal, school psychologist, school counselor or social worker, instructional coach, and intervention specialist.

Through building-level collaboration, the PST was able to bring a different perspective to student support and the monitoring of student progress. There was little opportunity for students to fall through the cracks thanks to the layered support structure in place; essentially, determining which students received certain interventions was left neither to the classroom teacher nor to the collaborative team alone. The PST met on a weekly basis and served two primary roles.

1. A place to proactively support teams that needed additional ideas for students who weren't progressing at a rate to meet grade-level expectations by the end of the school year

2. A way to determine if individual students weren't progressing and to begin looking into the possibility of a special education assessment

When a student from a specific classroom struggled, we expected the entire collaborative team to work together to meet his or her needs. If the collaborative team had exhausted all ideas, the team came to the PST as a united front for the benefit of all. This was an amazing and powerful change to the previous structure; it mandated proactive collaboration, but it also sent the message that we were in this together, and no teacher would be left on his or her own.

During the PST meeting, we analyzed data, received input, and determined the direction for helping a particular student. When appropriate, we placed students in a specific intervention and put them on a six-week rotation. During the six-week period, the PST and the collaborative team closely monitored the student, documenting any successes or failures. If it was clear that the intervention wasn't meeting the student's needs, a PST member and the collaborative team met to make necessary changes to the instruction or to implement a completely different intervention; we refused to wait for six weeks to change an intervention.

Developing the PST enhanced our ability to create a transparent culture that stresses the importance of relying on one another to ensure student learning for all. Working collaboratively, sharing effective strategies, engaging in dialogue when we didn't have a solution, and moving our focus from teaching to learning provided opportunities to our students that we wouldn't have been able to provide previously.

Our Extension Process

Initially, we primarily used WIN time to intervene for students who were falling behind and who we struggled to consistently meet the needs of throughout the day. Once we secured an effective process for those who struggled, we were able to also provide extensions for students who were craving to be challenged.

The professional development that teachers received on reading focused on coaching students to fill the gaps they had as readers but also to get the students to the next reading level and continue to grow. Teachers created student book clubs and began implementing ideas from resources such as *Reciprocal Teaching at Work* (Oczkus, 2010) to have students work interdependently and use high-level questioning and discussion techniques as they moved through the book. This approach became a great avenue for extending student learning. Students were also able to access mobile computer labs and tablets to work independently on skills in both mathematics and reading through different standards-aligned programs. Thus, individualized goal setting became an important piece of the core instruction; it translated extremely well to WIN time, when students worked to grow as readers beyond their present level. In fact, many of our students were able to move to reading levels we were never able to coach them to before, because our structure didn't allow for this type of individualized monitoring and instruction.

Washington began to realize that the work we did to learn and grow professionally not only raised its basic proficiency on the state assessments but also gave students what they needed when they needed it. Great core instruction opened opportunities to do things we would not have been able to accomplish previously. By reducing the number of students who needed interventions, because we taught the content more effectively the first time around, we were able to utilize our resources (people and materials) to develop activities and projects designed to engage students and truly make school more enjoyable for everyone involved.

Our Celebrations

Many of the changes implemented at Washington didn't take place immediately but occurred after several years of working to establish a PLC culture at the school. Attempting to put this structure in place in the very first year would have been quite challenging. It took time to convince people that what they do as educators truly makes a difference, but it proved itself true as they began tasting success. It was critical that we first became proficient in the way we functioned as a PLC before we were able to reach the levels of success for our students.

The teachers at Washington worked harder than they ever had, and it was taxing; we had to find ways to get through those challenging times when it felt like a person couldn't do one more thing. We began focusing on ways to celebrate the little things. We had the typical types of celebrations—holiday parties, afterschool gatherings, and so on—but we also chose to celebrate what was happening in our school and celebrate one another.

A simple but effective celebration took place during our building leadership team (BLT) meetings. All collaborative teams were required to submit an action plan of the work they were doing to ensure student learning. During our BLT meetings, we shared our action plans with the group. At first, there were many uneasy feelings and a fear that we weren't doing things correctly, but as time passed, the teams started to see the amazing things their colleagues were doing to ensure student learning and began acknowledging the great work of their peers. They also began borrowing ideas from one another, and as Charles Caleb Colton (1837) once said, "Imitation is the sincerest form of flattery" (p. 113). People appreciated the work of their colleagues and felt appreciated when others began asking questions and using the ideas that had been successful with their students.

Students were also working at levels they hadn't previously reached. We needed to keep their spirits and motivation up, so we celebrated their work by installing television monitors in the hallways. When students achieved a new level in reading, had amazing growth in their assessments, or were simply doing the right things behaviorally, we photographed them and displayed it on the monitors for everyone to see. There may be nothing more exciting to a student than to see his or her image on the television, while at the same time being acknowledged for his or her hard work and dedication for everyone to see. Through independent goal setting around reading levels and learning targets in mathematics, students became more invested in their own learning and were eager to share their successes.

As a principal, my conversations while visiting classrooms or walking down the hall completely changed and also became opportunities for celebrations with students. A student would say, "Mr. Remmert, I moved to a new reading level today," or "I have almost mastered counting money." Staff members would frequently stop me to share their success with a particular student or ask me if I'd visited the data wall lately to see the latest movement. The change in culture was remarkable, but it did not happen overnight or without growing pains.

By looking in the mirror instead of through the window and being transparent about how we were meeting the students' needs, our students achieved at levels we couldn't have imagined a few short years before. Through the amazing dedication of a school staff that understood we had a moral obligation to ensure high levels of learning for everyone, we created a school climate in which students would not be allowed to fail.

The process of meeting every student's needs never ends. It was a six-year learning curve at Washington, and there still is much to learn and be done. Functioning as a PLC means you never arrive at the finish line—there is always room for improvement. Every school year brings new staff, new students, and new challenges, and we must always focus on continuous improvement to ensure student learning for all.

References and Resources

Abbott, C. J., & McKnight, K. (2010). Developing instructional leadership through collaborative learning. *Journal of Scholarship and Practice, 7*(2), 20–26.

Ainsworth, L. (2003). *Power standards: Identifying the standards that matter the most.* Denver, CO: Advanced Learning Press.

Allington, R. L. (2008). *What really matters in response to intervention: Research-based designs.* Boston: Pearson.

Bailey, K., & Jakicic, C. (2012). *Common formative assessment: A toolkit for professional learning communities at work.* Bloomington, IN: Solution Tree Press.

Buffum, A., Mattos, M., & Weber, C. (2009). *Pyramid response to intervention: RTI, professional learning communities, and how to respond when kids don't learn.* Bloomington, IN: Solution Tree Press.

Buffum, A., Mattos, M., & Weber, C. (2012). *Simplifying response to intervention: Four essential guiding principles.* Bloomington, IN: Solution Tree Press.

City, E. A., Elmore, R. F., Fiarman, S. E., & Teitel, L. (2009). *Instructional rounds in education: A network approach to improving teaching and learning.* Cambridge, MA: Harvard Education Press.

Colton, C. C. (1837). *Lacon: Or, many things in few words: Addressed to those who think.* London: Longman, Orme, Brown, Green, & Longmans.

DuFour, R., DuFour, R., Eaker, R., & Many, T. W. (2010). *Learning by doing: A handbook for professional learning communities at work* (2nd ed.). Bloomington, IN: Solution Tree Press.

DuFour, R., & Fullan, M. (2013). *Cultures built to last: Systemic PLCs at work.* Bloomington, IN: Solution Tree Press.

Dweck, C. (2006). *Mindset: The new psychology of success.* New York: Ballantine Books.

Edmonds, R. (1979, October). Effective schools for the urban poor. *Educational Leadership, 23.*

Fisher, D., & Frey, N. (2010). *Enhancing RTI: How to ensure success with effective classroom instruction and intervention.* Alexandria, VA: Association for Supervision and Curriculum Development.

Hattie, J. A. C. (2009). *Visible learning: Synthesis of over 800 meta-analyses relating to achievement.* New York: Routledge.

Hattie, J. A. C. (2012). *Visible learning for teachers: Maximizing impact on learning.* New York: Routledge.

Marzano, R. J., & Pickering, D. (2011). *The highly engaged classroom.* Bloomington, IN: Marzano Research Laboratory.

Muhammad, A. (2009). *Transforming school culture: How to overcome staff division.* Bloomington, IN: Solution Tree Press.

Oczkus, L. D. (2010). *Reciprocal teaching at work: Powerful strategies and lessons for improving reading comprehension* (2nd ed.). Newark, DE: International Reading Association.

Scherer, M. (2001). How and why standards can improve student achievement: A conversation with Robert J. Marzano. *Educational Leadership, 59*(1), 14–18.

Serravallo, J., & Goldberg, G. (2007). *Conferring with readers: Supporting each student's growth and independence.* Portsmouth, NH: Heinemann.

Sharratt, L., & Fullan, M. (2012). *Putting FACES on the data: What great leaders do!* Thousand Oaks, CA: Corwin Press.

Wiliam, D. (2011). *Embedded formative assessment.* Bloomington, IN: Solution Tree Press.

 **Brian K. Butler** is the principal of Mason Crest Elementary in Fairfax County, Virginia. Mason Crest is a Title I school with over thirty-two languages spoken. Brian is the former principal of Mount Eagle Elementary School and former assistant principal of Lemon Road Elementary, both in Fairfax County. He is also a former counselor, physical education teacher, and athletic coach.

To be an effective administrator, Brian draws from strong beliefs in effective communication, servant leadership, and team and capacity building. In his roles as a school administrator, a counselor, a teacher, and an athletic coach, he has emphasized the power of teamwork over the success of individuals.

During his tenure in Fairfax, Brian has been named as a finalist for Principal of the Year, and he received the Nancy F. Sprague Leadership Award, a commendation of excellence for being a nominee for Fairfax County's Outstanding First-Year Principal.

Brian played professional basketball in the European League as well as Division I basketball at The George Washington University, where he earned a bachelor's degree in speech communications. He earned a teacher's certification in physical education and a master's degree in school counseling, both from George Mason University, and an administrative endorsement from the University of Virginia. Brian is also an educational consultant, as well as a Solution Tree Associate. He and his wife Kathleen have two amazing daughters, Alison and Emily.

To learn more about Brian's work, follow @bkbutler_brian on Twitter.

To book Brian K. Butler for professional development, contact pd@solution-tree .com.

Collaborating in the Core

Brian K. Butler

As we review this chapter, two words stand out in our minds—*intentional* and *inclusive*. Mason Crest Elementary School in Annandale, Virginia, utilizes a very intentional program of professional development to ensure that all teachers continue to learn, have a common vocabulary, and have common expectations. The process of developing the school schedule was very intentional (built around three non-negotiables) as well as inclusive (created in total collaboration with the staff). The use of specialists and their support of the school's overall mission are also very intentional and inclusive.

It should also be noted that the school has an equally intentional focus on the use of data, both formal and informal. In addition to frequent data discussions after major assessments, the school uses substitutes to release teachers once every six weeks for a more extensive three-and-a-half-hour data discussion that focuses on progress monitoring and follow-up planning for individual students. Mason Crest is equally intentional and inclusive in its approach to adult learning, through co-teaching, observation, and reflection. As a result, we understand why teachers frequently remind themselves, "The answer is in the room."

My professional life changed the day I walked into Carolyn Miller's office to interview for the job of assistant principal. Although I had been in education for over sixteen years, I did not know of the PLC at Work process until that day. In the interview, she asked me a number of questions about working together with others, sharing practices, being transparent, and focusing on the learning of both the adults and the students. All of those were very important, but the statement that stuck out to me the most was this:

> My ideal school is to be able to open the front door and have my grandchildren, Justin and Ashley, walk into any classroom and choose their teacher. And I should be able to feel comfortable with whomever they may choose. (C. Miller, personal communication, July 20, 2004)

Fortunately she hired me, and I immediately came to know such a school and quickly understood why she made that statement. I have since been privileged enough to have served as the principal of two Title I schools. If any school wishes to become a high-performing PLC at Work, the responsibility to ensure that every single student learns at high levels cannot be placed on the shoulders of an isolated teacher. To be frank, that practice is a recipe for failure. It has to be a coordinated, purposeful, and embedded process of adult professional development and learning.

Creating and sustaining a culture of collaboration does not happen by accident. In order to ensure high-quality Tier 1 core instruction, the staff at Mason Crest participate in multifaceted, ongoing, job-embedded professional learning and development in mathematics and reading. If our school's mission is to ensure high levels of learning for *all* students and adults, adults must be provided with the training to perform collectively at high levels. As Anthony Muhammad (2009) writes, "Educators who adopt egalitarian idealism as the center of their educational paradigm must cultivate professionalism as well. In order to achieve an end, a person must have conviction, but that conviction must be buttressed with skill" (p. 41). A major part of realizing our vision and honoring our mission is learning together. As a staff, we take on-site courses, including a mathematics course and a balanced literacy course, to build common knowledge, common language, and common expectations around how we plan to move forward in a clear, unified way. These courses are incredibly helpful and are truly our anchors, but they are only the tip of the iceberg in regard to professional development at Mason Crest. We take our cue from Richard DuFour, Rebecca DuFour, Robert Eaker, and Tom Many (2010) by focusing the bulk of our ongoing professional development on learning by doing through grade-level collaborative team meetings. These teams are made up of classroom teachers and support staff working with students at each grade level. The focus of this collaborative time may change, but team members are collectively responsible for learning together in order to support Tier 1 core instruction for all of our students.

So how do we ensure high-quality Tier 1 core instruction for *all* students through focused, ongoing, job-embedded professional learning and development? This chapter will highlight the following four components.

1. Master schedule creation

2. Common knowledge, common language, and common expectations in literacy and numeracy

3. The purposes of Mason Crest grade-level team meetings (planning for learning, data discussions with progress monitoring, and co-teaching, observations, and reflections)

4. Deeper ongoing learning

Master Schedule Creation

As DuFour and DuFour (2012) write:

> If principals hope to foster a collaborative culture, it is imperative that they create schedules that provide time for teachers to co-labor with their teammates. . . . [They] must be creative in finding ways to provide time for teachers to collaborate while students are at school without increasing costs or losing significant amounts of instructional time. (p. 19)

In order for our teams to have adequate instructional time to embed targeted small-group instruction into daily plans and to plan, analyze data, and learn from each other, there are specific structures in the school's master schedule that need to be in place. These structures provide uninterrupted time for teams to do their work.

In August, before the school year began, we invited teachers to participate in developing the instructional block schedule. We invited all teachers to participate but asked that we have at least one representative from special education, English for speakers of other languages (ESOL), physical education, art, music, library, advanced academics, and technology, as well as our content specialists (reading and mathematics). From that open invitation, we had about thirty teachers come together to work on the schedule. This diverse group provided varying points of view and allowed us to think creatively and flexibly. It also resulted in a schedule that was supported throughout the school. Before we began the work, we outlined some non-negotiable components. These non-negotiables have their foundation in district requirements for instructional time but were enhanced for our school and the needs of our students and staff. All grade levels *must* have the following.

- Two hours of daily uninterrupted language arts instruction
- Ninety minutes of daily mathematics instruction
- One hour of common planning time at least four days a week

These uninterrupted blocks of instructional time allow teacher teams to work with small groups of students who may need additional time and targeted support or opportunities to extend learning if they have already mastered an idea or concept. Therefore, we do not have a separate intervention or extension time built into our schedule. Another goal and challenge to this process was to stagger the instructional time blocks in order to maximize the use of support staff working in multiple grade levels. Another struggle we encountered was the timing of the specials block so that our students with special needs could be included in their age-appropriate physical education, library, art, and music classes. Throughout the process, we made compromises to ensure that the structure of our instructional block schedule supported our mission and vision. See figure 3.1 for an example of our schedule.

The specials section on the schedule depicts the time our students go to physical education, art, music, and the library. This is our common planning time for each grade-level team. This schedule would not be possible without the full support of our specialist team, made up of the librarian and physical education, music, and art teachers, who understand how critical they are to the overall mission of our school. Not only is the content of their specialty area important to the students, but they understand how important the structure of the schedule is in allowing adult learning in our school to occur. Finding time in the day for the specialist team to meet is an ongoing challenge. In 2013, they had a common planning time each week to meet as a team; however, in 2014, their built-in meeting time was limited to time that they scheduled on their own.

The process of arranging specials in each grade level to allow classroom teachers one hour of common planning time requires several days of meetings and working through different ideas in order for the schedule to work. Our team of specialists is a true example of *where there is a will, there is a way*. Although we encountered obstacles, we all had the can-do attitude that helped us problem solve and move forward. At one point, we hit a road block, and our music teacher, Celia, said, "Let's start over!" Instead of giving up and saying, "This isn't possible," we persevered until a solution was found. In the end, Celia said:

> I am always honored to be a part of the master schedule group. Allowing us to create the entire school's schedule confirms your belief in the importance of specialist teachers and makes me feel like I'm integral in the school's community. (C. Boltz, personal communication, October 15, 2013)

Ultimately, we created a system for all students to have access to these specialty areas and to optimize the use of the instructional time available to students and teachers throughout the day.

With this schedule, the structure is in place for teams to do their work. Building and sustaining the culture of collaboration comes with doing the work and building common language, knowledge, and expectations.

Time	K	1	2	3	4	5
9:00						
9:15	Morning Meeting				Specials 9:15–10:15	Word Study 9:15–9:25
9:25	Reading 9:30–10:50	Science or Social Studies 9:30–10:00	Mathematics 9:30–11:00	Science or Social Studies 9:30–10:15		Reading 9:25–10:35
9:35						
9:45						
9:55						
10:05						
10:15		Writing 10:00–10:40		Specials 10:15–11:15	Mathematics 10:15–11:45	
10:25						
10:35						Writing 10:35–11:25
10:45						
10:55	Writing 10:50–11:30	Reading 10:40–12:15				
11:05			Lunch 11:00/05–11:30/35			
11:15						
11:25				Mathematics 11:15–12:45		Specials 11:25–12:25
11:35	Lunch 11:30/35–12:00/05		Recess 11:35–11:55			
11:45					Lunch 11:45/50–12:15/20	
11:55			Writing or Word Study 11:55–12:55			
12:05	Recess 12:05–12:25					
12:15		Lunch 12:15/20–12:45/50				
12:25	Transition and Bathroom Break				Recess 12:20–12:40	Lunch 12:25/30–12:55/1:00
12:35						
12:45				Lunch 12:45/50–1:15/20	Word Study 12:45–12:55	
12:55	Mathematics 12:35–1:55	Recess 12:50–1:10	Specials 12:55–1:55		Reading 12:55–2:10	Recess 1:00–1:20
1:05						
1:15						
1:25				Recess 1:20–1:40		Science or Social Studies 1:25–2:15
1:35						
1:45				Word Study 1:40–1:50		
1:55	Specials 1:55–2:55	Mathematics 1:15–2:45	Reading 1:55–3:15	Writing 1:50–2:35		
2:05						
2:15						Mathematics 2:15–3:50
2:25					Writing 2:10–2:55	
2:35				Reading 2:35–3:50		
2:45		Transition and Bathroom Break				
2:55	Science or Social Studies 2:55–3:50	Specials 2:55–3:55			Science or Social Studies 2:55–3:50	
3:05						
3:15			Science or Social Studies 3:15–3:50			
3:25						
3:35						
3:45						

Figure 3.1: Sample Mason Crest instructional blocks.

Common Knowledge, Common Language, and Common Expectations in Literacy and Numeracy

Our first step in developing common knowledge, common language, and common expectations was to create a literacy course and a mathematics course. As part of our collective commitments, the entire staff agreed to participate in both courses:

> In order to honor and advance our shared purpose, vision, and goals, we pledge to honor the following collective commitments. We will:
>
> - Be positive contributing members of the schoolwide team as we work interdependently to achieve shared goals and demonstrate mutual accountability.
>
> - Identify and teach the agreed-upon essential outcomes, adhere to the curriculum pacing established by the team and help our students discover what they can do with that knowledge.
>
> - Create common formative assessments and administer them according to the team's agreed-upon timeline.
>
> - Use the results from our common assessments to improve our individual and collective practice and to meet the needs of all of our students.
>
> - Contribute to an effective system of intervention and extension.
>
> - Agree to a common language about behavioral expectations, model that behavior, and consistently reinforce our expectations for all of our students.
>
> - Establish a positive relationship with each student.
>
> - Engage in open frequent two-way communication among all stakeholders, provide families with ongoing information about their children, and offer specific ideas and materials to help families become full partners in the ongoing education of their children.
>
> - Embrace shared responsibilities and help others grow in their leadership responsibilities.
>
> - Contribute to a culture of celebration by acknowledging the efforts and achievements of our students and colleagues as we continually strive for even greater success.
>
> - Consider all points of view and come to our work each day as the best versions of ourselves.
>
> - Examine all of our practices in light of their impact on learning. We will continue to refine our literacy and math instructional practice by using a balanced literacy and the investigations math approach. All general education, special education, reading and ESOL teachers will be Balanced Literacy and Developmental Reading Assessment (DRA2) trained, will engage in professional development regarding the Mathematics Investigations curriculum as well as Advanced Academics. (Mason Crest Elementary School, 2014)

The mathematics and language arts courses each consisted of five three-hour sessions that took place in our school. We scheduled some of these sessions during the preservice week before the school year started, and the others were scheduled on Mondays during our countywide professional development time. These courses communicated our philosophy of teaching and learning while introducing key best practices common to both language arts and mathematics. Some of these practices included setting up the classroom environment to allow for teacher-led guided instruction, cooperative learning experiences, and purposeful student communication. Our focus was to create an environment that was student centered rather than teacher centered so students have the ability to internalize their learning, explain their thinking, and learn from each other. We also spent time introducing the tools and resources we would be using throughout the year.

The literacy course focused learning around the components of balanced literacy (Harvey & Goudvis, 2005), which included:

- Delineating shared reading, guided reading, and independent reading

- Creating a literacy-rich classroom environment

- Understanding grade-level standards in order to design a pacing guide for focus lessons

- Planning for and managing guided reading groups based on student needs (Serafini, 2001)

- Holding students accountable for independent reading

The mathematics course focused learning around the pedagogy, content, and components of a mathematics workshop (Van de Walle, Karp, & Bay-Williams, 2012), which included:

- Creating the physical and cultural classroom environment

- Identifying facilitation techniques

- Defining formative and summative assessment

- Writing and evaluating effective tasks

Since Mason Crest's literacy and mathematics specialists taught these courses, this foundation was continually built on in team meetings.

The Purposes of Mason Crest Grade-Level Team Meetings

There are three main categories of team meetings that occur on a regularly scheduled basis for different purposes at Mason Crest: (1) planning for learning, an instructional delivery model; (2) data discussions with progress monitoring; and (3) co-teaching, observations, and reflections. Our language arts and mathematics specialists facilitate our meetings. If a school does not have a specialist to facilitate the meetings, team members can rotate facilitation duties. It is important to ensure that the team understands and adheres to a focus on the PLC critical questions. Although we do have a specialist who facilitates our various grade-level mathematics and language arts team meetings, the members of the team all participate, share ideas and resources, and pitch in to make products that the team will need to accomplish their work.

Planning for Learning: An Instructional Delivery Model

For mathematics planning meetings and language arts planning meetings, each grade-level team meets once a week with the respective content-area specialist. These planning meetings are a cornerstone of learning by doing and are therefore an expectation for all grade-level teams. They are attended by grade-level classroom teachers, ESOL teachers, special education teachers, technology specialists, and advanced academics resource teachers, who support that team. Teams leave the meeting with at least one week's worth of lessons with differentiated resources, strategies, and plans for assessment. Brief conversations around a best practice, article, or video occur during these meetings in order to build shared knowledge around a strategy or resource.

We know of schools that accomplish the same goal without content-area specialists. As noted previously, these school teams share the wealth by having grade-level team members take turns facilitating the planning meetings. In fact, we do not have content-area specialists in social studies and science, so the classroom teachers divide roles as to who will be responsible for what parts of these particular planning meetings. It may take a little more time without a content-area specialist to facilitate, but it is definitely doable. Because we are a Title I school, we have some funds available to pay for these positions. We believe it is important for schools to focus on the human resources that they do have and not allow what they do not have to derail this process. It can be done but may take a bit more creativity. Our motto when confronted with any kind of challenge is, "The answer is in the room."

Lessons are developed based on our state standards, county curriculum, and pacing guides. The team identifies the content that is essential for all students to learn (Marzano, 2003) and commits to teaching it. All teams use a common lesson-planning format for every content area. Lessons begin with a link to prior knowledge, followed by a focus lesson delivering new content, guided practice differentiated for student needs, and a reflection about the new content learned and a connection to future learning.

The LEARN Lesson Plan Model (Link, Engage and Educate, Active Learning, Reflect, Now and Then) is a way for teachers to structure lesson plans. It was developed by Fairfax County Public Schools in 2005 and draws from research collected by John Bransford and the National Research Council (2000) and from Robert Marzano, Debra Pickering, and Jane Pollock (2001). Primarily, it aims to connect new knowledge to prior knowledge, increase students' metacognition, and increase their ability to transfer knowledge to novel situations. See figure 3.2 (page 60) for a sample LEARN template.

During common planning time, we create plans using a tool called Microsoft OneNote—a virtual binder that stores our collection of lessons and allows multiple users to access our plans. As we develop documents, resources, tables, charts, and visuals for each lesson, we save them in a shared folder. They are linked into OneNote's virtual binder to ensure all team members have easy access to the curriculum that they committed to deliver. This archived collection gives us the ability to refine lessons from year to year. For example, after reflecting on past plans, we realized that in order for our English learners to access the grade-level content, we needed to discuss and set a language goal emphasizing content-area vocabulary within our lessons.

Collaborative lesson planning allows us to differentiate instruction by creating and utilizing resources such as leveled texts, tiered tasks, effective questioning techniques, and instructional and student choice menus to meet the needs of all of our students. We strategically group and, at times, flexibly group students across classrooms. We explicitly discuss structures we introduced during the language arts and mathematics courses to allow teachers to successfully manage the classroom while working with small groups of students.

During this planning, teams also work to create common formative assessments based on the skills and strategies teachers covered during the lessons. These assessments can include exit tickets, checklists, rubrics, and end-of-unit tests. Teachers give these assessments frequently and use them to gather evidence *for* student learning in order to make instructional decisions throughout the unit of study (Stiggins & Chappuis, 2012).

Many people ask, "How can this all be accomplished in a one-hour planning session?" As Jenn, our mathematics specialist, said:

> I was in a meeting the other day, and it was clear that a few of the teachers not only didn't know some of the content, but they were really not confident in what they were about to teach. So what is the solution? Do some math problems on Monday with the whole team. Make a plan to fill out the co-teaching planning guide. Be encouraging in meetings and accept that we have to support each other to get better. (J. Deinhart, personal communication, October 21, 2013)

Link
The teacher begins the lesson by making a connection to recent learning, something the students learned yesterday, the day before, or within the last week.
(Three to five minutes)
Engage and Educate (Focus Lesson)
The teacher presents a whole-group lesson based on the school system's program of studies, which is aligned to the state standards and student assessment information. The learning objective or outcome is stated. Teachers plan these lessons beginning with the end in mind.
(Ten to twenty minutes)

Active Learning (Small-Group Time)		
Small-Group Lesson	*Small-Group Lesson*	*Small-Group Lesson*

Reflection (Sharing)
The teacher facilitates a brief discussion about what the students learned based on the stated outcomes. The teacher might ask questions, or students may share in pairs or write in journals.
(Five to ten minutes)
Now and Then
The teacher ends the lesson by making a connection to long-term learning. This is something that the students learned last month or before and may connect to other content areas. The teacher may also make a connection to what the students will learn tomorrow.
(Three to four minutes)

Source: Adapted from Fairfax County Public Schools, 2005.

Figure 3.2: LEARN—An instructional delivery model.

A great deal of work can be done when all team members participate and contribute to the discussion and workload. It takes time to learn mathematics and literacy content and pedagogy, and the teachers' learning continues to build over the course of weeks, months, and even years. Week by week, teachers produce lesson plans that support the needs of all learners while collecting data on student learning. They then use these data to discuss progress. See figures 3.3 and 3.4 (pages 62–63) for examples of a week's worth of lesson plans for both mathematics and language arts, each developed in a one-hour planning meeting.

Data Discussions With Progress Monitoring

During data discussions, we are constantly looking at both formal and informal assessment data. Stacey, our reading specialist, shared that in reading,

> informal data include exit tickets, running records, anecdotal notes, verbal questioning, checklists and some of the formal data we collect and use are Developmental Reading Assessment (DRA), DRA progress monitoring, Developmental Spelling Assessment (DSA), division-wide quarterly tests, team developed common assessments which are a mix of multiple choice items and "show your work" items which are all based on standards taught, as well as the use of rubrics. (S. Duff, personal communication, October 12, 2013)

Similarly, Jenn shared that in mathematics,

> we administer preassessments (usually fewer than ten questions) to give us information about what our students already know and where the biggest misconceptions are before we start a unit. We give exit tickets throughout the course of a unit that take on a variety of forms: tasks, multiple-choice questions, or even a recording sheet from a game. These help us gauge student understanding so that we can adjust our teaching practices and form targeted groups for guided instruction. We give performance assessments that are more open tasks. Students can use a variety of strategies to show their thinking, and there is often more than one correct response. We use a rubric to score this type of assessment. Our end-of-unit assessments mirror the test language, format, and rigor of the end-of-the-year state assessments. This assessment is cumulative, so each unit assessment also includes question items from previously taught units. This allows us to reassess when we have provided additional time and support but also helps us keep students from losing content knowledge over the course of the year. (J. Deinhart, personal communication, October 15, 2013)

We have two scheduled opportunities for teams to work through an in-depth data discussion and, as a result, make plans for student learning.

	Day 1	Day 2	Day 3	Day 4	Day 5
Objective	Place value through the 100,000s	Subtraction with regrouping	Comparing larger numbers	Rounding numbers through the 1,000s	Rounding numbers through the 1,000s
Link to Prior Knowledge	Build and name a model with base ten blocks.	Which place value did we need to regroup?	Look at real-life visuals of things in 100,000s.	Show a model of 239,472.	Mix and match word form with standard form using the SMART Board.
Focus Lesson	Build numbers in 10,000s and 100,000s using the SMART Board.	How can we see what is happening in the algorithm using base ten blocks?	Name this number: Model with pictures of larger numbers on the posters using the SMART Board.	Rounding on a number line: Which number is it closer to?	What are all the numbers that round to 3,400 when rounded to the nearest hundred? Sentence frames: This number is between _____ and _____. This number rounds to _____.
Active Learning	Two-day workshop Modeling large numbers: • Stamping numbers • GLOG for making numbers • Base ten riddles Teacher group— Differentiated guided instruction Subtraction with regrouping		Comparing numbers: • Naming numbers in more than one way • Building the bigger number	Must Do: Rounding whole numbers Choices: • Mix and match • Number-line game	Must Do: Rounding task Choices: • GLOG • Mix and match • Number-line game
Reflection	Exit ticket: Solve number riddle, and recognize a model.	Can you say this number in more than one way? Can we build it, draw it, and say it?	Exit ticket: Compare large numbers.	Name at least three numbers that would round to 360 when rounded to the nearest 10.	Exit ticket: Round numbers using test-like questions.

Figure 3.3: Sample weeklong mathematics lesson plan.

	Day 1	**Day 2**	**Day 3**	**Day 4**	**Day 5**
Objective	Readers use context clues in fiction to figure out what words mean.	Readers use context clues in nonfiction to figure out what words mean.	Readers use context clues in functional formats to figure out what words mean.	Readers can visualize to help them understand what a word means.	Readers think about how strategies help them as they read.
Link to Prior Knowledge	Review sorting of noun, verb, and adjective.	Make a t-chart for fiction and nonfiction.	Review how functional formats are organized differently than other texts.	Review strategies for figuring out words.	Show one sentence and practice visualizing to understand the meaning.
Focus Lesson	Shared reading of a fiction text using context clues Model of using context clues—highlight the use of parts of speech	Shared reading of a nonfiction text using context clues Model of context clues in informational texts	Shared reading of a functional format using context clues Model of context clues in real-world texts	Modeled use of visualization to help you figure out what a word means Anchor chart: I see I hear I feel I smell I taste What I already know	Modeled response for visualizing Sentence frames: I read _____. I visualized _____. This helped me because _____.
Active Learning	Guided reading groups Response day! In their response, underline the noun, circle the verb, and put a box around an adjective.	Guided reading groups Give students a nonfiction passage that is on their reading level.	Guided reading groups Give students functional formats and have them use the context clue chart.	Guided reading groups or independent reading	Students complete reading response. Guided reading groups or independent reading
Reflection	Exit ticket: Give students a sentence to check knowledge of noun, verb, and adjective.	3-2-1 Three words you figured out Two pieces of evidence you used One meaning you figured out	Students share their anchor charts on the SMART document camera.	Students share a word they figured out by visualizing in their independent reading.	Students share their reading response with a partner or with a small group.

Figure 3.4: Sample weeklong language arts lesson plan.

1. One-hour meetings in which teams look at recent common assessment data

    - These are scheduled as needed on Monday afternoons during our professional development time in addition to our one-hour team meeting times scheduled during the school day.

    - All teachers supporting the grade level are present.

    - During these meetings, we adjust student groupings for targeted instruction.

2. Three-and-a-half-hour meetings after a major mathematics or language arts assessment

    - These are scheduled every six weeks.

    - These meetings take place during the school day, and substitute teachers provide coverage for classroom teachers.

    - All teachers supporting the grade level are present (classroom teachers, content specialists, special education, and ESOL teachers).

    - During these meetings, we regroup students for targeted supports and extensions, and refine teachers' schedules to reflect the new student groupings.

Progress-monitoring meetings are part of the three-and-a-half-hour data discussions. During this portion of the meeting, we document each student's small-group supports and create an individual plan and goal for the student. The goal is to be reached within the next six weeks. At the end of six weeks, we review each student's goal and revise the plan.

Jenn explains data discussions and progress monitoring as follows:

> We have a data discussion meeting roughly once a month on Monday afternoons to discuss common assessment data and to think through what our kids know, understand, and are able to do based on their results on exit tickets, checklists, rubrics, and unit tests. In addition, every six weeks we have meetings to discuss data from larger scale assessments which leads into a progress-monitoring discussion where we take a deeper look at student progress, set goals, and develop individual plans for each child. For each of these data discussions, we start the meeting using a data analysis protocol (Marshall, 2009). The protocol will help us think through the first common assessment that the students will be taking. The first assessment will be given on October 4th and we will have a meeting within a few days of the assessment in order for the data to be useful. When we meet, we will take the results of the assessment and, through the use of the protocol, answer the following questions. (J. Deinhart, personal communication, October 15, 2013)

First, teams must answer the following three questions.

1. Which of our students need additional time and support to achieve at or above proficiency on an essential learning?

   List the students who were not proficient and areas in which they struggled.

2. What is our plan to enrich and extend the learning for students who are highly proficient?

   List the students whose learning needs to be extended based on consistently high scores on varied assessments, and develop a plan to address these needs.

3. What is an area in which my students struggled?

   Look for trends in your own class data to identify objectives where student performance was less than 70 percent. Ask teammates who had success in some of these areas to share strategies and resources that were effective in helping students achieve.

   If you identify a grade-level weakness, reflect on the students' misconceptions by analyzing their work.

Once we have answered these questions, we create an instructional plan that allows us to revisit the identified objectives while still moving on to the next unit of study. We choose resources or create new ones that will give our students additional practice and, in some cases, a different approach to learning the material. We also allocate time in the upcoming unit to spiral back to objectives that need reteaching. This can take the form of an entire lesson or as tasks and games that can be incorporated into other lessons. Additionally, we create three grouping scenarios that support our students' learning needs.

1. **Purposeful partners:** Create an opportunity to communicate with a peer during classroom discussions, problem-solving activities, and games.

2. **Homogeneous groups:** Allow teachers to address a specific skill during guided instruction.

3. **Heterogeneous groups:** Provide students with a rich cooperative learning experience when a teacher is not directly involved with the instruction.

The final step is to record our plans in the progress-monitoring notes for each individual student. These notes identify the following.

- Teachers providing additional support on the targeted skill that the student needs

- Number of minutes and times per week the student will receive guided instruction

- Teacher-to-student ratio of the group

- Duration in weeks that we will give this support

- Individual student goal and the assessments the teacher used to monitor and measure student progress

See figure 3.5 for a sample mathematics progress-monitoring chart.

The literacy team takes a similar approach to data discussions with progress monitoring. Stacey explains the process that grade-level teams work through to group students and develop individual instructional plans:

> During progress monitoring, the team analyzes reading assessments to determine an instructional reading level as well as a focus for instruction for each student. Then they make groupings for guided reading. The diagram [figure 3.6, page 68] is an example of a third-grade teacher's guided reading schedule. The shape of the box indicates students who are reading below, at, or above grade level. The below-grade-level students are met with more often and in a smaller student to teacher ratio. At times, students are flexibly grouped between classrooms in order to provide them with the group that best fits their needs, as shown by the gray shading of their box. This also allows teachers to meet with more groups rather than each teacher meeting with a student individually or in a group of two because they have no one else that has similar needs. (S. Duff, personal communication, October 15, 2013)

The Developmental Reading Assessment (DRA) is an assessment that analyzes students' fluency, comprehension, and accuracy. Each grade level has an end-of-the-year benchmark. The students in the following figure are in third grade; they are expected to come into third grade at a DRA 28 and leave at a DRA 38.

Once we make the groupings, our reading specialists Jacquie Heller and Stacey Duff lead the third-grade team in developing a reading plan for each student. Using Microsoft OneNote, they also explain and document a summary of the data-discussion progress monitoring meeting to the rest of their grade-level teammates. When talking about our student Lucy, you would hear the following.

- According to the DRA given in September, Lucy is reading at DRA 18, which is well below the third-grade beginning-of-the-year benchmark of DRA 28.

- Lucy's goal is to be a DRA 38 by the end of the year which is the third-grade benchmark.

Mathematics Assessment Data (Baseline Score) and Concerns (Unit common assessments, performance tasks, exit tickets, and problem-solving tasks)	Time and Support in Core Instruction (LEARN)	Who	Frequency	Length	Duration	Ratio	Additional Assessments	Goal
SEPTEMBER AND OCTOBER Unit 1: 78%	Guided Instruction	Koeppel Lipsett or Deinhart	1x 4x	60 min. 30 min.	6 weeks 6 weeks	1:4 1:4	Exit tickets, anecdotal notes	80 percent or higher on unit 2 assessment
NOVEMBER Unit 2: 65% Needs more time to develop fraction concepts, particularly equivalents	Guided Instruction	Koeppel Lipsett	1x 4x	60 min. 30 min.	6 weeks 6 weeks	1:4 1:4	Fraction task and exit ticket	80 percent or higher on mid-year assessment
FEBRUARY Mid-Year Assessment: 63% Focus on subtraction with regrouping and multistep problem solving	Guided Instruction	Koeppel Lipsett Deinhart: Subtraction Group	1x 4x 1x	60 min. 30 min. 25 min.	6 weeks 6 weeks 6 weeks	1:4 1:4 1:6	Exit tickets Anecdotal notes on progress with subtraction strategy	80% or higher on spring assessment
APRIL Spring Assessment: 73% Very close to her goal; she is getting more consistent with her strategies	Guided Instruction	Koeppel Bagnall	1x 4x	60 min. 30 min.	6 weeks 6 weeks	1:4 1:4	Exit tickets, technology item practice	Pass Proficient on end-of-year assessment (SOL)
End-of-Year State Mathematics Assessment Score - Pass Proficient 407								

Figure 3.5: Sample mathematics progress-monitoring chart.

Visit go.solution-tree.com/rtiatwork for a reproducible version of this figure.

	Monday	Tuesday	Wednesday	Thursday	Friday
Guided Reading Block 1	Flexible time for test preparation group and word-study groups based on previous assessments	Murphy DRA 28 Fluency Lucy DRA 28 Fluency Johnny DRA 30 Fluency Ezzie DRA 28 Fluency TJ DRA 28 Fluency	Lou DRA 20 Decoding Zoey DRA 20 Decoding Maddie DRA 20 Decoding	Lou DRA 20 Decoding Zoey DRA 20 Decoding Maddie DRA 20 Decoding	Lou DRA 20 Decoding Zoey DRA 20 Decoding Maddie DRA 20 Decoding
Guided Reading Block 2		Lucky DRA 30 Summary Leo DRA 28 Inferences Bruno DRA 28 Main Idea Olivia DRA 30 Summary	Griffith DRA 34 Inference Tessa DRA 38 Main Idea Reese DRA 34 Inference Bella DRA 34 Main Idea Monroe DRA 38 Inference Linda DRA 38 Summary	Lucky DRA 30 Summary Bruno DRA 28 Main Idea Leo DRA 28 Inferences Olivia DRA 30 Summary	Murphy DRA 28 Fluency Lucy DRA 18 Fluency Johnny DRA 30 Fluency Ezzie DRA 28 Fluency TJ DRA 28 Fluency

Key: Developmental Reading Assessment = DRA

Figure 3.6: Sample ELA progress-monitoring chart.

- She needs to focus on decoding and monitoring comprehension, especially retelling using vocabulary from the text.

- The plan for Lucy is to receive guided reading instruction in the core from Ms. K. two times per week for twenty minutes each session for six weeks in a group with a teacher-to-student ratio of 1:6.

- Mrs. D. will provide additional guided reading support focusing on retelling two times per week for twenty minutes each session for six weeks in a group with a reduced teacher-to-student ratio of 1:2.

- Our goal for Lucy is to have her read instructionally at DRA 24 by our next meeting in November.

- Lucy's progress will be monitored through running records and anecdotal notes of her retellings.

As you see in figure 3.7 (pages 70–71), Lucy's progress was continually monitored, and the plan reflected the team's response to her instructional needs. You'll notice this is the same format as the mathematics progress-monitoring chart. By year's end, Lucy was on grade level with a DRA reading level of 38.

We realized that originally we had not documented a critical piece of information in our progress-monitoring charts—the student-teacher ratio. This information is now included so that we can monitor the intensity of support that some students require.

Once the planning is in place, the focus turns to teaching and reflection.

Co-Teaching, Observations, and Reflections

If our school vision is to meet the needs of all learners by *planning* collaboratively, then we also need to *teach* and *reflect* collaboratively. Through the process of team planning, co-teachers make decisions on how and what students will learn, thereby sharing ownership and accountability for the learning of all (Murawski, 2010).

The collaborative relationship begins at the grade-level planning meeting. Initially co-teachers commit to an additional weekly time to define co-teaching roles for certain lessons, specific moves the teacher will make throughout the lesson, and the grouping of students for guided instruction. In time, as the co-teacher relationship deepens with shared trust and responsibility, co-planning begins to take place within the collaborative team meetings. This eliminates the need for before- or after-school planning. The co-teachers achieve the objectives decided in the grade-level team weekly planning meeting, though the path might differ from class to class.

Language Arts Assessment Data (Baseline Score) and Concerns	Time and Support in Core Instruction (LEARN)	Who	Frequency	Length	Duration	Ratio	Additional Assessments	Goal
SEPTEMBER AND OCTOBER • DRA 18 • Decoding and monitoring comprehension—omits words without self-correcting • Needs to work on retelling and comprehension skills (connections)	Guided reading	Katie Stacey	2x 2x	20 min. 20 min.	6 weeks 6 weeks	1:6 1:2	Running record (One time per week)	Read independently, and retell at DRA 20 Instructional level = DRA 24
NOVEMBER • Exceeded goal • Progress-Monitoring DRA 28 • District quarterly assessment: 57 percent • Able to decode; great expression • Needs to add details to retell • Needs to work on higher-level questions	Guided reading	Katie Stacey	2x 2x	20 min. 20 min.	6 weeks 6 weeks	1:6 1:2	Anecdotal notes on retelling and using detail	Instructional DRA 30; retell a DRA 28 story using details from the text.
FEBRUARY • Partially met goal (nonfiction still at DRA 28) • Great at decoding; needs to work on retelling and higher-level thinking skills	Guided reading	Katie Stacey	2x 2x	20 min. 20 min.	6 weeks 6 weeks	1:6 1:2	Anecdotal notes during guided reading group; additional leveled reading assessments	Instructional DRA 30 with nonfiction text Instructional at a DRA 34 fiction text

Language Arts Assessment Data (Baseline Score) and Concerns	Time and Support in Core Instruction (LEARN)	Who	Frequency	Length	Duration	Ratio	Additional Assessments	Goal
APRIL • Passed nonfiction progress monitoring at DRA 30 • Did not pass fiction at DRA 34 • Better at retelling • Needs to add details	Guiding reading	Katie Stacey	2x 2x	20 min. 20 min.	6 weeks 6 weeks	1:6 1:4		Instructional at a DRA 34 fiction text Retell a DRA 34 story with details from the text.
End of Year Passed DRA 38	Monitor at the beginning of next year to check for summer retention or regression.							Met year-end goal! DRA 38!

Figure 3.7: Sample language arts progress-monitoring chart.

*Visit **go.solution-tree.com/rtiatwork** for a reproducible version of this figure.*

Co-teachers also spend time after teaching the lesson to reflect on student learning using informal assessments, such as exit tickets and anecdotal notes from observations. It is through these reflections that they are able to make future instructional decisions and refine their co-teaching relationship.

Figure 3.8 depicts the co-teaching models (Murawski, 2010) we currently practice.

Teachers make decisions about which type of grouping to use based on the objective being taught and on the number of teachers available to co-teach. Co-teachers look at these models during their planning meetings and stage their lessons. Student seating and teacher roles and placement are based on the learning goals of the lesson. For example, teacher placement could be for English learners, advanced learners, or students struggling with behavior. For instance, whenever students struggle either with an advanced concept or a grade-level objective, we are able to scaffold the student learning by using various co-teaching models.

Previously, we asked our specialist teachers to support classrooms without providing them with the structures and information needed to understand co-teaching and best practices for inclusion. We now embed co-teaching discussions into our planning meetings. Specialists are a part of the planning meetings and often co-teach with classroom teachers.

By deepening our understanding of different co-teaching models and having specific time to co-plan we not only are more effective in our instructional approaches but we are realizing the power of the relationships that are developed as we work together. As one Mason Crest teacher put it,

> If you had asked me before working at MCES, I thought I had been co-teaching! Co-teaching is on another professional level, and it involves trust in your co-teacher and an element of risk taking on your own part. You have to be comfortable sharing not only your students, but the instruction as well. One teacher in isolation does not know best. (Mason Crest Teacher, personal communication, October 15, 2013)

While we learn from each other in the co-teaching setting, we also schedule times for teams to observe other teams in order to build common language and practices. Just as we scaffold learning for students, we scaffold adult learning through a cyclical process. Observation allows for abstract ideas that originate in planning meetings to become concrete and helps build the capacity of our teachers to implement best practices effectively. As Albert Bandura (1977) notes:

> Learning would be exceedingly laborious, not to mention hazardous, if people had to rely solely on the effects of their own actions to inform them what to do. Fortunately, most human behavior is learned observationally through modeling: from observing others one forms an idea of how new behaviors are performed, and on later occasions this coded information serves as a guide for action. (p. 22)

One Teaches / One Supports

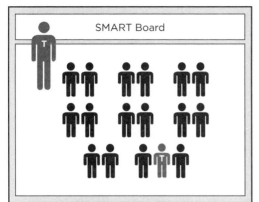

Team Teaching

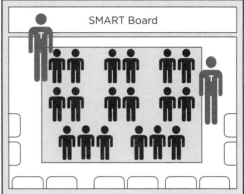

Parallel Teaching

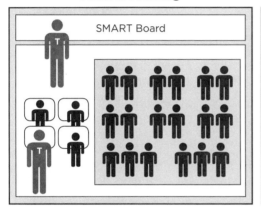

Guided Instruction

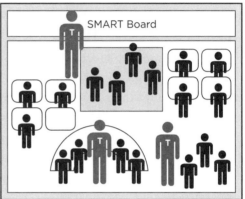

Source: Jenn Deinhart, 2013. Used with permission.

Figure 3.8: Co-teaching models at Mason Crest.

How do we make this happen? Teams meet during a common planning time and discuss which team they will observe and for what purpose. The mathematics or literacy specialist also briefs the observing team about the lesson it will observe. Although we are fortunate enough to have specialists, teams can engage in this process without them. Classroom teachers, resource teachers, and instructional assistants can create blocks of time for each other in order to engage in this observation and reflection process. For example, a mathematics resource teacher could begin the focus lesson so that the classroom teacher can go observe a colleague.

Each observing team member uses an observation form or checklist to record details from the observation (see figure 3.9). The team may have also decided on a certain purpose of the observation that they are trying to collectively or individually achieve, such as teacher talk, behavior, management of class or materials, differentiation, co-teaching, classroom organization, and so on. After the observation is complete, the observing team reconvenes to discuss findings. The data the team records on the observation form or checklist drive the reflection conversations, which usually include dialogue around teacher affirmation, new questions, and takeaway items or ideas to try. The specialists act as a link between the observing and presenting teams, should there be any questions or ideas to communicate. Often the observing teams will seek out the presenting team if they have any further questions or comments about the observation.

Our language arts and mathematics specialists then fold the findings or goals into future planning meetings so there is a cycle of continued growth in best practices.

If the schedule doesn't allow for teacher observation within the classroom, we videotape lessons and save them in a shared folder for all teachers to access. The reflection process around these videos is the same. Specialists, mentors, or teacher leaders can also scaffold adult learning in this manner as requested by individual teachers or to help new teachers understand the process.

The video camera and taping of on-site courses, team meetings, and classroom lessons at Mason Crest are powerful tools. We use videos as an opportunity to be reflective about our practice. They allow us to archive our work, and staff members who may not have had the opportunity to be part of that particular professional development session can view it at a more convenient time. We have many requests to visit Mason Crest, but when other school teams are unable to visit, they can see what our planning meetings look like by viewing a particular grade level's planning meeting in either mathematics or language arts.

Deeper Ongoing Learning

Just as we encourage our students to continually seek new knowledge and diversify their learning, we strive for the same for our staff. We continue to seek opportunities to build shared knowledge, and one way to do that is through book studies. In order to solidify the belief that all students can and will learn at high levels, we collectively read and discussed Carol Dweck's (2006) book *Mindset*. To achieve our mission, teachers must believe that all students can increase intelligence with perseverance and necessary supports. Similarly, the staff read the book *Implementing RTI With English Learners* (Fisher, Frey, & Rothenberg, 2011) to build shared knowledge around the needs of our English learners. We have a diverse student population with over thirty-one home languages represented, and this book helped our staff understand how we can respond to our English learners' needs rather than having our ESOL team work in isolation.

In addition, each year that staff members return to Mason Crest, they agree to a collective commitment to participate in shared professional development. After

Instruction	Evidence Observed
☒ Use strategies that capture and maintain student interest.	I am interested in learning more about how she organizes her groups. I also noticed that the kids seem to know what is expected of them in the workshop.
☒ Record student thinking with anchor charts.	Is it part of the routine that students show their thinking using a place value chart?
☐ Engage students during whole-group instruction with accountable talk:	

☒ Turn and talk.
    ☐ Restate what a friend said.
    ☐ Add on.
    ☒ Make a connection.
    ☐ Agree or disagree.
    ☐ Explain your thinking (how you know).
    ☐ Represent ideas with tools.
    ☐ Listen actively.
    ☒ Ask questions.
    ☐ Look for patterns.
	How does she use the SMART board as a station and still communicate to students where they go in the workshop?

☒ Use whole-group, small-group, independent, and partner instruction effectively.	I noticed that when students were on the carpet for the focus lesson and the reflection, they have turn and talk partners. Was that intentional? Are they the same partners every time?
☐ Provide all students the opportunity to use tools, visuals, vocabulary support, and sentence frames to aid in building content knowledge.	
☒ Use differentiation techniques to meet student needs such as:	I think we might be able to use the parallel task that we saw kids working on with some of our learners. Can we talk at planning about how to adopt it to meet our kids' needs?

☒ Parallel and tiered tasks
    ☒ Menus
    ☐ Choices
    ☐ Open tasks
    ☐ Leveled questioning	

Figure 3.9: Teacher observation tool.

*Visit **go.solution-tree.com/rtiatwork** for a reproducible version of this figure.*

participating in a mathematics course and balanced literacy course our first year since opening, the entire staff participated in a course to develop a common understanding of the philosophy of differentiation our second year. New staff members have a full-day orientation before other staff return; along with the different team meetings, they receive one-on-one coaching with a mathematics specialist, reading specialist, and staff mentor. Through co-teaching we give all staff members opportunities to observe best practice, which reinforces everything that was taught in the original courses. We choose this topic not only because of student diversity in language and culture but also due to a vast range of student readiness and learning profiles. The staff participated in the course, which a teacher team at our school developed, for over fifteen sessions throughout the year during contract hours on student early-release Mondays. In this course, we addressed a multitude of topics, including the following.

- Co-teaching models
- Identified English language proficiency levels
- Concept-based learning
- Strategies for differentiation, such as tiered tasks, parallel tasks, and choice menus
- Management and routines for a workshop model
- Multiple intelligences and student interest
- The evaluation of differentiation quality

Staff members increasingly implement these key ideas into their daily instruction throughout the year.

As we grow and welcome new staff members to our team, it is imperative that they understand the culture and structure of our school. It is an expectation that all new teachers participate in a preservice week, during which our teacher leadership team familiarizes new teachers with the way we do business. In addition, these teachers are expected to meet one-on-one with our language arts and mathematics specialists for weekly coaching. Any other teacher in the building needing additional coaching also has the opportunity to meet in this one-on-one setting.

According to one of our new fifth-grade teachers, Christina:

> These meetings have helped me fine-tune the plans created as a team to best meet the needs of all learners in my classroom. We plan co-teaching lessons and guided reading lessons for groups that are shared, as well as talk about different strategies for extension and intervention. These meetings provide me with time to deeply explore the needs of my students in conjunction with the curriculum and understand the best methods of implementation for the plans we have created. (C. Hunt, personal communication, October 15, 2013)

The support that each teacher receives—no matter who they are—is consistent yet, like the students', is also differentiated to support their learning and development. This individual coaching is a perfect example of targeted support for new teachers to ensure they have a clear understanding of curriculum, instruction, and assessment.

Our process at Mason Crest Elementary School is very reflective in nature. This individual and collective reflection is an integral part of our learning and professional development. Collaboration continues at Mason Crest in the core for all staff in order to ensure high levels of learning for all students. Our multifaceted approach to professional learning and development is our rudder, which will help us continue on the right path on this difficult but awesome journey. We have no choice. As Austin Buffum, Mike Mattos, and Chris Weber (2012) state, it's "a moral responsibility we owe to every child" (p. xiv).

Writing my chapter was by no means accomplished in isolation. I would like to thank some extraordinary educators, Diane Kerr, Jenn Deinhart, Jessie Bagnall, Morgan Huynh, Stacey Duff, Jacquie Heller, Tracey Hulen, and Leslie Leisey for the time that they spent assisting me in writing this chapter. Nick Vanderhye, Melissa Bergen, Celia Boltz, Brigitte Fontaine, and Donna Sheridan are as selfless as they come, and their work on our schedule is the engine that drives this process. Carolyn Miller, Ken Williams, and Lillie Jessie have been wonderful with their constant encouragement of me. The entire staff at Mason Crest should be proud of the work we are doing on behalf of all children.

References and Resources

Bandura, A. (1977). *Social learning theory*. Englewood Cliffs, NJ: Prentice Hall.

Bransford, J. D., National Research Council Committee on Developments in the Science of Learning, & National Research Council Committee on Learning Research and Educational Practice. (Eds.). (2000). *How people learn: Brain, mind, experience, and school*. Washington, DC: National Academies Press.

Buffum, A. G., Mattos, M., & Weber, C. (2012). *Simplifying response to intervention: Four essential guiding principles*. Bloomington, IN: Solution Tree Press.

DuFour, R., & DuFour, R. (2012). *Essentials for principals: The school leader's guide to professional learning communities at work*. Bloomington, IN: Solution Tree Press.

DuFour, R., DuFour, R., Eaker, R., & Many, T. W. (2010). *Learning by doing: A handbook for professional learning communities at work* (2nd ed.). Bloomington, IN: Solution Tree Press.

Dweck, C. S. (2006). *Mindset: The new psychology of success*. New York: Random House.

Fisher, D., Frey, N., & Rothenberg, C. (2011). *Implementing RTI with English learners*. Bloomington, IN: Solution Tree Press.

Harvey, S., & Goudvis, A. (2005). *The comprehension toolkit*. Portsmouth, NH: Heinemann.

Marshall, K. (2009). *Rethinking teacher supervision and evaluation: How to work smart, build collaboration, and close the achievement gap*. San Francisco: Jossey-Bass.

Marzano, R. J. (2003). *What works in schools: Translating research into action*. Alexandria, VA: Association for Supervision and Curriculum Development.

Marzano, R. J., Pickering, D. J., & Pollock, J. E. (2001). *Classroom instruction that works: Research-based strategies for increasing student achievement.* Alexandria, VA: Association for Supervision and Curriculum Development.

Mason Crest Elementary School. (2014). *Mason Crest staff collective commitments* (Unpublished document). Annandale, VA: Author.

Muhammad, A. (2009). *Transforming school culture: How to overcome staff division.* Bloomington, IN: Solution Tree Press.

Murawski, W. W. (2010). *Collaborative teaching in elementary schools: Making the co-teaching marriage work!* Thousand Oaks, CA: Corwin Press.

Serafini, F. (2001). *The reading workshop: Creating space for readers.* Portsmouth, NH: Heinemann.

Stiggins, R., & Chappuis, J. (2012). *An introduction to student-involved assessment* for *learning* (6th ed.). Boston: Pearson.

Van de Walle, W., Karp, K. S., & Bay-Williams, J. M. (2013). *Elementary and middle school mathematics: Teaching developmentally* (8th ed.). Boston: Allyn & Bacon.

 **John Wink** is the director of curriculum, instruction, and assessment for Tatum ISD in Tatum, Texas. He was previously the principal at Gilmer Elementary School in Gilmer, Texas. Prior to coming to Gilmer Elementary School, he served as high school principal at Hallsville High School in Hallsville ISD (a PLC model school district) from 2008 to 2011. Under his leadership, the campus moved from acceptable status to exemplary status in two years. Each academic distinction earned was the direct result of each school's collaborative efforts to create instructional and intervention supports that guaranteed learning for all students.

To learn more about John's work, visit www.leadlearner2012.blogspot.com or follow @JohnWink90 on Twitter.

To book John Wink for professional development, contact pd@solution-tree.com.

Making Mid-Unit Interventions as Easy as 1-2-3

John Wink

Editors' Note

While this chapter serves as yet another example of a school that recognizes interventions begin in the classroom, it also provides an example of the "right kind of thinking." Beyond creating a schedule that gives teachers time to collaborate and intervene, Gilmer Elementary also learned how to use the 1-2-3 process to promote deep discussion and reflective practice, which has resulted in improved student achievement. In addition, this same process and open communication are extended to discussions with specialists and interventionists regarding students receiving Tier 2 and Tier 3 interventions.

Gilmer Elementary School in Gilmer, Texas, is a rural school that serves 1,051 students in early childhood through grade 4. The school's demographics are 72 percent white, 16 percent Hispanic, and 12 percent African American, and 70 percent of the school's students receive free or reduced lunch. The school experienced success by becoming a Texas Education Agency Recognized campus in 2009 and 2010, but in 2011, the school received an Academically Unacceptable rating from the Texas Education Agency due to reading performance in one subgroup. I became principal in the fall of 2011, and in my second year, the campus moved from unacceptable status to being in the top 20 percent of all elementary schools in the state of Texas by earning all three academic distinctions on the new State of Texas Assessments of Academic Readiness test in 2013. Gilmer experienced dramatic improvement in student achievement between 2011 and 2013. To fulfill our campus mission, "One Exceptional Team + One Exceptional Goal = One's Exceptional Future Success," teacher teams set high academic standards in the belief that all kids can learn, and they initiated a focused and collaborative effort among all staff members, parents and the community to engage and challenge students to learn the things they needed to learn. (Jensen, 2009, p. 151)

To make this mission a reality, teams created norms for working together interdependently, so they could produce rigorous assessments, targeted and specific mid-unit interventions, engaging extension opportunities for all students, and a guaranteed and viable curriculum as defined in *Leaders of Learning* (DuFour & Marzano, 2011). They also used the 1-2-3 intervention process, based on the work of Austin Buffum, Mike Mattos, and Chris Weber (2012), to revolutionize how they approached core instruction and interventions as teacher teams. A culture of collaboration ultimately created the difference in student achievement.

Finding Our Focus on Learning

The Gilmer campus leadership team, along with the guidance and support of district administration, began the 2011–2012 school year focused on improving student achievement in reading and mathematics performance. The first step was to create collaborative time within the school day during which teachers in the same grade could collectively focus on learning. To meet the criteria for successful collaboration, "it had to be frequent, during the time that the faculty were paid to be on campus, and it had to be mandatory for every staff member to participate" (Buffum et al., 2012, p. 40).

Within each team, members established norms to maximize individual contributions. Teachers shared the responsibility of creating one common plan with everyone's contributions. This plan also included common interventions. Since 2011, these roles and responsibilities have been the backbone of creating aligned instruction, rigorous assessments, and prescriptive classroom interventions.

With respect to intervention, the campus sought to create a new mindset. Although Gilmer had experienced success in the past (2008–2010), the campus discovered a systemic deficit in mid-unit interventions. This deficit contributed to excessive and unnecessary student referrals to Tier 2 intervention settings. As a result of bypassing mid-unit interventions and overloading intervention staff with too many students, many student needs were not addressed, which ultimately caused the campus to receive a rating of Academically Unacceptable. The campus leadership team wanted to strengthen interventions by first establishing a campuswide mindset that intervention begins in the classroom. Second, they wanted to create a system of interventions where students were guaranteed "additional time and support regardless of who their teacher might be" (DuFour, DuFour, Eaker, & Many, 2010, p. 97). Third, campus leaders wanted to build capacity within each team to collaboratively create and provide targeted mid-unit interventions in every classroom every day. Last, the intended byproduct of this collective effort in designing mid-unit interventions was that Tier 2 interventions were reserved exclusively for students who were continually unsuccessful in Tier 1 instruction.

When the state of Texas changed its state testing from the TAKS test (Texas Assessment of Knowledge and Skills) to a more rigorous STAAR test (State of Texas Assessments of Academic Readiness) in 2012, Gilmer began creating a more rigorous curriculum. Teachers and leaders developed a scope and sequence map that best prepared students to master the most critical state standards. Once the scope and sequence map was in place, teams began the arduous task of writing a new and more rigorous curriculum. One week at a time, teacher teams used Richard DuFour, Rebecca DuFour, Robert Eaker, and Tom Many's (2010) four critical questions as a framework to create highly effective instruction and challenging common assessments.

1. What do we expect students to learn?

2. How do we know they are learning it?

3. How do we respond if they do not learn?

4. How do we respond when they have already learned?

The best intervention is good core instruction; therefore, collaborative time is essential to align teachers' understanding of the standards. As DuFour and colleagues (2010) note, "A school characterized by weak and ineffective teaching will not solve its problems by creating a system of timely interventions for students" (p. 111). Failure to align teachers' understanding of the rigor necessary to master critical learning targets guaranteed more students would fail and require intervention support. Thus, giving students access to the same curriculum at the same common time was imperative to ensure that all students learned.

Rebuilding a Schedule

From 2011 to 2013, teacher teams began the process of designing highly effective core instruction by framing out each week of instruction two weeks in advance, which required meeting often. During the first year, teachers collaborated every other day but quickly found that they needed more time to meet in collaborative teams. Per state law, every teacher must have conference time to do work; thus, we do not use conference time for collaboration. Because of the visionary leadership of Gilmer ISD Superintendent Rick Albritton, in 2012–2013, all campuses in the district were guaranteed a forty-five-minute conference time and a forty-five-minute time during which every teacher could collaborate with his or her peers to focus on the four questions and so on. Figure 4.1 illustrates how this planning time was incorporated into Gilmer's schedule for third and fourth grade by overlapping these sessions with specials. Visit **go.solution-tree.com/rtiatwork** to download a whole sample schedule.

Third Grade		Fourth Grade	
8:00–10:15 a.m. **(8:15–9:00)**	Homeroom Instruction (Enrichment)	8:00–10:20 a.m. (8:15–9:00)	Homeroom Instruction (Enrichment)
10:15–10:40	Switch Class Instruction	10:20 a.m.–12:10 p.m.	Switch Class Instruction
10:45–11:25	Collaboration and Specials	12:10–1:00	Lunch and Recess
11:25 a.m.–12:15 p.m.	Lunch and Recess	1:00–1:45	Conference and Physical Education
12:15–12:55	Conference and Specials	1:45–2:25	Collaboration and Specials
1:00–3:15	Switch Class Instruction	2:30–3:15	Switch Class Instruction

Figure 4.1: Gilmer Elementary schedule for third and fourth grade.

Within this collaborative time, teachers agree on the products or evidence that students will generate to demonstrate mastery of the standards. Teachers then plan in advance for students who fail the initial learning of the concept and design independent extension activities for students after they learn the concept.

Table 4.1 shows how teacher teams aligned Tier 1 instruction during their daily forty-five-minute collaborative meeting. Since teachers were building a new curriculum one week at a time, it was crucial for teachers to spend the bulk of their time developing common instructional outcomes.

Table 4.1: Gilmer Elementary School Collaborative Planning Topics

Day	Purpose	Product
Monday	Preplanning (Two weeks in advance)	Teachers discuss high-leverage skills that will be taught in two weeks. They develop a common understanding of the standard and what students must do to demonstrate mastery. Teachers leave the meeting and independently begin to add ideas, resources, and activities to the common plan that will be finalized the following week.
Tuesday and Wednesday	Planning	Teachers review the preplanning document from the previous week and discuss the resources and activities that had been added to the plan. They model lessons to better align common instruction.
Thursday	Assessment	Teachers write common assessments and formative assessments.
Friday	RTI day	Teachers discuss individual students who continue to struggle despite mid-unit interventions.

While this basic collaborative framework structured blocks of time for teams to create common instruction and assessments, teams had to be flexible with collaborative time to ensure two things. First, members had to create a curriculum that was *guaranteed*—one that all teachers taught and all students learned. Second, teams had to ensure that there was viability or "enough instructional time available to actually teach the content identified as important" (DuFour & Marzano, 2011, p. 91).

In order to successfully build this guaranteed and viable system, Gilmer had to implement a pyramid of interventions.

Planning Instruction and Interventions

As a part of collaborative planning, teachers strengthened core instruction by discussing common misconceptions that students developed when they initially learned the new concept. From there, teachers operated with a preventative mindset to create immediate responses during direct instruction when students displayed the common misconceptions (see figure 4.2). In other words, teachers didn't wait for students to fail. Using prior experience from working with students or from the teacher's personal experience in teaching content, teachers anticipated obstacles that students would face during initial learning of a concept and responded before misconceptions transformed into unbreakable habits.

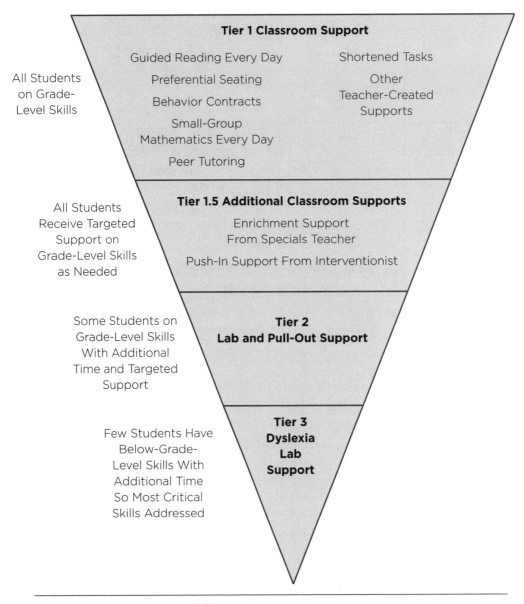

Figure 4.2: Gilmer's pyramid of interventions.

In addition to preparing for common misconceptions, teachers became familiar with prerequisite skills needed to master every new skill. As they designed instruction, teachers reviewed the standard from the previous grade and used it as the starting point for new instruction. To deepen their knowledge of the prerequisite skill, teachers collaborated once a month with the teacher team from the previous grade level. The monthly meeting was held in place of the traditional afterschool faculty meeting.

The setting for mid-unit interventions with the teacher included small-group instruction, guided reading, and individual conferencing. To document student progress, teachers maintained anecdotal records as qualitative documentation of their intervention efforts. In addition to mid-unit interventions with the teacher, the teams also created interventions that did not require the teacher's direct support. Peer tutors, use of manipulatives, shortened tasks, and lower-level reading tasks with or without technology support were just a few of the mid-unit interventions we tried. According to the research of Dylan Wiliam (2012), "peer tutoring can be almost as strong as one-on-one instruction from a teacher" (p. 134). In these peer-tutoring opportunities, tasks were specific to the essential skills that needed reinforcement with repetition and practice.

To further support students in Tier 1 instruction, administrators built time into the schedule for teachers to provide enrichment support, which became known as Tier 1.5. Tier 1.5 interventions differ from Tier 2 interventions in that personnel provide additional support (rather than more time) to students during regular core instruction in the student's regular classroom. For example, interventionists provide supports in the classroom from 8:00 a.m. until 10:00 a.m. They assist teachers by modeling lessons for them, helping them strengthen core instruction, and working with individual students who need additional support. In addition, elective physical education, music, and art teachers assist teachers for forty-five minutes per day in the regular classroom. Specials teachers support the classroom teacher by helping students with assignments or by reading with individual students while the classroom teacher pulls specific students for small-group instruction. The intent of this support is to use these specials teachers to support students in the Tier 1 setting, build relationships with all students, and encourage them in their efforts to learn.

Thanks to the pyramid of interventions, students were being served in a multitude of ways. However, teams did not have a systemic method to reflect on interventions that were in place before prescribing new ones. Creating the pyramid wasn't enough; the tiers also had to be monitored for success.

Monitoring and Improving Instruction and Interventions

With the many intervention options to support students and the many personnel involved in the intervention process as a whole, it was difficult to monitor and gauge the success of interventions, which lacked specificity. Students were receiving supports for every skill rather than the most critical skills. As a result, teachers abandoned or prescribed interventions based on assumptions rather than on data, and it was unclear which interventions they implemented with fidelity.

Campus administration lacked a systematic way to determine if Tier 1 instruction and interventions were guaranteed and viable before making a referral for Tier 2 interventions. Teachers worked hard to design highly effective instruction and rigorous assessments but struggled with initial steps of responding in the classroom with specificity when students were unsuccessful in learning high-leverage standards or meeting proficiency on their reading levels. The systemic ambiguity led to mixed results in interventions and uncertainty as to which Tier 1 and 2 interventions were the most effective for individual students. Lack of clarity resulted in students continuing to lag behind peers and increased teacher frustration with the campus intervention system and the campus as a whole.

The missing piece was collaboration. Buffum et al. (2012) write, "At its core, RTI is about creating a collective response when students need additional support, rather than leaving this response up to each individual teacher. This process is predicated on the staff having the time necessary to work together" (p. 39). Thus, teacher teams needed to do two things: (1) respond when teachers exhausted all of their individual knowledge and expertise to close learning gaps with individual students in the classroom and (2) respond when students receiving Tiers 2 and 3 interventions still were not making growth.

Response for Individual Teachers

Teachers needed to tap into the collective expertise of their peers to improve the mid-unit interventions that were tried or develop more targeted and specific academic and behavior interventions. Teachers were experiencing similar problems with individual students, but there wasn't a focused process for them to plan together for individual students. Teams needed to have collaborative discussions to strengthen their responses to unforeseen gaps, enhance instructional efficacy, and increase every teacher's instructional capacity. These discussions would also ensure that all efforts had been made to respond to the student's specific deficits before making a recommendation for additional time and support in Tier 2 interventions.

Response for Students

Often, students receiving Tier 2 support failed to demonstrate progress in Tier 1 instruction. As a result, teachers experienced difficulty in observing noticeable growth from struggling students on a daily basis, but when the students worked with the interventionist for thirty minutes every other day, the student was able to demonstrate appropriate reading or mathematics behaviors. Essentially, the interventionist's strategies did not always transfer back into the classroom. Thus, classroom teachers had to work with interventionists to address students' problems with Tier 1 instruction, and interventionists had to share strategies that were taking root in the small-group or individualized setting. The hope of the conversation was that strategies would move from being compartmentalized by the schedule to becoming coordinated by design. As Richard DuFour and Robert Marzano (2011) note, "A collective and systematic approach to interventions requires effective communication between all those who contribute to the intervention process" (p. 178).

To fill these needs, Gilmer used the 1-2-3 process, adapted from the research of Buffum et al. (2012).

Learning the 1-2-3 Process

When designing highly effective instruction, aligned assessments, and preventions for struggling students, teacher teams have a macro view of what all students need to learn in Tier 1 instruction, but the teams also need a concise and precise manner to respond to students who are unsuccessful after initial instruction. The 1-2-3 process guides teacher teams to take a more focused micro view so they can pinpoint causal factors that contribute to an individual student's failure to learn and, more importantly, understand the reasons why interventions failed to close learning gaps. It helps teachers problem solve within their collaborative team using the following three steps.

1. The teacher identifies the student in need of support and the greatest obstacle affecting his or her learning.

2. The teacher describes two interventions that have been tried and the student's response to each intervention.

3. The team helps the teacher revise current interventions or develop new interventions.

The process forces teacher teams to ascertain if mid-unit interventions were implemented with fidelity before seeking Tier 2 or 3 supports.

Step 1: Identify the Student's Greatest Area of Need

Isolating the causes of failure, identifying individual strengths, and providing evidence of student learning are the foundational parts of step 1. In some cases, students struggle with academic deficits, while others struggle with disciplinary issues. DuFour and Marzano (2012) write, "Without greater clarity regarding what is causing the failure, teachers will be unable to intervene effectively" (p. 178).

To begin the process, the teacher must identify the largest factor presently affecting a specific student's learning. To support his or her prognosis of the student's difficulties, the teacher is required to provide samples of student work or behavior logs to the team. Products of student work help the teacher team identify student potential, which in turn helps the team better determine if the teacher needs to change core instructional practices or classroom management procedures.

Step 2: Describe Results of Current Interventions

DuFour et al. (2010) note that "effective intervention will be characterized by differentiation and precision. Intervention will offer a setting and strategies that are different from those that have already proven to be ineffective for the student" (p. 111). Thus, in step 2, the teacher shares the two most prevalent mid-unit interventions that have been tried. When describing the interventions, it is important for the teacher to describe how the intervention was delivered to address the problem, the time frame in which the intervention response was made, the frequency and duration of the intervention, and the student's response to the intervention.

Too often, students fail to respond to mid-unit interventions because the teacher failed to address the cause of the problem, the intervention was the same as the initial instruction, or the intervention wasn't administered regularly over a long period of time. The reason that the teacher is asked to list two interventions that have been tried is because the team needs to know if mid-unit interventions have been tried with fidelity. By listening to current interventions that have failed, teams possess one more piece of information to help them create more targeted and specific interventions.

Step 3: Teamwork

Once the team members know more about the student, interventions that have been tried, and the results of the teacher's hard work, they are now ready to support. In step 3, team members ask clarifying questions about the student or the implementation of the interventions. Knowing more about the interventions tried and the student helps the team focus its response on generating ideas for more prescriptive interventions. Bill Ferriter, Parry Graham, and Matt Wight (2013) remind us that "while it is important to create an initial list of interventions, it is also important to provide teacher teams with some flexibility to innovate" (p. 71).

At this point in the process, the team members have many options. They can revise current interventions to make them more effective or recommend new interventions that would better address the student's needs. For example, consider a student with reading difficulties who is not responding to small-group instruction due to peer distraction. A logical response would be to pull the student individually at a time without distractions to see if he or she responds positively. Or, if a student fails to understand how to solve mathematics problems, the teacher team could create a specific graphic organizer that helps the student scaffold his thinking in respect to problem solving.

There will be times when the teacher team has no solutions and needs assistance. Teams should feel comfortable encouraging the teacher to seek assistance from the interventionist, counselor, or administrator. At Gilmer, interventionists, counselors, and administrators participate in teacher team planning meetings on at least a week-ly basis so that lines of communication are open and coordination of interventions supports both teachers and students.

The 1-2-3 Schedule

To make the process effective, teachers should collaborate in groups of three to four to maximize time and participation. Since time is a team's most valuable asset, teams should structure collaborative time so that all teachers can solicit ideas and support from peers about struggling students. Focused team time also allows members to provide help to fellow colleagues who are experiencing difficulty with specific students. Thus, at its very core, the 1-2-3 process guarantees learning for all students by encouraging all teachers to both seek support and give support to one another. A sample agenda might look like this:

- **First ten minutes**—Teacher 1 seeks support for a student in her class.

- **Second ten minutes**—Teacher 2 seeks support for a student in his class.

- **Third ten minutes**—Teacher 3 seeks support for a student in her class.

- **Fourth ten minutes**—Teacher 4 seeks support for a student in his class.

If time is a limitation, there are many opportunities for teachers to have 1-2-3 meetings throughout the day. Teachers can meet at lunch, during their conference, or at the end of the day. The beauty of the 1-2-3 process is that teachers have flexi-bility to hold a meeting at any time or any place as long as they can meet with fel-low teachers for support. Teachers can have a 1-2-3 meeting whenever they can get together. Scheduling is often a barrier for the traditional RTI process, but the 1-2-3 process eliminates the hassle of paperwork and setting times to meet.

The 1-2-3 Process Form

The 1-2-3 process form (figure 4.3) serves as formal documentation of the results of mid-unit interventions over time and helps the team determine if the student needs to be referred to the campus intervention team for additional supports. In addition, it "allows flexibility and problem solving while also helping teams ask the right questions and complete the work efficiently" (Buffum et al., 2012, p. 41).

Student Name: _____ Date: _____ Teacher: _____	

1	Referring Teacher Responsibilities
	
	  a. Name one student who struggles in academics or behavior.
	  b. Name the biggest issue that prevents the student from learning.
	  c. Share samples of student work or data.

	Notes

2	Referring Teacher Responsibilities
	
	  a. Name two classroom interventions that have been tried.
	  b. Describe the frequency of the interventions used.
	  c. Describe the student's response to the interventions.

	Notes

3	Team Member Responsibilities
	
	  a. Ask questions about the student behavior or learning.
	  b. Recommend interventions that could be tried to help the student.

	Notes

Figure 4.3: The 1-2-3 process form.

Visit **go.solution-tree.com/rtiatwork** *for a reproducible version of this figure.*

Using the 1-2-3 Process in All Tiers

During the 1-2-3 process, the teacher should allow two to three weeks for interventions to work. If the student continues to show the same difficulties after this time, the teacher should meet with his or her team a second time before recommending the student for Tier 2 support. If a student is struggling with his greatest area of need, the teacher team devises new interventions to be tried for the next two to three weeks. If the student does not respond to the interventions, teachers will meet again with the teacher team, an administrator, and an interventionist. The purpose of this meeting is to see if any new mid-unit interventions can be tried or if the student should be referred for Tier 2 interventions.

For students being served in Tier 2 or Tier 3 settings, teachers and interventionists can use the 1-2-3 process to better coordinate support. Students receiving Tier 2 supports often have multiple areas of need, and the 1-2-3 process can assist by helping teachers find support from Tier 2 personnel to create new strategies to implement in Tier 1 instruction. This coordinated effort between Tiers 1 and 2 strengthens the response because aligned common language and methodologies give the student an advantage in closing learning gaps.

For example, consider a student who failed to grow in his reading during Tier 1 instruction because he always stopped and looked to his homeroom teacher for support when he came across an unfamiliar word. In the Tier 2 lab setting, the student didn't look to the interventionist for support and was successful when reading unfamiliar words. The difference was not found in the talent of each teacher but rather in the level of support the teacher gave. The classroom teacher gave support to the student too quickly, while the interventionist guided the student to decide which reading decoding strategy would help him read the unfamiliar word. Once both teachers used the same response that best helped the student decode unfamiliar words, the student raised his reading level more rapidly in the coming weeks. It's good to note that teachers do not need to have a 1-2-3 process meeting about their Tier 2 students unless those students continue to fail; this is more a matter of checking the 1-2-3 form to make sure everyone is on the same page and is addressing the greatest area of need.

Finally, for students who have massive learning gaps, the 1-2-3 process can be used to seek immediate assistance through Tier 2 and Tier 3 supports. There are times when students come to school with gaping holes in their learning and seem to fail every learning task they are given. In these situations, the 1-2-3 process can be skipped at the start to seek additional support, but it shouldn't be left out altogether. With these types of rare situations, administrators, interventionists, and teachers should work collaboratively to define the student's greatest areas of need, create targeted interventions within each tier, and develop a communication plan to ensure that all tiers that serve the student reinforce the interventions.

Throughout this process, monitoring data is an important task in order to keep everyone on the same page. At Gilmer, teacher teams create common assessments that are aligned to essential standards. With these common assessments, teams can gather data across classrooms to determine the effectiveness of instruction as well as mid-unit interventions. In addition to common assessment data, students are also regularly monitored for mid-unit interventions based on the following data points.

- Reading levels including fluency, accuracy, and comprehension
- Reading, writing, and mathematics performance on common assessments and benchmarks
- Beginning-of-year assessments
- Writing rubrics
- Benchmark tests
- State standardized tests (STAAR)
- Report card grades

Teachers gather data cumulatively for every student using an Excel spreadsheet. Teachers update the file each time new assessment data are available, and campus administrators update changes to Tier 2, Tier 3, and special supports so everyone is on the same page. Through this process, school leaders use "relevant, timely data to frame the dialogue to transform classroom practice" (Pijanowski, 2008, p. 45).

If students continue to not respond to mid-unit interventions, and the teacher team has exhausted the 1-2-3 process, the team and the interventionist can begin push-in support, which is Tier 1.5. With this method, interventionists provide support in the classroom and work with the classroom teacher to ensure that instruction is maximized for all students. Interventionists assist by modeling instruction for teachers, providing feedback to help teachers improve their instructional practices, or guiding teachers in their efforts to respond to struggling students. As Wiliam (2011) notes, teacher "feedback should cause thinking," and it "needs to direct attention to what's next rather than focusing on how well or badly the student did on the work" (pp. 127, 128).

If instructional supports for the teacher are unnecessary, interventionists work directly with struggling students in the classroom setting to help the teacher close specific learning gaps while gathering formative data that help the teacher drive instruction and the interventionist drive Tier 2 interventions.

Conquering Concerns by Cultivating Trust

As with any new procedure, questions and skepticism were prevalent at Gilmer. The implementation of the 1-2-3 process yielded basic concerns, such as the following.

- How do we provide quality mid-unit interventions in a classroom of twenty-two students and keep instruction moving forward for all students?

- With respect to preparing all students to be successful on a standards-based state test, how do we determine which skills are high leverage?

- What is the purpose of Tier 2?

- What happens if we don't have enough time to talk about every student?

- How do we develop trust?

Providing Quality Mid-Unit Interventions While Moving Instruction Forward

This concern is common when teams begin to allocate time for mid-unit interventions in the classroom. Buffum, Mattos, and Weber (2009) write, "Two challenges that teacher teams face when upgrading the quality of their teaching within the Tier 1 program are classroom management and the selection of quality activities that students can complete independently" (p. 75). To address this issue, Gilmer teachers use planning time to create instructional and classroom management plans to ensure all students are engaged successfully in independent learning activities while teachers pull specific students for additional support.

To guarantee good classroom management, teachers use Randy Sprick's program CHAMPs (conversation, help, activity, movement, participation) to set classroom management expectations for working and learning so students do not engage in disruptive behavior while the teacher provides additional Tier 1 support to their classmates (Sprick, Garrison, & Howard, 1998). With respect to instructional plans, students are given relevant and challenging activities that all students can complete independently or with a partner while the teacher provides intervention support. The key to making time for mid-unit interventions is that the teacher must provide students with meaningful work and clear expectations for learning and behavior, and they must make students accountable for completing the work successfully.

Determining Which Skills Are High Leverage

Gilmer teachers had to come to grips with the fact that while every standard was important, only certain skills were critical for future years of learning. The most critical skills that teachers agreed every student must master were reading on grade level, reading comprehension, mathematics fluency, and mathematics problem solving. By focusing on these high-leverage skills, more students were successful, and ultimately, standardized test scores rose in one year by 6 percent in reading and 11 percent in mathematics. The staff used the SMART goal process developed by Anne Conzemius and Terry Morganti-Fisher (2012) to determine the greatest areas of need. This process helps campuses quickly determine the next steps in meeting the instructional needs of all children.

Discovering the Purpose of Tier 2

Gilmer teachers now recognize that Tier 2 intervention was not created to replace Tier 1 instruction. Rather, Tier 2 remediates students in the most critical skills not mastered on common formative assessments. Tier 1 instruction is essential to ensure that students learn the high-leverage skills. When teams refer students for Tier 2 interventions without guaranteeing the fidelity of Tier 1 instruction, the entire system will eventually become overwhelmed. Therefore, teacher teams must ensure that all students receive high-quality Tier 1 instruction so that Tier 2 is reserved for the select few who continue to fail. It's also important to note that some students will have deficits of more than one grade level. In these cases, teachers, interventionists, and administrators must collaboratively design specific interventions from all three tiers to close years of deficits while ensuring that students continue to learn current standards.

Talking About Every Student

While campus administration understands that multiple students may be struggling, there is simply not enough time to discuss every student. The 1-2-3 process addresses the struggling student, and the collaborative process yields intervention strategies that can be tried with students who have similar problems. In this way, the collaborative process solves problems that go far beyond the scope of the meeting.

Developing Trust

Trust is a critical piece that has to be developed with every decision, setback, and success. Janet Hale and Michael Fisher (2013) describe trust within the implementation process as follows: "Teachers need to be given social and emotional permission to be learners with their colleagues and administrators. . . . It is imperative that participants feel comfortable admitting when they do not know necessary information or lack certain abilities" (p. 11). Similarly, Michael Murphy (2009) describes the implementation phase with respect to teachers: "In reality, too many teachers perceive a side-by-side conversation with a school-based specialist as risky" (p. 17).

At Gilmer, campus administrators and specialists had to constantly improve relationships with every conversation. Initially, conversations were superficial and on low-risk topics, but as trust grew between administrators and teachers, discussions began to broach difficult topics that initially were virtually impossible to mention. Relationships improved further when teams and administrators kept the focus on student learning and identifying instructional practices that contributed to student learning. The key to building relationships was much like building a house: one brick at a time.

Getting to the Heart of Learning

Gilmer strives to guarantee that every student learns from every staff member every day in every way possible. This can only occur when all students are exposed to highly effective instruction, which means that all students learn as a result of its work. All staff members understand that initial instruction will not always be effective for every student the first time it is delivered; therefore, teachers must have focused dialogue to prepare for failure before it happens. They believe that their collaborative discussions help one another respond more effectively when preplanned interventions fail to address a student's learning deficits. Since time is the most precious resource available, teacher teams employ a focused process to help them collaborate about the most important topics that impact learning. While the PLC culture serves as a vehicle to design high-quality instruction and assessments, the 1-2-3 process serves as the litmus test to ensure that the RTI process is implemented with fidelity.

References and Resources

Buffum, A., Mattos, M., & Weber, C. (2009). *Pyramid response to intervention: RTI, professional learning communities, and how to respond when kids don't learn.* Bloomington, IN: Solution Tree Press.

Buffum, A., Mattos, M., & Weber, C. (2012). *Simplifying response to intervention: Four essential guiding principles.* Bloomington, IN: Solution Tree Press.

Conzemius, A., & Morganti-Fisher, T. (2012). *More than a smart goal: Staying focused on student learning.* Bloomington, IN: Solution Tree Press.

DuFour, R., & Marzano, R. J. (2011). *Leaders of learning: How district, school and classroom leaders improve student achievement.* Bloomington, IN: Solution Tree Press.

DuFour, R., DuFour, R., Eaker, R., & Many, T. W. (2010). *Learning by doing: A handbook for professional learning communities at work* (2nd ed.). Bloomington, IN: Solution Tree Press.

Ferriter, W. M., Graham, P., & Wight, M. (2013). *Making teamwork meaningful: Leading progress-driven collaboration in a PLC at work.* Bloomington, IN: Solution Tree Press.

Hale, J. A., & Fisher, M. (2013). *Upgrade your curriculum: Practical ways to transform units and engage students.* Alexandria, VA: Association for Supervision and Curriculum Development.

Jensen, E. (2009). *Teaching with poverty in mind: What being poor does to kids' brains and what schools can do about it.* Alexandria, VA: Association for Supervision and Curriculum Development.

Murphy, M. (2009). *Tools and talk: Data, conversations, and action for classroom and school improvement.* Oxford, OH: National Staff Development Council.

Pijanowski, L. (2008). Striking a balance: Georgia district adds assessments and transforms classroom practice. *Journal of Staff Development, 29*(4), 43–46.

Sprick, R., Garrison, M., & Howard, L. M. (1998). *Champs: A proactive and positive approach to classroom management.* Eugene, OR: Pacific Northwest.

Wiliam, D. (2011). *Embedded formative assessment.* Bloomington, IN: Solution Tree Press.

Susan B. Huff, EdD, retired as principal of Spanish Oaks Elementary School in Utah after thirty-four years in public education. Previously, she was principal of Santaquin Elementary for two years and of Westside Elementary for eight years. Susan was a classroom teacher for eighteen years and also worked for two years at a university with preservice teachers. She started working with her staff to implement PLC at Work concepts at Westside Elementary, a Title I school in Nebo School District. Westside was transformed from the lowest-performing school in the district to a school in which students perform well on standardized and criterion-referenced tests. She continues her work as a consultant helping schools with improvement efforts.

In 2002, Susan received the Utah Association of Elementary School Principals Rookie of the Year Award and, in 2004, the Utah Elementary Reading Principal of the Year Award from the Utah Council of the International Reading Association. In 2006, the National Association of Elementary School Principals named her Utah's National Distinguished Principal. In 2012, Susan was honored with the Alumni Achievement Award from Brigham Young University for her service to the field of education.

She earned a doctor of education degree from Brigham Young University.

To book Susan B. Huff for professional development, contact pd@solution-tree .com.

Teaming Up in Tier 1

Susan B. Huff

This chapter, while reinforcing much of the thinking in previous chapters, introduces some new thinking that led to success. With the loss of the school's full-time literacy coach, the school staff did not simply say, "We can't do that any longer." Instead, they actively recruited parents and community members and taught them how to deliver effective interventions. They also looked at how they could regroup students with like needs for interventions among the grade-level team of teachers. This is an example of the right kind of thinking that separates schools that things happen to from schools that makes things happen.

Another important aspect of this chapter is similar to the moral taught in Aesop's fable "The Goose That Laid the Golden Eggs." In too many instances, schools that reduce their caseload of special education students are rewarded by reduced staffing of the very team that was part of the school's success. Again, the principal and the school did not allow this fact, which was beyond their control, to stop or slow their efforts to help all students become successful. They simply found another way to get there.

Editors' Note

Nestled in the mouth of Spanish Fork Canyon in Utah is Spanish Oaks Elementary School, with 640 students, 35 percent of whom receive free or reduced lunch. This suburban school was built in 2001 to support the housing growth in Spanish Fork. Before my appointment as principal at Spanish Oaks, I had previously been the principal at two Title I schools in the same district and helped them transform into professional learning communities. In addition to the obvious difference in demographics (90 percent Caucasian at Spanish Oaks), the most striking difference between Spanish Oaks and the other schools in which I had led PLC work was that every student at Spanish Oaks lived in a house—some with grandparents or double-bunked with another family—but nonetheless, each student lived in a house. This was a distinct contrast to my previous Title I schools where many of the students lived in trailer parks or apartments, which contributed to greater mobility. After working for ten years in Title I schools with so much more diversity, I anticipated that perhaps PLC work at Spanish Oaks would somehow look different. I soon found that PLC concepts are the same for any school. Every school has students who struggle with behavior or who struggle to learn new concepts. It was clear that many of the things we had implemented with success at the Title I schools would also help struggling students at Spanish Oaks.

From Good to Great

On the surface, our school performance was good when we looked at our school-wide data as compared to other schools in the district and state. However, at Spanish Oaks, good was the enemy of great (Collins, 2001). We were good, but we knew we could be better. In a PLC, data must have a basis of comparison (DuFour, DuFour, Eaker, & Many, 2006), but we needed a basis of comparison that created a more accurate picture of how our school was performing in comparison to schools most like us. Measuring our data against those from schools with comparable demographics created the sense of urgency we needed; it was clear we had work to do! We created grade-level alert lists of students who had not been proficient on the previous year's state test so teams could know right at the beginning of the year who they should monitor. We embarked on a journey to identify nonproficient students by name and standard or learning target and to provide targeted interventions for those students so they could reach proficiency on essential knowledge and skills.

During my first year as principal at Spanish Oaks in 2009, we completed a book study using *Learning by Doing* (DuFour et al., 2006) to build shared knowledge about PLCs across all teams. We communicated information to staff through a weekly principal-created bulletin, which then freed up bimonthly faculty meetings to devote to our book study. First, teachers read a chapter. Then, we used various learning protocols, like jigsaw (see figure 5.1), to process the content and apply what we learned.

Teams were making great progress continuing to improve PLC implementation, but we had a recurring problem. Though teachers were doing an effective job identifying students through team-made common formative assessments who needed more time and support, they were continually asking where they could send their students for intervention. They asked, "Who is available to help my students?"

Directions for principal: Assign all participants to read the chapter ahead of time and to mark or highlight any ideas that resonate with them. Divide the chapter into four sections that are approximately equal in length, and have participants mark these sections in their individual books. Divide participants into groups of four (you could have tables of four). Direct each person in the group to take a numbered slip of paper—1, 2, 3, or 4. Print the following steps for each table.

Book: *Learning by Doing*

Chapter: Chapter 1, "A Guide to Action for Professional Learning Communities at Work"

Process:

1. Pick a slip of paper from the table (1, 2, 3, or 4).

2. Partner with a person from another table who has your same number (sit together so you can talk).

   - Five minutes—Discuss with your number partner your section of chapter 1. What are the key ideas? What will you share with the larger group at your table?

   - Five minutes—Return to your original group of four. Share your big idea with the rest of the table (in order 1, 2, 3, 4).

   - Ten minutes—Move to another table with new people. Anyone can share insights from any of the numbered sections.

Figure 5.1: Jigsaw protocol for faculty book study.

Although our school did not have the additional intervention resources that Title I schools have, I shared some strategies my previous schools used to provide more time and support that did not require additional funds. For example:

- For small-group reading instruction in leveled text, group outliers (extremely low- or high-achieving students) across the team of grade-level teachers to make the necessary number of leveled groups manageable.

- Using preassessment data, group students based on need across the grade-level team of teachers in short-cycle flexible groups for differentiated instruction.

- Group students by need across the grade-level team of teachers (by learning target or standard) for intervention.

- Train community volunteers to provide targeted interventions or skills practice.

- Group all students in the grade level with one or two teachers on the team (for a group presentation, an assembly, or an educational video on a topic students are studying) to free the rest of the teachers on the team to pull students for short time segments of intervention.

Even with the introduction of these ideas, we needed a new mindset at Spanish Oaks. So in 2010, we chose *Pyramid Response to Intervention* (Buffum, Mattos, & Weber, 2009) as our book study, again using learning protocols to process the content (see figure 5.2). The World Café is an example of one of the protocols we used to extend learning. A café ambiance is created with colorful tablecloths (butcher paper) on each table and a small vase of flowers or a candle in the center, along with a mug filled with colorful markers. Snacks and beverages may also be provided to extend the café theme. With this book study, however, we added something different. As teams discussed each chapter in the faculty meeting, they made a plan of what they would *implement* from that chapter. Then, during the following faculty meeting, each team reported on what teachers had tried and what results they found. This was a great strategy for spreading what is known as "positive deviance" (Sparks, 2004) throughout the school—identifying intervention processes that were working for some teams and then spreading those practices across the school.

Our first big breakthrough came as we were discussing chapter 3, "RTI Models." We read that "regular classroom teachers often offer students a second, and even third, iteration of core reading and math instruction during leveled instructional time" (Buffum et al., 2009, p. 34). I wrote in my book margin, "We're not doing enough in Tier 1!" This was a common insight that came from our faculty discussion. We had been exploring Tier 2 options without first examining what was happening in Tier 1. The pattern for practice at our school had been "Teach it, and if students don't get it, find somewhere to send them until they get it." But with shrinking school resources and increases in class sizes with budget restraints, it became evident that teams needed to hold up the mirror and decide what they could do as a team to help their struggling students. Teams began generating ideas of how to improve Tier 1 instruction and provide more time and support for struggling students using the resources within the team.

To help teachers improve student learning, in 2011, we studied Jan Richardson's (2009) *The Next Step in Guided Reading* along with *The Continuum of Literacy Learning* (Pinnell & Fountas, 2007). In 2012, we studied *Elementary and Middle School Mathematics* (Van de Walle, Karp, & Bay-Williams, 2010) to help us improve mathematics instruction. We explored ways to differentiate mathematics and literacy instruction to increase mastery of content as well as students' efficacy and ownership of their own learning (Tomlinson, 2008).

Directions for principal: Assign all participants to read the chapter ahead of time and to mark or highlight the ideas that resonate. Assign one table host per table (teacher with the next upcoming birthday or teacher with the longest or shortest hair). Top each table with butcher paper.

Book: *Pyramid Response to Intervention*

Chapter: Chapter 5, "Learning CPR"

Process:

Round 1—Fifteen minutes

1. For three minutes, write a list in a corner of the butcher paper tablecloth what you think are strengths about our school's response to learning emergencies (consider the attributes of normal CPR: it is urgent, directive, timely, targeted, administered by trained professionals, systematic); make another list of areas in which we could improve.

2. Share your lists with your table group (start with the teacher most recently hired and then go clockwise). Brainstorm with your group any other possible items to add.

Round 2—The table host remains (one teacher); all others move to another table of their choice.

3. Review what the previous group listed on the butcher paper tablecloth. Respond or add to the list on the tablecloth. The table host summarizes any insights that the previous group discussed.

Round 3—The table host remains; all others move to a third table of their choice.

4. Review what the previous groups listed on the butcher paper. The table host shares any insights that the previous groups discussed.

   Discuss with your grade-level team and then record what your team will implement from this chapter by our next faculty meeting in two weeks. (Be prepared to share with the rest of the faculty the results of your efforts.)

I'm a table host; what do I do?

- Remind people at your table to jot down ideas.

- Remain at the table when others leave, and welcome travelers from other tables.

- Briefly share key insights from the prior conversations so others can link and build using ideas from their respective tables.

Source: The World Café Community, 2002.

Figure 5.2: World Café protocol for faculty book study.

In his research on increasing student learning, John Hattie (2012) finds that teachers make a profound difference when they have a "mind frame in which they see it as their role to evaluate their effect on learning" (p. 18). Our school's common book studies empowered teachers with this mind frame as teachers increased their knowledge of "a range of learning strategies with which to supply the student when they seem not to understand" (Hattie, 2012, p. 19). Teachers increased their abilities to assess student learning, apply multiple learning strategies when students experience difficulty learning, and provide descriptive (not just evaluative) feedback to students. Hattie (2009) also finds that teacher collaboration is one of the most powerful strategies to increase student learning. But teachers need specific coaching to learn how to interpret evidence about the effect of their actions and need to be shown methods to help them gain these effects (Hattie, 2012). Teacher teams worked together to acquire new knowledge and skills through our book studies, and then they coached each other on how to interpret data to improve student learning for their collective students. In my own dissertation research (Huff, 2007), I found a pattern that gave educators both the *will* and *skill* to improve student learning. As educators participate in professional development and gain knowledge with personal effort and energy, they acquire skill. That cycle of learning can be continually repeated to increase the skill level: participate, learn, apply. During this cycle of learning, when educators experience even a small degree of success, they acquire will to do the work. Then comes the enthusiasm, persistence, courage, and desire that translate to internal motivation to increase student learning. The leadership work of principals (Huff, 2007) thus becomes facilitating professional development and helping teachers apply what they learn to acquire skill, then structuring success experiences and empowering teachers in their roles as evaluators of learning to acquire will.

The Obstacles

As we continued with our book study of *Pyramid Response to Intervention*, it became apparent that we needed to look closer at Tier 1 first and then consider how we could provide additional time and support in Tiers 2 and 3. Were we maximizing our existing resources within each team? Were we differentiating initial instruction in ways that supported varying student needs? Were we utilizing collaboration time to identify new and effective strategies that teachers could adopt as part of their Tier 1 instruction? Teams began brainstorming how they could improve Tier 1 instruction and capitalize on the individual strengths and talents of each team member to improve student learning for their collective students. They started bringing their best instructional ideas to share and started planning for differentiated instruction at weekly team collaboration for the concepts they would be teaching next week, according to their team's curriculum map.

We also recognized the following obstacles that could derail our efforts to increase student learning.

- Decreased funding for resources, including continuing loss of support staff

- Increased class sizes because of district and state budget cuts

- Lack of sufficient time for planning and collaboration

- Individual teacher autonomy that did not support collaboration

- Adding intervention time plus new curriculum to fit into an already tight school schedule

- No district universal screening for mathematics

Although some obstacles seemed beyond our control, there was one large obstacle to improving student learning that was completely within our sphere of influence: our school schedule.

The School Schedule

Thoughtful, careful attention to schedules is significant work for schools serious about improving student learning. School schedules can either promote student learning or detract from it; there is no neutral ground. In October 1999, seven weeks after the school year had begun, I was appointed principal at Westside Elementary—a Title I school that, at that time, had the highest percentage of free and reduced lunch in the district, the largest percentage of English learners, high mobility, and was the lowest-performing school in the district (which we happily turned around). In my first few weeks there, I became keenly aware of the significance of the school schedule. What I observed is but one example of how a schedule might detract from student learning.

While I was visiting a third-grade classroom, I noticed one student kept watching the clock. Throughout Mrs. Smith's whole-class lesson, Tyler continually watched the clock, completely unengaged in the lesson. Promptly at 10:00 a.m., Tyler respectfully stood up and left the classroom to go to his Title I reading intervention on the other side of the building. I was still in the classroom when Tyler returned thirty minutes later. In the meantime, Mrs. Smith had given directions for independent literacy activities and had transitioned to small-group guided reading lessons at the back table. Tyler walked respectfully back into the classroom; he looked at Mrs. Smith, but she was engaged with the small group. He glanced at the whiteboard to check for any indication of what he should be doing. He perused the room to see what the other students were doing. Then, he quietly sat down in his seat and began playing with the contents of his pencil box. Whoa! Here was one of our struggling readers who had missed the whole-class literacy lesson because he was clock-watching, missed his small-group guided reading lesson because Mrs. Smith had called back his reading group while he was out of the room, and missed independent literacy practice because he was gone when the directions were given. Here was one of our most impacted students who had the most fragmented schedule—one that would never give him the *extra* time and support he needed to close the gap between his current level and grade-level reading. It became very clear we needed to tackle the school schedule by eliminating instructional disruption for essential standards at Tier 1. Changing the school schedule requires a specific mindset: putting student needs first over adult convenience and ensuring all students remain in class for critical Tier 1 instruction in essential standards.

There is no intervention that can replace solid Tier 1 instruction in schools. A strong Tier 1 includes structures that support learning and maximize teacher effectiveness. It also includes teachers with the will and skill to make a difference, research-based instructional strategies that produce results, and effective schedules and structures. In fact, tackling the school schedule to improve student learning was my first order of business at each of the three schools where I was appointed principal.

In our PLC journey at Spanish Oaks, each team created a common grade-level schedule, grade-level curriculum maps, and team-made common formative assessments. We identified essential standards for mathematics and language arts using Doug Reeves's (2005) criteria of whether they have endurance, create leverage, and are essential for the next level of instruction. We marked these standards in the curriculum maps using the respective Common Core State Standards dot notation (see figures 5.3 and 5.4, pages 109–110). Each team had one hour of weekly collaboration time built into the school day with our district's early release of students on Wednesdays, which allowed teams to collaborate on curriculum and analyze student common formative assessment data together.

Once all of these foundational structures were in place, we could explore new scheduling options to provide additional time and support to help struggling students. We divided our scheduling structures into three categories: (1) intervention schedule, (2) reading structures, and (3) mathematics structures.

Intervention Schedule

At the beginning of every school year, it was always a struggle to develop the pull-out schedule for both special education and Tier 2 services (special education resource, speech therapy, counseling, and Tier 2 interventions, including computer-assisted learning, reading tutoring, and skills tutoring). Because coordinating schedules between classroom teachers and pull-out services so that students did not miss instruction on essential learnings was such a challenge, it was usually not until the

	Story Selection	Comprehension	Fluency	Grammar	Decoding	Vocabulary Strategies	Target Vocabulary
Week 1	*Because of Winn-Dixie*	Story structure (RL.4.5) Summarize	Rate	Complete sentences	Vowel/consonant/vowel (VCV) syllable pattern	Prefixes: re-, un-, dis-	comfort, mention, mood, properly, intends, consisted, positive, advanced, peculiar, talent
Week 2	*My Brother Martin*	Author's purpose Monitor and clarify	Phrasing Pauses	Subjects and predicates	Open and closed syllables	Prefixes: in-, im-, il-, ir-	injustice, numerous, segregation, nourishing, captured, dream, encounters, preferred, recall, example
Week 3	*How Tía Lola Came to (Visit) Stay*	Cause and effect Visualize	Accuracy	Kinds of sentences	VCCV syllable pattern	Using context	welcomed, sensitive, observes, unspoiled, prepared, negative, honor, included, glances, encouragement
Week 4	*The Power of W.O.W.*	Theme (RL.4.2) Analyze and evaluate	Intonation	Simple and compound sentences	VCV and VCCV syllable patterns	Prefixes: non-, mis-	assist, burglaries, innocent, scheme, regretfully, misjudged, suspect, favor, speculated, prior
Week 5	*Storm Along*	Understanding characters (RL.4.3) Infer and predict (RL.4.1)	Expression	Nouns	Homophones	Using a dictionary	yearning, memorable, betrayed, condition, seafaring, shortage, tidal, outcast, foaming, horrified
Week 6	*Once Upon a Cool Motorcycle Dude*	Compare and contrast (RL.4.9) Infer and predict	Expression	Verbs	Common consonant patterns Digraphs	Suffixes: -y, -ous	rescue, hideous, exploding, battle, wealthy, refused, invisible, hired, immense, warrior

Source: NGA & CCSSO, 2010a, p. 12. Adapted from Houghton Mifflin, n.d.

Figure 5.3: Sample page from Spanish Oaks fourth-grade language arts curriculum map.

Ratios and Proportional Relationships

Time	CCSS	"I Can" Statement for Learning Targets
Weeks 1–2	6.RP.1	I can understand the concept of ratios. I can use ratio language to describe a ratio relationship. I can make a table of equivalent ratios relating quantities.
Weeks 3–4	6.RP.2	I can use rate language. I can understand the concept of unit rate. I can solve unit rate problems.
Weeks 5–7	6.RP.3c	I can find the percent of a quantity as a rate per 100. I can solve problems involving finding the whole, given the part.
Week 8	6.RP.3a	I can find the missing values in a table. I can plot pairs of values onto a coordinate plane.

The Number System

Time	CCSS	"I Can" Statement for Learning Targets
Weeks 9–10	6.NS.1	I can interpret quotients of fractions. I can compute quotients of fractions. I can solve word problems involving division of fractions.
Week 11	6.NS.3	I can add, subtract, multiply, and divide multidigit decimals.
Week 12	6.NS.4	I can find the greatest common factor of two whole numbers greater than or equal to 100. I can find the least common multiple of two whole numbers greater than or equal to 12.
Week 13	6.NS.4	I can use the distributive property to express a sum of two whole numbers 1–100.
Week 14	6.NS.5, 6.NS.6a, 6.NS.6b	I can use positive and negative numbers to represent values in real-life situations. I can understand that positive and negative numbers are opposite values. I can understand that an opposite of an opposite is the same value. I can graph a four-quadrant coordinate plane. I can understand that the sign of a number in an ordered pair indicates its quadrant location.

Source: NGA & CCSSO, 2010b, pp. 42–44.

Figure 5.4: Sample page from Spanish Oaks sixth-grade mathematics curriculum map.

third week of school that we actually started providing pull-out services. We needed a schedule that kept students in the classroom during critical instructional times so that our most impacted students did not have the most fragmented day—so that interventions supplemented regular education instruction on grade-level essential standards and did not supplant it. Thus, we tackled the school schedule to build an intervention schedule that supported learning.

At Spanish Oaks every May, the special education teachers and I sat down to build the special education resource schedule for the upcoming year, which we then shared with all the staff before school ended. We followed these six steps to create grade-level time blocks that we could use for either Tier 2 interventions for regular education students or for special education pull-out services.

1. As IEPs came due, we were careful to align reading, writing, and mathematics intervention times to thirty-minute time blocks to facilitate scheduling; all interventions occurred on the hour or half hour.

2. In May, special education teachers prepared lists of students by grade level and content served, which were rolled forward to the next year so we could see how many groups would be needed in each grade level for each special education content area. For example, if we had twelve students in fourth grade receiving mathematics special education, we would need two fourth-grade mathematics groups, or if we had five students in third grade receiving reading special education, we would need one third-grade reading group.

3. Every grade-level team collaborated and agreed on a common grade-level schedule. We examined those grade-level schedules and wrote on our master schedule all possible times when students would not miss essentials and could leave that grade level for intervention—where students would not miss mathematics instruction, science in fourth through sixth grades (because science is tested on the year-end test), specialty classes, recess, or any of the literacy block except during the small-group guided reading time (see figure 5.5, page 112). We agreed that students would always receive guided reading from the regular education teacher, but they could be pulled out for thirty minutes during that one-hour guided reading block when they would have been working on independent literacy activities (which students reading below grade level typically struggle to complete anyway). In some cases, we asked grade levels

Time	Fourth-Grade Schedule	Adapted Schedule for Fourth Graders Receiving Interventions
9:00–9:30	Opening, cursive, journal, daily preparation, check mathematics review	* Fourth-grade special education mathematics pull-out (or Tier 2 intervention)
9:30–10:00	Shared reading, writing, grammar	
10:00–10:30		
10:30–11:00	Guided reading and independent literacy activities	* Fourth-grade special education reading pull-out (or Tier 2 intervention)
11:00–11:30		Guided reading for special education students in regular education classroom
11:30–12:00	Lunch	
12:00–12:30	Intervention and extension block	
12:30–1:00	Specials: library, physical education, computers, art	
1:00–1:30	Mathematics	
1:30–2:00		
2:00–2:15	Recess	
2:15–3:05	Science and social studies rotations	
3:05–3:15	Teacher read-aloud	

* Special education resource students are pulled out from class during these times, but other fourth-grade students can also be pulled out of class during these blocks for Tier 2 interventions, speech, counseling, or other services. The biggest scheduling challenge is for students receiving more than two interventions. For example, a fourth-grade student who receives special education mathematics and reading and, in addition, has speech and counseling services, would go to speech therapy at 2:30 p.m. on Mondays and counseling at 2:30 p.m. on Tuesdays during social studies, but would then remain in class Wednesday through Friday for science, which is a protected block because it is tested at the end of the year in fourth grade.

Figure 5.5: Sample fourth-grade schedule with accompanying intervention adaptation.

to slightly tweak their schedule to make pull-out times work. For example, the schedule would not work if every grade level in the school had guided reading at the exact same time or every grade level in the school had mathematics at the exact same time.

4. Because every grade level had a common schedule, we pulled students from all classes on a specific grade level at the same time for each specific content intervention. This meant that students' availability to be pulled out dictated our special education teachers' schedules. This also meant that all of our special education teachers had to be willing and able to teach any grade level—whatever the schedule dictated, where in the past they had specialized in either upper or lower grades only. This created an additional challenge for special education teachers because the grade levels they served often varied from year to year. Within any given year, special education teachers' workloads were not greater as far as the total number of groups they served, but they sometimes needed to create new support materials and become familiar with a new grade-level curriculum as the grade levels that they individually served changed from year to year.

5. We made a scheduling template in half-hour increments that included a column for each special education teacher. It then became a giant puzzle. We started filling in the template with the most challenging grade level that served the most students or with the grade level that had the fewest time options for interventions. Whatever time slots were left after every assignment was scheduled became the resource teacher's testing and preparation time.

6. The schedule was then shared with all teachers so that teams knew as school ended when their students would be leaving the classroom in the coming year for special education or, for that matter, any other intervention.

Now, because the schedule is ready, special education services begin the second day of school, rather than sometime after the third week of school. The special education template allows for any student in that grade level to be pulled out for any service—not just special education. For example, students could be pulled out of a grade level during the scheduled special education time for resource, speech, counseling, computer-assisted intervention, or reading tutoring—for either Tier 2 or Tier 3 intervention—because regular education teachers know they cannot teach essential standards during this time. This strategic schedule maximizes the time that regular education teachers have all of their students in class. The biggest challenge is planning the schedule for a student who has more than three interventions, so we tackle that early on in the planning stage.

Holt Elementary, a Title I school I have been mentoring in PLC implementation, used this same thinking process to develop their master school schedule with three strategic intervention times per day for each grade level so that students do not miss instruction in essential skills while they are receiving special education services or Tier 2 interventions (figure 5.6). At Holt, students can receive interventions, including special education services, at three time blocks per grade level.

- The first is during half of the guided reading hour (when they would be doing independent literacy activities, but not during their guided reading group time with the classroom teacher).

- The second is during the flex block of social studies, art, music, or PE. All students go to "specials" classes of art, music, PE, computers, and library weekly with the specials teacher while the regular education teacher has a preparation block. The flex block is for the curriculum that is left for the regular education teacher to cover because the specials teacher is not able to cover all of each specials curriculum in a once-a-week time period.

- The third is during Tier 1 writing instruction for a few students. If a special education student has IEP goals in reading, mathematics, *and* writing, it is difficult to schedule three intervention time blocks in the grade-level schedule where students are not receiving Tier 1 instruction in essential skills, so these few students receive Tier 1 writing instruction and special education writing services during the same time block. The special education teacher teams or coordinates with the regular education teacher.

Holt's special education resource schedule in figure 5.7 (page 118) coordinates with their master schedule. This schedule is used for two special education teachers *with* a half-day self-contained class. With limited special education resources and because there were only a few special education students in some grade-level content areas, some grade levels were combined for services.

At Spanish Oaks, as we got better each year at meeting student needs in Tiers 1 and 2, the number of special education students decreased, because we both had fewer referrals and because students were discontinued from special education since they were now on grade level. The mixed blessing was that while we decreased the number

	9:00	9:30	10:00	10:30	11:00	11:30	12:00	12:30
1st	LA2 Shared reading	LA4 Guided reading w/ independent literacy activities		LA3 Writing	LA1 Literacy access skills		Lunch 11:40–12:20	10 min. teacher read-aloud before math
2nd	LA2 Shared reading	LA4 Guided reading w/ independent literacy activities		LA3 Writing	½ LA1 Lit. access skills	Lunch 11:20–12:00	Specials (teacher prep)	
3rd	LA1 Literacy access skills	LA2 Shared reading	LA4 Guided reading w/ independent literacy activities		Math 1		Math 2	Lunch 12:20–1:00
4th	LA4 Guided reading w/ independent literacy activities		LA2 Shared reading	Math 1		Math 2	Lunch 12:00–12:40	
5th	Math 1		Math 2	LA4 Guided reading w/ independent literacy activities		½ LA1 Lit.	Lunch 11:50–12:30	
6th	Math 1		Math 2	LA2 Shared reading	½ LA1	LA4 Guided reading w/ independent literacy activities		Lunch 12:10–12:50
*Kinder-garten		Resource				Lunch 11:30–12:10		

Figure 5.6: Holt Elementary School master schedule.

Continued ⊐

Grade Level	12:30	1:00	1:30	2:00	2:30	3:00	3:20–3:25
1	Math 1		Math 2	Specials (teacher preparation)	Recess 2:30–2:45	Social studies, science, art, music, physical education, health	Cleanup
2	Social studies, art, music, PE, health	Math 1		Recess 2:00–2:15 / ½ LA1 Literacy	Science	Math 2	Cleanup
3	(Lunch)	Social studies, art, music, PE, health	LA3 Writing	Specials (teacher preparation)	Recess 2:30–2:45	Science	Cleanup
4	½ LA1 Literacy access skills	Specials (teacher preparation)	LA3 Writing	Social studies, art, music, physical education, health	Recess 2:30–2:45	½ LA1 Literacy / Science	Cleanup
5	Specials (teacher preparation)	Social studies, art, music, PE, health	LA3 Writing	Science / ½ LA1 Literacy / Recess 2:15–2:30	Social studies, art, music, physical education, health	LA2 Shared reading	Cleanup
6	(Lunch) / ½ LA1	LA3 Writing	Specials (teacher prep)	Recess 2:00–2:15 / Science 2:15–2:50		Social studies, art, music, physical education, health 2:50–3:20	Cleanup
*K		Resource					Cleanup

Language arts (LA) 1: Literacy access skills—forty minutes (Word work, fluency, and vocabulary)

LA2: Whole-class shared reading in basal text with skills instruction—thirty minutes

LA3: Learning to write—thirty minutes

LA4: Small-group guided reading—one hour for three twenty-minute leveled groups per day

(Special education writing goals are met during grade-level writing time for some grade levels, as special education teachers team with regular education.)

Math 1: Mathematics lesson and practice

Math 2: Mathematics intervention or extension

Special Education Resource Pull-Out Times or Tier 2 Interventions: Three per grade level

"Specials" include art, music, PE, computers, and library

* Kindergarten schedule varies; some half-day and some full-day classes

Source: Adapted from Holt Elementary, 2014.

	Teacher A	Teacher B
9:00–9:30	Self-contained resource	Fourth-grade reading
9:30–10:00		Kindergarten and first-grade mathematics
10:00–10:30		Second-grade and third-grade mathematics
10:30–11:00		First-grade and second-grade writing
11:00–11:30		Fifth-grade reading
11:30–12:00		Sixth-grade reading
12:00–12:30	Lunch	Lunch
12:30–1:00	Second-grade reading	Kindergarten reading
1:00–1:30	Third-grade reading	Fifth-grade and sixth-grade writing
1:30–2:00	Testing or prepping	Third-grade and fourth-grade writing
2:00–2:30	Fourth-grade mathematics	Testing or prepping
2:30–3:00	Fifth-grade mathematics	
		Sixth-grade mathematics (2:50–3:25)

Source: Adapted from Holt Elementary, 2014.

Figure 5.7: Holt Elementary School special education resource schedule.

of students needing special education services, our district cut our number of special education teacher positions and sent those teachers to other schools. We went from three full-time teachers to one and a half teachers over three years as the number of resource referrals was reduced and the number of students in special education decreased as they met their IEP goals. We had to adjust our resource schedule accordingly.

Tight district budgets and the scarcity of resources create a dilemma for schools: our focus is to help all students learn at high levels, but unfortunately there are no financial incentives for schools to remediate students from intervention services because schools often lose the resources that have helped them be proactive and preventative—they are punished for being successful. Resolving this dilemma will help schools continue to improve student learning rather than spiral through improvement cycles as resources come and go.

Reading Structures

As soon as students are identified as reading below grade level, the grade-level team makes a plan to provide more time and support for these struggling readers. This plan always includes daily small-group differentiated guided reading lessons for students reading below grade level, while students reading on or above grade level may receive guided reading only two or three days per week. In addition to the extra time and differentiation the grade-level team is doing, this individual student intervention plan also includes any of the other structures described in this section or Tier 2 pull-out interventions, prioritized by need across the school. Once students reading below grade level are flagged by teachers for intervention, the principal, literacy coach, and school facilitator make recommendations on who should initially receive Tier 2 pull-out interventions, giving priority to first- and second-grade students for early intervention. These interventions include computer-assisted learning (Imagine Learning, SuccessMaker, Waterford) or individual reading tutoring (Star Tutoring, First Steps, Early Steps) with a highly trained paraeducator. Students are assigned to interventions in the time slots the intervention schedule generates. The draft is then given to teams for their input; they make revisions and generate a final list.

Because each grade-level team has a common schedule, and teachers pace together, it is possible for teams to share students across the grade level when and where it promotes learning of essential standards. Each grade level has a one-hour block for small-group guided reading. Student reading data drive the structure of this hour for each team. Reading groups are flexible and fluid; individuals move up levels as soon as they are ready. Regular education teachers assess their below-grade-level students weekly through ongoing running records. In addition, the entire school is formally assessed by classroom teachers three times each year using the Fountas & Pinnell Benchmark Assessment System (BAS), which categorizes reading into lettered levels (Fountas & Pinnell, 2008). By examining their reading data, teams determine the appropriate time to use the following structures: grouped outliers, double guided reading, or a combination of supports.

Grouped Outliers

When there are small numbers of students at either end of the reading continuum (high or low), these outliers may be grouped across the team for small-group reading instruction, since every teacher on the team has the same scheduled time for guided reading. For example, if one first-grade teacher has two students reading on level M in the BAS, and another first-grade teacher has one student on level M, those three students could form one reading group. Because first graders are expected to be on level I by the end of first grade and level M is the expectation for mid third grade, level M for first graders is advanced. These high readers may have guided reading only three times per week from one of the teachers, freeing up both teachers to spend more time with struggling readers. Another example from fifth grade, where the BAS end-of-year expectation is level U, is a teacher who has one student reading on level M and another fifth-grade teacher who has two students reading on level M (mid third grade level). Those three students could form a group that would receive guided reading every day from one of the teachers. Although the first and fifth graders in these examples are all reading on the same level, they would never be grouped together because their needs are very different. The first-grade group is advanced, while the fifth-grade group is struggling and requires more time and support with strategic instruction to accelerate learning.

Double Guided Reading

Typically in the one-hour guided reading block, each teacher works daily with three groups for about twenty minutes each. When students are not in a group reading with the teacher during this block, they are engaged in independent literacy activities, or they may leave the classroom for special education or other interventions either before or after their guided reading group. Using the previous example, the fifth-grade group of three students reading on level M could receive guided reading every day from both teachers—twenty minutes from one teacher, then twenty minutes of independent literacy activities, and finally twenty minutes from the other teacher during the hour-long guided reading block, thus having two sessions of guided reading each day—in other words, double guided reading—as a Tier 2 intervention. This would give those students ten sessions of guided reading per week, while fifth-grade students reading on level Z (above grade level) might only receive two sessions per week. During the other three days of the guided reading block, level Z students would engage in literature circles and reading and writing assignments using their guided reading books.

Double guided reading has been especially effective for Spanish Oaks's second-grade team. This team chose to group all of their students—not just the low students—across the team. They assess all students reading below grade level on a weekly basis with ongoing running records, and they assess students on or above grade level on a monthly basis. All students reading below grade level receive two guided reading lessons daily from two different teachers. Every Wednesday, the team has a working lunch for which they bring their students' current reading levels and discuss who needs to move up a level and who is struggling, and then they brainstorm what to try and regroup any students who are ready to move up. Because they have been doing this for three years, they do all of this and eat their lunches in only thirty-five minutes. Anything they are not able to complete during their working lunch just carries over to our schoolwide PLC collaboration time later that day. On Wednesdays, students throughout our district are released forty-five minutes early for teachers' one-hour PLC collaboration time after school, and the second-grade team continues its collaborative work in the school library, alongside all of our school teams, as they analyze the results of their team-made common formative assessments, plan for students who are not yet proficient, and look ahead on their curriculum maps at what they will be teaching in the next week.

Students reading on or above grade level still receive guided reading in challenging books on their instructional reading level during the one-hour block, but they have more time with independent literacy activities than students who receive double guided reading.

Combination of Supports

When students are still not making reading progress, the literacy coach recommends or administers additional assessments that target potential problem areas, and then a new plan is created. We have also consulted with literacy coaches from other schools to help us diagnose and prescribe when we are stuck. One fifth-grade student was great at comprehension—he passed all grade-level assessments—but fluency was a problem. We tried unsuccessfully to determine how to help him, so we asked a literacy coach from another school to consult with us. She looked at our assessments and immediately diagnosed a serial order problem. She then suggested some intervention strategies for the classroom teacher to try, which soon fixed the problem.

Some students need just a little help to become proficient in reading, while others may need a lot of help. Although we have not labeled our interventions in specific tiers because the line between Tier 2 (some help) and Tier 3 (a lot of help) is fuzzy, we do have a continuum of reading supports with increasing intensity that are in addition to the extra time and differentiation from the classroom teacher or from the grade-level team.

- Students in primary grades who are just slightly below grade level or who don't get help with home reading are invited to participate in peer tutoring; they come for thirty minutes before school each day and read with a trained older student, and a paraeducator supervises them.

- Computer-assisted learning is the next level of support; students work with computer programs for thirty minutes daily before school or during one of the grade level's intervention blocks.

- For the next level, parents or community volunteers are trained as tutors to work with individual students two to five days per week on reading during an intervention block.

- Double guided reading from grade-level teachers is the next level of intensity.

- Double guided reading coupled with daily tutoring by a highly trained paraeducator increases intensity further.

- If a student is still not making adequate reading progress after these interventions, the teacher presents a case study at monthly literacy collaboration with the grade-level team, the principal, and literacy coach. That team reviews the interventions and the results and then collaborates to make suggestions for the next level of support, which may include additional diagnostic testing by the literacy coach. This next level of intervention consists of daily one-on-one reading instruction from a certified teacher—usually the classroom teacher—following the prescription generated in the literacy collaboration. This individual ten- to fifteen-minute instruction may happen before school, during the guided reading block, when the rest of the class is silently reading, when one or two teachers on the team are instructing the entire grade level (for music, physical education, or an educational video on the science unit), freeing other teachers on the team for intervention, or when a paraeducator supervises the class during independent or routine work time.

There is no funding for a specialist in our school to provide this intense intervention, so we work with our existing resources. As the principal, I also work with one student wherever there is the greatest need. For example, I worked with the lowest reader in second grade. He was still reading on a BAS level C at midyear second grade, where he had ended first grade. I read with him three to five times a week (as my schedule allowed) for fifteen minutes for a year and a half; at the end of his third-grade year, this student was reading on grade level.

The most intensive support involves special education resource pull-out services from a highly trained special education teacher, which he or she may couple with one of the less intense interventions listed previously that the literacy collaboration team identifies.

Mathematics Structures

Every grade level has daily mathematics instruction and practice for one hour for all students. Special education support is in addition to this instruction. Intervention is always in addition, not in place of, classroom instruction in essential standards. Each team has a common schedule, follows a team-made curriculum map, gives team-made common formative assessments on essential standards within the same window of time, discusses student data, and forms a team response when students don't learn the first time and require additional time and support to master key concepts. There are several methods we use at Spanish Oaks to allow for such support, including intervention and extension blocks, leveled mathematics groups, and collaboration for differentiation.

Intervention and Extension Blocks

At all three of my schools, our teams had generated grade-level schedules that included a thirty-minute intervention and extension block for mathematics—from two to five times per week, depending on need. Although it was difficult to carve out this time, each team accepted the challenge while still honoring our school expectation of two and a half hours for upper-grade literacy, three hours for lower grades, and one hour for mathematics instruction and practice. For example, the entire fourth grade has mathematics from 1:00 p.m. to 2:00 p.m., and from 12:00 p.m. to 12:30 p.m., students are regrouped across the team for mathematics intervention or extension (see figure 5.5, page 112). Students who were not proficient on the team's latest common assessment of an essential learning are grouped for additional instruction on that concept from one teacher on the team—typically the teacher whose students performed best on the assessment overall. The proficient students of the teacher now designated for intervention are divided across the other classes on the team for extension. Proficient students receive extensions in the same content as the students receiving intervention during that time.

The intervention and extension blocks are primarily for mathematics because the literacy block for each grade level includes one hour for small-group guided reading, which structurally allows for differentiation.

Leveled Mathematics Groups

Our fifth- and sixth-grade teams first started using unit preassessment data to group students for differentiated initial instruction in that unit. For teams with three teachers, one teacher teaches a larger high group, one a middle group, and one a smaller group of students who lack prerequisite skills as the preassessment indicates. These groups are fluid and flexible, and students are regrouped with every new preassessment. The strongest teacher for each particular unit typically teaches the group that needs accelerated learning to become proficient; thus, teachers rotate levels they teach during the year. Because the team is pacing together by following the team curriculum map, students can easily move from one class to another as needed— even during the instructional unit. All students still take the same team common assessments during the same window of time, no matter which group they are in. This is very different from the traditional ability grouping that was once common in schools, in which teachers group students by academic ability for instruction in unchangeable groups; therefore, students who struggle often have lower expectations. Students who struggle need accelerated learning on grade-level essential standards—not "dumbed down" instruction and lowered expectations.

School-based action research drives our structures. In 2012, our fourth-grade team started the year with all four teachers teaching their own mathematics class. As they gave their team common formative assessments and identified students for the intervention and extension block, they were typically seeing three to four students from each class who were not yet proficient; the team felt that number was too high. Midyear, teachers decided to try the leveled mathematics groups that fifth and sixth grades had used with success.

Fourth-grade teachers designed their preassessment for the next unit from the third-grade foundational skills for those concepts and then created groups based on the preassessment data. They moved a couple of students even after instruction had begun from one class to another to better match the students' needs. Students who had lacked many of the prerequisite skills before unit instruction began reporting daily that they loved the success they were experiencing as instruction targeted their learning needs. These low-performing students were not getting "low" instruction; their learning was being accelerated to proficient. Similarly, the needs of higher-achieving students were being met through extensions on those concepts. When the team gave its common formative assessment to all students, only three students in the grade level were not yet proficient—a big change from the number of students who previously needed intervention. The team then made a plan to give more time and support to those three students to become proficient. Because their data indicated that classes with differentiated instruction and varied levels of support were better for students, the team officially switched to this structure.

When the fourth-grade team shared its improved results with the rest of the school during our staff development, primary-grade teams decided to also try leveled mathematics groups. The first grade lost too much time with transitions, so teachers went back to teaching their own classes, but second-grade teachers got better results, so they continued. Action research!

Collaboration for Differentiation

In their weekly PLC collaboration, teams worked together to plan differentiated mathematics lessons. This was critical to student success as we transitioned to Common Core standards, especially when teams had to create new materials for concepts they had not taught previously. For example, when sixth-grade teachers were teaching dependent and independent variables in mathematics, they worked as a team to write the same real-world launch they would all use in their leveled mathematics classes. Then, they collaborated on instructional ideas they would use during the coming week for each of the three leveled mathematics classes: (1) the class that would need extensions, (2) the middle group, and (3) students who would need their learning accelerated. All three groups completed the same rigorous exercises on a grade-level essential learning standard; only the instructional methods and support varied. All three groups of students were successful with this essential learning. Differentiation for struggling students was also facilitated as teams shared their common curriculum maps and their essential learning targets with special education and ESL teachers so that they could frontload instruction and vocabulary for a new unit and support classroom learning of essential standards. At Spanish Oaks, teams also shared grade-level common formative assessment results of essential learning standards with special education teachers to help them better meet students' needs.

Challenges to Overcome

Until 2010, Spanish Oaks had a full-time literacy coach who was a great mentor. She assisted teachers with instruction and assessment. She also kept us on track with our monthly literacy meetings and was highly skilled at diagnosing problems and prescribing strategies. As funding decreased each year, she had less time at our school—decreasing to about twenty days scattered throughout the year. With budget cuts, we also lost funding for Reading Recovery, our most effective first-grade intervention. In the past, we rarely had resource referrals for first graders because the Reading Recovery intervention was so effective. We learned that when it comes to intervention, money does make a difference! With budget cuts, we also had increased class sizes, which placed greater demands on classroom teachers. Although there are many factors schools *cannot* control (dwindling financial resources, changing school demographics, waning parent support), our school focused on the significant factors we *can* control; your school can do the same!

Actively recruit parents and community members as volunteers, and teach them how to provide interventions or skills practice. Build a school schedule that supports learning, and schedule interventions so that nonproficient students are in class for instruction in essential skills. Build a school culture of continuous improvement in teaching and learning with high expectations for all. Schedule collaborative team time for teachers so they can map the curriculum, select and use common formative assessments, examine student data, and plan a team response to provide additional time and support for nonproficient students. Share students with like needs across the grade-level team for differentiated instruction, intervention, or extension. Build shared knowledge among the school staff through common book studies and school-based staff development. Identify what is working in the school, and amplify that success to broaden it across the school. Finally, become even more collaborative, reflective, and thoughtful about the use of existing resources, such as time, people, money, and space.

Dr. Ellen J. Williams first introduced me to the concept of a professional learning community in November 2002 at CITES (Center for the Improvement of Teacher Education and Schooling) Principals' Academy, when she asked us participants to read Rick DuFour and Bob Eaker's seminal work, Professional Learning Communities at Work *(1998). Reading this book changed the course of my professional life; a few weeks after reading this book, we were having our first grade-level data meetings that started our PLC transformation. Later, as my doctoral chair, Dr. Williams suggested I frame my dissertation research around a PLC leadership concept. Ellen became my intellectual mentor, my colleague, and my treasured friend. She pushed me to become a better thinker and writer and to dig deeply into professional learning communities concepts through my own dissertation research. She also introduced me to Rick and Becky DuFour, who then invited me to join them in their work. I am forever grateful to Ellen Williams for starting me on this amazing learning path!*

I would like to acknowledge the dedicated staffs with whom I worked at Westside Elementary, Santaquin Elementary, and Spanish Oaks Elementary where the practices described in this chapter evolved through our collaborative efforts. They were willing to continue to learn alongside me on our PLC journey of reflective prac-tice—trying new strategies, testing them, and improving our collective practices. I treasure those people.

I thank Rick DuFour, Becky DuFour, and Bob Eaker for doing the hard work of school improvement and then writing about that process in clear, concise ways that we educators can understand and apply. Learning from the three Rs continues to be a source of motivation, passion, and understanding.

And finally, I sincerely thank Austin Buffum and Mike Mattos for their input and for allowing me to be part of this project. Pyramid Response to Intervention *and* Simplifying Response to Intervention *have greatly influenced me and countless other educators as we have sought ways to provide more time and support for struggling students in learning essential standards.*

References and Resources

Buffum, A., Mattos, M., & Weber, C. (2009). *Pyramid response to intervention: RTI, professional learning communities, and how to respond when kids don't learn.* Bloomington, IN: Solution Tree Press.

Collins, J. (2001). *Good to great: Why some companies make the leap—and others don't.* New York: HarperCollins.

DuFour, R., DuFour, R., Eaker, R., & Many, T. W. (2006). *Learning by doing: A handbook for professional learning communities at work.* Bloomington, IN: Solution Tree Press.

Fountas, I. C., & Pinnell, G. (2008). *Fountas & Pinnell Benchmark Assessment System.* Portsmouth, NH: Heinemann.

Hattie, J. A. C. (2009). *Visible learning: A synthesis of over 800 meta-analyses relating to achievement.* New York: Routledge.

Hattie, J. A. C. (2012). *Visible learning for teachers: Maximizing impact on learning.* New York: Routledge.

Houghton Mifflin. (n.d.). *Journeys Common Core: Scope and sequence, grade 4.* Accessed at www.hmhco.com/~/media/sites/home/education/global/pdf/scope-and-sequence/reading/journeys-common-core/Scope-and-Sequence-2014-Journeys-Gr4.pdf on July 30, 2014.

Huff, S. B. (2007). *Professional learning community leadership: A collective case study of principals acquiring the skill and will to transform their schools by continuous improvement in teaching and learning.* Doctoral dissertation, Brigham Young University, Provo, UT.

National Governors Association Center for Best Practices & Council of Chief State School Officers. (2010a). *Common Core State Standards for English language arts and literacy in history/social studies, science, and technical subjects.* Washington, DC: Authors. Accessed at www.corestandards.org/assets/CCSSI_ELA%20Standards.pdf on May 21, 2014.

National Governors Association Center for Best Practices & Council of Chief State School Officers. (2010b). *Common Core State Standards for mathematics.* Washington, DC: Authors. Accessed at www.corestandards.org/assets/CCSSI_Math%20Standards.pdf on May 27, 2014.

Pinnell, G. S., & Fountas, I. C. (2007). *The continuum of literacy learning, grades K–8: Behaviors and understandings to notice, teach, and support.* Portsmouth, NH: Heinemann.

Reeves, D. B. (2005). Putting it all together: Standards, assessment, and accountability in successful professional learning communities. In R. DuFour, R. DuFour, & R. Eaker (Eds.), *On common ground: The power of professional learning communities* (pp. 45–64). Bloomington, IN: Solution Tree Press.

Richardson, J. (2009). *The next step in guided reading: Focused assessments and targeted lessons for helping every student become a better reader.* New York: Scholastic.

Sparks, D. (2004). From hunger aid to school reform: An interview with Jerry Sternin. *Journal of Staff Development, 25*(1), 46–51.

Tomlinson, C. A. (2008). The goals of differentiation. *Educational Leadership, 66*(3), 26–30.

Van de Walle, J. A., Karp, K. S., & Bay-Williams, J. M. (2010). *Elementary and middle school mathematics: Teaching developmentally* (7th ed.). Boston: Pearson Education.

The World Café Community. (2002). *World Café protocol.* Accessed at https://archive.org/details/World-Cafe-Meetings on July 30, 2014.

Lillie G. Jessie is the award-winning, former principal of Elizabeth Vaughan Elementary School, a high minority, highly diverse, Title I school in Woodbridge, Virginia. The Prince William County School Board named a wing of the school in honor of Lillie in 2009.

While Lillie was there, Vaughan was a nationally recognized model professional learning community and serves as a visitation site for school divisions throughout the United States. Vaughan students consistently exceeded all Virginia Standards of Learning objectives. The school received the Title I School of Distinction Award from the Virginia Department of Education and Governor of Virginia's Board of Education Award for high achievement. It was also one of five schools internationally to be named a High-Flying School by the National Youth-At-Risk Conference.

Under Lillie's leadership, Vaughan received four School of Excellence Awards from Prince William County Public Schools. The school is featured on the All Things PLC site (www.allthingsplc.info) and in the videos *The Power of Professional Learning Communities at Work: Bringing the Big Ideas to Life*; *Collaborative Teams in Professional Learning Communities at Work: Learning by Doing*; and *Leadership in Professional Learning Communities at Work: Learning by Doing*.

Lillie is also a skilled presenter and trainer. She has conducted workshops throughout North America and has conducted training on the implementation of professional learning communities. She was one of seventeen principals to receive the *Washington Post* Distinguished Leadership Award in 1997, and she was named Principal of the Year for Prince William County Public Schools. She has also been named Supervisor of the Year. The Title I program under her supervision was cited as one of the best in the state of Virginia.

Lillie is a recipient of the Lifetime Educational Achievement Award, NAACP Community Service Award, Human Rights Commission Award, National Coalition of 100 Black Women's Eboné Image Leadership Award, and Prince William County Kathleen Seefeldt Community Service Award. She created the award-winning Martin Luther King Youth Oratorical Contest. She was also elected to represent the Occoquan District on the Prince William County, Virginia School Board in 2012.

Her contributions to the education and civil rights community were archived in the Library of Congress, George Mason University, and local libraries in Virginia at the Northern Virginia Civil Rights Archive Dedication Ceremony by Congressman Gerry Connolly. In addition, the Secretary of Education of the Commonwealth of Virginia appointed Lillie to the Governor's Standards of Learning Innovation Committee in June, 2014.

To book Lillie G. Jessie for professional development, contact pd@solution-tree.com.

Focusing on the "Principal" of the Thing

Lillie G. Jessie

Editors' Note

This chapter, by title, identifies the incredibly import-ant role of the principal in the process of helping each and every student realize success and learn at high levels. The chapter speaks about principal leadership in a very personal and human sense that goes beyond the creation of new structures. The author recognizes the importance of providing emotional as well as structural support to teachers and reminds us to take the time to build relationships.

We find the metaphor of glue holding the three intervention tiers together and making its surface smooth to be powerful. The glue spoken of here is the celebration of small wins plus compe-tent and compassionate leadership. We could not agree more with the statement "people are not moved by facts [alone]; they are moved by emotions!" We call that the *why* behind RTI.

Robert, a student who had never before spoken to an adult audience, introduced Mike Mattos without the use of notes. When he closed with, "At the bottom of every pyramid is a kid like me! We want to drop into learning, not out," he received a standing ovation. Some members of the audience later asked if Robert was one of my gifted students or if he was a "savant." Actually, he was a student who had been unsuccessful in another setting and whose parents transported him to my school for five years.

After Robert's great introduction, there was anticipation and excitement until Mike said, "If you came here to learn how to get good test scores, you are in the wrong place!" The audience response reminded me of the sitcom *Diff'rent Strokes*, in which Gary Coleman's character often said, "What you talking 'bout, Willis?"

You see, like most educators in this high-accountability culture, that *was* what they came for.

Mike Mattos and I believe that when your only focus as a principal is test scores, and you are the sole leader holding up your pyramid, your pyramid may collapse. When the foundational focus is on the Roberts and the teachers, however, high test scores will be a natural outcome. My experience has been that you just can't stop the growth. Thus, this chapter is about the foundational and emotional support necessary to make this process a high-yield, learning-producing structure.

That said, there also has to be a strong, visionary principal with a persistent belief in both the ongoing, quality assessments and the ability of students to learn at high levels. Teachers can become disenchanted or exhausted, making the support and belief of the presiding principal vital. Building a schedule is the easy part. Building *people* is by far the most challenging. Building both, according to Daniel Pink (2005), requires combining left-brain thinking, such as order, with right-brain thinking, which includes creativity and empathy. Here, we'll discuss building both.

First, I'll outline how Elizabeth Vaughan Elementary School, in Woodbridge, Virginia, became a model professional learning community by providing time for planning, interventions, and enrichment on a daily basis—all while growing personal relationships. Then, I'll discuss the three foundational elements needed to support Tier 1: (1) collective capacity and efficacy building, (2) vertical anchors, and (3) baseline supporters. I'll also describe the glue holding all three tiers together.

Vaughan Elementary

Vaughan, which was once a very middle-class school, became more diverse immediately after my arrival. A new school was built and most of the middle class population was reassigned to this more affluent school, which left us with highly transient, diverse, low-income students. This diversity was compounded by the influx of English as a second language (ESL) students. Since teachers had experienced the luxury of adequate test scores in the past, they saw no need to change their practices, which resulted in us making the front page of the local newspaper with a headline that read "Lowest Math Scores" in the county.

To move ourselves forward, we initially used Ron Edmonds's early effective schools research, which was later published by Larry Lezotte and Kathleen McKee (2002); but by 2001, the PLC research of Richard DuFour, Rebecca DuFour, and Robert Eaker became our primary source. Realizing that we must change, we decided to review our mission and vision statements with the help of teachers and parents and the aid of the original PLC video (DuFour, Eaker, & DuFour, 2007). When we asked ourselves what we wanted to see as an outcome of this change, we decided it was to have students leave us with a "college-going identity" (Savitz-Romer & Bouffard, 2012, p. 1). Thus, our final mission statement became "Excellence for All . . . Whatever It Takes!" and the vision statement became "We want them to see what they can be!" After that, everything we did in the building related to our mission and vision statements.

In addition, the scheduling research of Robert Canady and Michael Rettig (2008) served as the basis for our block schedule. We also looked at the meta-analysis findings of John Hattie (2009) and Robert Marzano, Debra Pickering, and Jane Pollock (2005). Adrian Gostick and Chester Elton's (2009) research on the importance of celebration and recognition was a valuable resource as well. The cultural and buy-in element included the findings of Lee Bolman and Terrence Deal (2001), Pink (2005), and John Kotter (2008). Our work in principal leadership incorporated the research of Douglas Reeves (2006), Richard DuFour (2007), and James Kouzes and Barry Posner (2007). A rich source of information on student efficacy was also gleaned from the research of Jeff Howard (2011) and Ron Ferguson (2007).

The Obstacles

We began sharing quarterly data upon my arrival in 1991. I called it the Day of Dialogue. The staff secretly called it Day of Death, Day of Dread, and so on. Anonymous staff members phoned the superintendent's office complaining that I was asking them to do what other schools were not required to do. I was also referred to as "the lady who required her staff to read books." I researched constantly to find a practice that supported the belief that all students can and should learn at high levels. Soon, I found what I frequently refer to as "this thing called PLC." Effective schools research confirmed learning for all *could* be done, but PLC research told us *how* to do it. We were the only school in the county to implement the PLC model in 2001. Reeves (2006) says that "behavior precedes belief" (p. 97) by leaders of change. That phrase became my silent mantra.

Despite stark and open resistance, we improved our scores dramatically. There is nothing like high performance to overcome obstacles and resistance. I was reluctant to fully embrace the term *PLC* until the staff attended the DuFours' summer institute for my school system in 2005. Staff members returned and asked, "Are we a PLC?" When I said yes, they said, "We knew it!" or "I told you so! We knew more than most of the teachers in the session."

The Schedule

We used Canady and Rettig's (2008) elementary block schedule, which lets specialists cover classes at a specific grade level, allowing that grade-level team to have forty-five minutes of uninterrupted planning time five days a week. (Visit **go.solution-tree .com/rtiatwork** to see a sample schedule.) Our grade-level teams scheduled three days for collaborative planning, one day for personal planning, and one day to share data with me in the High Expectation for Learning (High Ex) Center, our data room. Each week, a specific content area (language arts, mathematics, social studies, and science) was discussed using the four critical questions of a PLC (DuFour, DuFour, Eaker, & Many, 2010).

1. What do we expect students to learn?

2. How do we know they are learning it?

3. How do we respond when they do not learn?

4. How do we respond when they have already learned?

This type of schedule allows for more flexibility, since the usual five-day rotation is not the rule. Schools with enough specialists can have a six-day rotation schedule, which allows time for grade levels to engage in class-reduction strategies. For example, if every grade level receives at least one extra day of specialist coverage, it can use that time to respond to specific students' common assessment findings. Once we arranged our schedule to incorporate a sixth day of rotation, we allowed the individual grade levels to decide what to do with this extra time. Most used this time to send a mixed group of students, perhaps five from each class of twenty-five, to specials. This reduced their classes by five and allowed for intervention and extension. Some used this time to send students to what we called the "tall graph" teacher, who taught the objective in question most successfully (thus having the tallest bar on the bar graph). Due to this level of flexibility, the schedule is highly conducive to the interdependence we seek in a PLC environment.

The Data

When I reflect on my initial implementation of data-based monitoring (the Day of Dialogue), I realized that Steve Edwards, a national consultant, was right when he told my staff during a site visit: "One test is too much if it doesn't change instruction." Initially we did not have the right assessments. When you hear teachers say, "There are too many tests," they may be saying, "We don't have the *right* tests." Often, teachers—like my teachers initially—prepared assessments as an accountability measure rather than for their personal use in the classroom. Frequently, teachers sent test results to the principal's office, never using them to guide their practice.

Imagine what would happen if doctors conducted tests and sent them to the hospital administrator's office instead of using them immediately to meet the needs of their patients. If your life as a principal was anything like mine, those assessments could sit on my desk for days before I got back to teachers. I call these principals *data collectors*. They collect data, usually in beautiful binders, and often do nothing with them before sending them to the central office. That said, remember that an imperfect PLC or pyramid response to intervention (PRTI) structure can still generate very high performance. My advice is this: give yourself and your staff permission not to be perfect!

Instead of being data collectors, we moved to a system in which each grade level named an individual to act as the data cruncher. To keep everyone on the same page, we displayed the data findings from every grade level and special program on a data wall (see figure 6.1).

Source: Prince William County Public Schools, 2009. Used with permission.

Figure 6.1: The Vaughan Elementary data wall.

The quote on our data wall—"No one of us is as smart as all of us"—reminded the team we were all responsible for the school's success. Thus, once a week, I scheduled myself to be in the High Ex Center for the entire day. Richard DuFour frequently jokes about how little he gleaned from thirty-minute teacher observations. For a while, my question was, "What is he doing instead?" The answer, I now realize, is *monitoring results*. So, my role during that full day in the High Ex Center was to *listen* to teachers. They led the discussion, and boy could they lead! In fact, I made a point of never sitting at the head of the table—the teacher presenter assumed that position. They discussed their performance standing in a content area and provided solutions. Sometimes I provided additional insight or modified their plans, if needed. I then included these data chats in their formal evaluation. I finally got what DuFour meant: this process allowed me to know who my teachers were as *professionals*. Many became administrative leaders in the school system. If you grow people, your test scores will grow with them.

Talking to students is another great way to monitor results. For half a day each week, I met with a randomly selected group of students in the High Ex Center to talk about the curriculum. Anticipation was in the air, because no one knew whose name was going to be called. This was a way to actualize our mission statement. *All* should mean *all*. All students at Vaughan were called "Bright Ones"—so bright, in fact, we distributed sunglasses to those selected to attend and displayed their photos. I also had quarterly goal-setting meetings with the group of students who had moved beyond honor roll status and were candidates to have their names engraved in a brick on a specially designed walkway in front of the building. The students came up with the name "Brick Kids" and the phrase "Going for the brick!"

There is power in student self-regulation, according to Mandy Savitz-Romer and Suzanne Bouffard (2012), and I saw the evidence of that late in my tenure. On average, about thirty-five students became Brick Kids each year from 1992 to 2007. Once I began having personalized goal-setting sessions, the number jumped to sixty-one the next year. Finally, in my last year, we had 114 Brick Kids. Most of these students achieved Pass/Advanced performance on the state end-of-year assessment. The lesson we learned is better late than never! (Visit **go.solution-tree.com/rtiatwork** for a reproducible principal chat form and to access the full list of prevention strategies.)

The Interventions

We made most intervention decisions during the weekly common assessment meetings and at our weekly Day of Dialogue. The weekly meetings included every department in the school, as well as the specialists and administrative staff. These meetings allowed me to have a pulse on everyone in the building.

The block schedule provided forty-five minutes of planning time for each grade level and for specialists. Grade levels designated three days each week for grade-level planning, one day for individual or personal planning, and the remaining day for our weekly meetings. While specialists did not administer assessments, they were given information from grade-level teachers. With that information, the specialists provided enrichment units and responded to specific needs of grade levels. For example, when it was determined that the grade-level performance on "Measurement" was a concern, the three specialists designed units that supported the objective, using vocabulary aligned with the objective.

The weekly meeting allowed us to quickly identify students in need of support by name and helped us identify the small issues as well as the large issues. We used reading and mathematics assessments and cognitive and ESL measures to determine interventions. Every classroom was heterogeneously grouped but was also assigned a group of students in need of services from a selected specialist, such as the reading, Title I, ESL, special education, and so on. This was done at the request of teachers as a way of reducing classroom interruptions from numerous specialists. In addition to using common assessments developed at grade levels, each of these programs conducted assessments that were generated by the central office but useful to the team.

Teachers immediately retaught students who required support during regular classroom time or during the intervention or extension block. The five third-grade teachers, for instance, would divide themselves across this block—one teacher for reteaching or intervention, two for extension, and two for maintenance. The maintenance group included those students whose skills needed to be reinforced. Often teachers successfully teach an objective and wait until the end of the school year to review a plethora of skills that have been taught early during the school year, only to find that the students have forgotten what was taught. Our staff established times during the year to review the objectives in a systematic and timely manner. The reteaching groups included those who did not master the objective when it was taught initially.

Reading groups were spread across the grade level as well, allowing each teacher to have no more than three reading groups. These groups were fluid, so students moved between them as necessary throughout the year.

Our simulations included a pep rally for students, actual scheduled tests for each content area, and a sharing of our status with the entire school. So, in addition to ongoing common assessments and daily grade-level assessments, teachers gave simulation tests six weeks before the state test and shared the resulting data with the entire building during a celebratory data dinner. Why celebratory? Having data dinners created a non-threatening atmosphere for teachers and students, and accepting your current reality is one of the most powerful success tools. Waiting until the actual state test date to determine how your students will perform is too late. The final test results should never be a surprise. Simulating an actual test and responding to the results prior to the actual test is one way of doing this. It relieves the anxiety for teachers and students before the actual state scheduled date. High-performing schools understand the importance of everyone being on the same page.

While small schedule changes took place throughout the school year, major schedule changes occurred after the simulation test results were disaggregated and reviewed by grade levels. They then presented their findings to the entire school at a fun, themed data dinner. One theme was Data of Our Lives, with an Emmy for best presenter.

During simulation, teams reviewed grade-level score averages for grades 3 through 5 to determine where we were as a school. Some students needed small-group testing environments, while others needed read-alouds or breaks during the actual test. Teams provided this simulation information to all staff members prior to the state test. If a particular grade level was in trouble, we made schedule and support adjustments to include temporary reassignments of teachers if they had expertise in a certain area (even those from grades K–2, which were not required to take the state test). There was a sense of ownership and oneness in the building. Public sharing of data facilitates this necessary interdependence.

We also informed the parents of student needs and asked them to attend a six-week Saturday institute, where we provided them with information on how the end-of-year test works and how to best support their children in reading and mathematics.

The Monitoring Process

Our weekly common assessment meetings in the High Ex Center also helped us monitor student progress. Principal time with students provided information as well. All students had data notebooks that were monitored on a weekly basis by their teachers as well as by the principal and a team of teachers (visit **go.solution-tree.com /rtiatwork** to download a reproducible of this resource). Every Friday, teachers reviewed students' notebooks, and the principal and a team of teachers reviewed them during weekly meetings. Students in need of intervention six weeks prior to the end-of-year assessment met in the High Ex Center with me, my assistant principal Rachel English, and specialists.

Rachel and I reviewed the simulation results by asking each student the same open-ended question: "What happened?" We then classified the students into two groups: (1) those who *didn't* answer test items correctly upon review and (2) those who *couldn't* answer test items upon review. Each year, we got the same remarkable results. We classified only two or three students as *couldn't* and needing intervention. The remaining students just *didn't* answer correctly for reasons that included reading the question improperly, lack of confidence, and just downright guessing because they lack the skills in an area. These meetings allowed us to focus on these areas in a one-on-one setting.

Students also used self-monitoring techniques. To achieve a J curve (see figure 6.2), students learned how tests were scored at the state level. They understood terms such as *scaled scores*, *field items*, and *foils* (which are used by test designers to fool students, such as close rhymes—*field* versus *feel*—and similar-looking numbers—968 versus 698). They were also taught to count their correct answers in order to meet their goal, which we called the *counting strategy* (visit **go.solution-tree.com/rtiatwork** to download a reproducible of this resource).

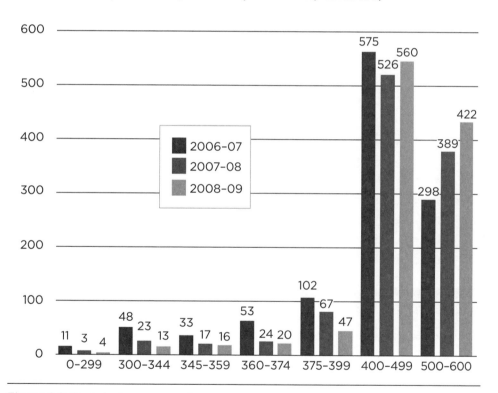

Figure 6.2: Sample J curve graph.

By monitoring student progress, and students' self-monitoring, student performance climbed, and the school reached its goal of achieving a J curve. The ones who take the test are often the last ones told how it works. Involve students, and your scores will soar.

The Extension Process

Our extension process spread beyond the walls of the classroom. Business partnerships and club participation provided real-world experience for students. For example, students could interview to become managers or tellers at the student-run bank, which was partnered with a local bank. The bank employees then taught students financial literacy. Students also authored two school-published books, and the staff authored one. The latter was done as a professional development project on memoir writing. The staff writers shared their writings with students, allowing them to apply a writing rubric to them.

Also, students who proved their use of test-taking skills on end-of-the-year assessments by justifying their answers on paper were given tickets for the annual ice cream truck visit. The reward was for thinking, not performance level or scores.

The Foundational Elements of Tier 1

Jeff Howard (1992), president of the Efficacy Institute, says, "Smart is not something you are. Smart is something you get." He says that once you convey to students—whether consciously or not—they are too dumb, they will prove you right. This idea of diminished innate ability rests with teachers themselves, who sometimes lower the standards in a sincere effort to eliminate some of the struggle (Howard, 1992). Carol Dweck (2006), David Shenk (2010), Ronald Ferguson (2007), Karin Chenoweth (2009), and Betty Garner's (2007) research support Howard's findings. There are three foundational elements supporting the pyramid to help combat these lower standards and ensure all students learn at high levels—(1) collective capacity and efficacy building, (2) vertical anchors, and (3) baseline supporters (see figure 6.3)—as well as the glue holding all three tiers together.

Collective Capacity and Efficacy Building

To me, leadership is the ability to get people to do what they would not normally do. According to Kouzes and Posner (2007), leaders are like architects; they have a picture in their mind's eye of what the results are going to look like before they've even started. They go on to say that if you want to get extraordinary things done, you must "enable others to act not by hoarding power [you] have but by giving it away" (p. 21). The goal is to have *many* people but *one* voice.

During monthly meetings, our focus was on short wins or tall-graph performers providing short-term interventions. At one point, when faced with the serious possibility of a pass rate of 25 percent or below on a fifth-grade writing test in three weeks, teachers from other grade levels were brought in temporarily. Instead of a 25

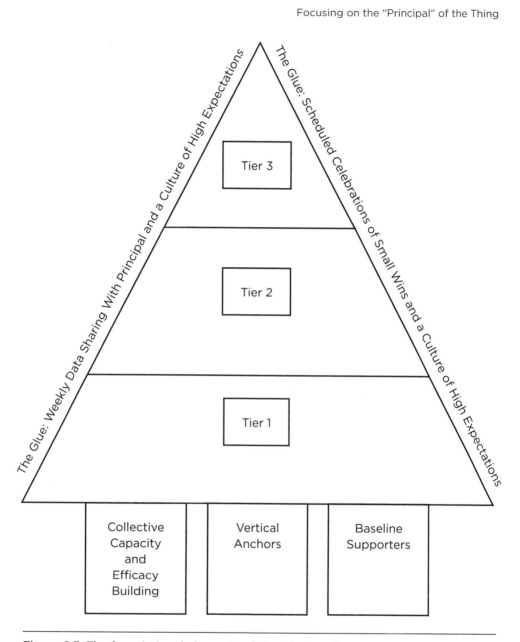

Figure 6.3: The foundational elements of Tier 1 instruction.

percent pass rate, we achieved an 87 percent pass rate. In a true PLC or RTI pyramid, sometimes you need to reorganize the people providing instruction instead of the schedule. This happens when there is shared vision in the school. Teachers don't see the number 25 percent. They see seventy-five students who will fail. By coming together and addressing the issue as one team, they made a difference.

Both teachers and students benefit from capacity building, since teachers' lack of self-belief can be passed on to students. Dennis Sparks (2005) reminds us that most educators do not see themselves as scientists, innovators, or problem solvers. He writes, "The intellectual and creative capacity of educators, particularly principals and teachers, to make significant improvements in teaching and learning is an underdeveloped and untapped resource" (p. xiii). Thus, capacity building is important for the morale of the whole school.

Capacity building reminds me of Cassie Erkens who—during my 2005 orientation as a Solution Tree PLC associate—said, "He who does the talking is doing the learning!" For instance, my third-grade team once came to me and said, "Our kids are just not motivated; they have the skills but don't seem to care!" I asked, "What do you plan to do about it?" and waited for them to do the talking. Finally I heard, "We could have a night where we brought all of those students together, told them and their parents that we believed in them and that we *expect them* to pass." They called the event the Achievable Dream. Our affirmation of students read:

- We believe that you are capable of achieving your goals with the guidance and support from your parents and school.

- We believe, if you utilize your test-taking strategies, that you will do well on the standards of learning and testing.

- We believe in your ability to do your best!

In addition, we sent invites home for parents. They said, "We believe your child can pass." The result was standing-room-only attendance at the event.

Previously, I had noticed one teacher who had a very personal way of speaking directly to selected students during honors assemblies. She would say, "John, you came to me last week and said, 'Mrs. Clarke, I know I can do it,' *and you did!*" I selected her to make personal statements of belief that night directly to students with their parents standing next to them. There was not a dry eye in the room. She also wrote and sang a song to the students. I had no idea she possessed such a gift. During Mike Mattos's presentation in our school system, he said a high level of performance is bigger than a test score. This is what I think he meant: it is about demonstrating belief in your staff and allowing them to pass that belief on to their students.

Vertical Anchors

Vertical anchors include systematic monitoring, schedule flexibility, and schoolwide sharing of practices and data. These anchors keep everyone on the same page.

Sharing data publicly should be seen as an opportunity to ask for help. This decision was pivotal to our success; it allowed everyone to take ownership. Bolman and Deal (2001), experts in educational leadership, call it authorship. Consider the teachers who viewed footage of one of our fourth-grade teacher data discussions—they were moved to tears. One said, "They look so, so professional! That's who I wanted to be when I became a teacher." Another response was, "They are laughing!" Yes, they were laughing because it was their data. It is analogous to home ownership versus rental—when a person owns something, he or she puts more pride and effort into making it appealing to others.

Baseline Supporters

In the end, a schedule is just an object on paper; people make it real, including teachers, specialists, support staff, the principal, students, and parents. Everyone involved in a school can provide baseline support in Tier 1. Every individual in the school needs to know and embrace the mission and vision of the school. "Excellence for all . . . Whatever it takes" had to become real for us. Our teachers at each grade level were constantly reminded that our mission was excellence, not mediocrity, and that we said *all*, not some. Finally, we were committed to do whatever it took to achieve our goal.

I contend that you can have the most sophisticated schedule in the universe, but when that schedule belongs to you alone as a principal, sooner or later your beautifully drawn schedule with all of its bells and whistles will become simply another thing you have to do, and eventually your pyramid will collapse or die a slow death due to lack of use.

Kotter (2008) warns that a lack of urgency is the number one reason people do not buy in to the vision and mission of businesses. He also cautions that a false sense of urgency is even worse and more difficult to see. These are staff members who just pretend to be engaged and are not really part of the baseline needed to support the school. These are the people who walk fast, talk fast, look very busy, and have thousands of PowerPoint slideshows. They have notebooks filled with pretty graphs, but they don't use any to guide instruction. They present false tall graphs to cover up their shortcomings. They may even have a library of professional books, but if you look closely, there is none of what I laughingly call "air between the pages," because they have not read them.

When this situation happens, your leadership team needs assurance that you will have the courage to step up to the plate and make a painful decision, which sometimes includes relieving or reassigning an individual. This is one part of what DuFour (2007) calls *tight and loose leadership*. I have had to do this a few times in my career. Allen Bell, a former teacher and now an assistant principal, often referred to what happens in true PLC schools as "the good, the bad, and the sometimes downright ugly." Most teacher leaders are professionals and will take care of challenges themselves. They do, however, expect you to take care of the dependent people who expect others to carry their loads.

The Glue

Glue is needed to seal the three tiers together and smooth cracks in the pyramid surface. Without it, negativity and low staff engagement can invade the structure. This glue is both the provision of time to conduct data sharing and the celebration of small wins.

Weekly data chats with teachers allow principals to see who is supporting the pyramid, who needs help, and who is demonstrating a false sense of urgency. Waiting a full quarter to discuss data with teachers is similar to waiting months before you repair a small leak in the roof. It does not go away. In fact, it gets bigger. Small leaks of negativity and wrong thinking can invade and result in a flood later. You can be more positive and responsive when you respond to small student losses. For instance, I recall when a small unnoticeable lack of curriculum alignment in our instruction for the state writing predictor became a flood on the day the results came in. We were so proud of our diligence to time on task that we failed to do what Richard DuFour often refers to as the "right work." We were excited when the test results packet arrived—to the point of being downright giddy—but when we saw the results, we were devastated. It was the first and only time that I saw four adult teachers cry out loud. I vowed to never have that happen again. Yet there was a positive side to this reaction: I knew these teachers would never allow this to occur a second time. Their emotional response told me they saw themselves as the owners of the poor results. Your final results should never be a surprise—it is as simple as that.

It is important to celebrate as well. I cannot tell you how many times I have heard the phrase "Don't forget to celebrate success" as a casual reminder. I have even heard my colleagues respond with, "I'm just not good at that!" Yet, Marzano (2012) lists it as number three in his forty-one research-based strategies.

Gostick and Elton (2009) have researched the importance of recognition in the workplace for years and have worked with over a million people. They say recognition is effective because it answers a universal human need. We all want to matter to those we work with. They say there is no accelerant with more impact than purpose-based recognition. Communication combined with recognition of strategically important behaviors takes your mission and vision off the wall and puts them into the hearts and minds of your people, which is exactly where you want them to be.

We found several ways to celebrate at Vaughan. As a staff, we used a fun, themed meal when sharing data with the entire staff. This approach conveyed that it was safe to share your successes and your temporary failures here—we've got your back. This atmosphere also encouraged interdependence.

We held pep rallies as well, where all students and teachers wore self-designed thinking caps because, as noted previously, thinking instead of test scores was our focus. Students were rewarded for thinking while testing (such as justifying answers on paper, using scratch paper for mathematics, and maintaining a record of the number they got right during the test). In addition, Fridays ended with celebratory songs over the intercom, and sometimes I marched down the hall with the Bright Ones. In addition, I awarded a principal cup to a deserving staff member weekly, since I wanted the students *and* staff to end the week on a high note. These cups were given to individuals who made small contributions behind the scenes or to those who exceeded expectation. I asked the staff if they wanted to select the recipient, and they said, "No, we like it better when you do it and when it is a surprise . . . Our kids go crazy when our name is called." I wasn't sure teachers appreciated these demitasse cups until they returned one to me as a retirement gift.

Not all celebrations were events. For instance, our brick sidewalk engraved with the names of honor roll students is front and center when you enter the school. Students return as adults to see their brick and even bring relatives on holidays. Kent Peterson and Terrence Deal (2009) remind us that physical space can create a sense of mission and purpose for students and staff. Every piece of wall art in our school is related to the mission and vision of creating a college-bound atmosphere. In addition, our High Ex Center induced envy in visiting educators. For me, creating a professional environment for teachers to share their work was as vital as creating a surgical suite in a hospital. Treat your staff like the professionals they are!

Conclusion

At the end of the day, when we grow *people* like the Roberts of the world, test scores will follow. I frequently use the phrase, "People are not moved by facts; they are moved by emotions!" If your only way of improving performance is to say, "We've got to get these test scores up or you are fired," staff members will eventually drift away because they will either get tired of hearing this test-score mantra, or you will become exhausted, sit down and stop holding up the pyramid, or hold it up alone. There has to be something about you as a principal that makes people want to follow your leadership. When that happens, your schedule will move from being a written document to a vehicle for student improvement.

As Robert's father said on behalf of Vaughan parents:

> Mrs. Jessie has lived her *Life Lit by Some Large Vision* [Davis, 2006] that I can never fully address or appreciate. We thank you for . . . being a champion of our children and celebrating their individual uniqueness and diversity while at the same time uniting them with a sense of collective purpose and pride. We thank you for pursuing high achievement—and striving valiantly, daringly, and greatly. (R. Davenport, personal communication, January 31, 2011)

Notice that Robert's father did not say, "Thank you for those high test scores." He could have, since they went out of their way to have Robert attend Vaughan instead of their neighborhood school, but instead he focused on the energy and pride Vaughan emanates thanks to our baseline supporters. Instead he referenced vision. Principals must have a vision that is obvious and contagious so others will embrace it and follow. How can teachers follow you if you do not know where you are going? That was the greatest compliment I could have received.

It is very difficult for negativity to invade your pyramid structure when you have so much positive energy shielding the people, programs, and ideas you have inside. Gostick and Elton's (2009) research finds that with competent leadership, celebration, and recognition act as accelerants. So, the "principal" of it all is that, at the end of the day, the glue is you!

References and Resources

Bolman, L. G., & Deal, T. E. (2001). *Leading with soul: An uncommon journey of spirit* (Rev. ed.). San Francisco: Jossey-Bass.

Buffum, A., Erkens, C., Hinman, C., Huff, S., Jessie, L., Martin, T. L., et al. (2008). *The collaborative administrator: Working together as a professional learning community.* Bloomington, IN: Solution Tree Press.

Buffum, A., Mattos, M., & Weber, C. (2009). *Pyramid response to intervention: RTI, professional learning communities, and how to respond when kids don't learn.* Bloomington, IN: Solution Tree Press.

Canady, R. L., & Rettig, M. D. (2008). *Elementary school scheduling: Enhancing instruction for student achievement.* Larchmont, NJ: Eye on Education.

Chenoweth, K. (2009). *How it's being done: Urgent lessons from unexpected schools.* Cambridge, MA: Harvard Education Press.

Davis, O. (2006). *Life lit by some large vision: Selected speeches and writings.* New York: Atria Books.

DuFour, R. (2007). In praise of top-down leadership. *American Association of School Administrators, 64*(10), 38–42.

DuFour, R., DuFour, R., Eaker, R., & Many, T. W. (2010). *Learning by doing: A handbook for professional learning communities at work* (2nd ed.). Bloomington, IN: Solution Tree Press.

DuFour, R., Eaker, R., & DuFour, R. (2007). *The power of professional learning communities at work: Bringing the big ideas to life* [DVD]. Bloomington, IN: Solution Tree Press.

Dweck, C. (2006). *Mindset: The new psychology of success.* New York: Random House.

Ferguson, R. F. (2007). *Toward excellence with equity: An emerging vision for closing the achievement gap.* Cambridge, MA: Harvard Education Press.

Garner, B. K. (2007). *Getting to "got it!": Helping struggling students learn how to learn.* Alexandria, VA: Association for Supervision and Curriculum Development.

Gostick, A., & Elton, C. (2009). *The carrot principle: How the best managers use recognition to engage their people, retain talent, and accelerate performance.* New York: Free Press.

Hattie, J. A. C. (2009). *Visible learning: A synthesis of over 800 meta-analyses relating to achievement.* New York: Routledge.

Howard, J. (1992). *Schools that work: The research advantage, videoconference #7, preparing students for work in the 21st century.* Oak Brook, IL: North Central Regional Educational Laboratory.

Howard, J. (2011, October 8). *An attribution primer.* Accessed at www.efficacy.org/Portals/7/Article_Downloads/Writings_by_dr_jeff_howard/AnAttributionPrimer.pdf on March 25, 2014.

Kotter, J. (2008). *A sense of urgency.* Boston: Harvard Business School Press.

Kouzes, J., & Posner, B. (2007). *The leadership challenge* (4th ed.). San Francisco: Jossey-Bass.

Lezotte, L., & McKee, K. (2002). *Assembly required: A continuous school improvement system.* Okemos, MI: Effective Schools Products.

Marzano, R. J. (2012). *Becoming a reflective teacher.* Bloomington, IN: Marzano Research Laboratory.

Marzano, R. J., Pickering, D., & Pollock, J. (2001). *Classroom instruction that works: Research-based strategies for increasing student achievement.* Alexandria, VA: Association for Supervision and Curriculum Development.

Peterson, K. D., & Deal, T. E. (2009). *The shaping school culture fieldbook* (2nd ed.). San Francisco: Jossey-Bass.

Pink, D. H. (2005). *A whole new mind: Moving from the information age to the conceptual age.* New York: Riverhead Books.

Reeves, D. B. (2006). *The learning leader: How to focus school improvement for better results.* Alexandria, VA: Association for Supervision and Curriculum Development.

Savitz-Romer, M., & Bouffard, S. M. (2012). *Ready, willing, and able: A developmental approach to college access.* Cambridge, MA: Harvard Education Press.

Shenk, D. (2010). *The genius in all of us: Why everything you've been told about genetics, talent, and IQ is wrong.* New York: Doubleday.

Sparks, D. (2005). *Leading for results: Transforming teaching, learning, and relationships in schools.* Thousand Oaks, CA: Corwin Press.

 **Merrilou Harrison** is an educational consultant who also is the dean of the College of Education and Psychology for Heritage University. Merrilou draws from her success with the PLC at Work model to share passionate and practical information. With many years of experience, Merrilou has taught and been an administrator at every grade level. Her presentations, workshops, and trainings contain strategies that empower educators to play an active role in the success of *all* students.

As a principal at Gilbert Elementary in Yakima, Washington, a featured school on the All Things PLC site, Merrilou faced significant challenges. This low-performing urban school enrolled 525 students, including a high percentage of youth at risk. This urban school was 61 percent minority students, 75 percent students of poverty, 22 percent special education students, and 25 percent second language learners. Merrilou led her staff in building a PLC to ensure all students received the time and support necessary to succeed.

To learn more about Merrilou's work, follow @MerrilouH on Twitter.

To book Merrilou Harrison for professional development, contact pd@solution-tree .com.

Working in an RTI Construction Zone

Merrilou Harrison

Editors' Note

Throughout this chapter, the author refers to the role of the Instructional Leadership Team (ILT), and in doing so makes an important point. As John Kotter (1996) states, "Putting together the right coalition of people to lead a change initiative is critical to its success" (p. 57). During each step of Gilbert Elementary School's journey, the ILT helped guide the change process in partnership with the collaborative teacher teams. Instead of first imposing a structure or schedule, the ILT asked the right questions, eventually leading to a complete system of interventions.

One of the most important distinctions drawn by the questioning of the ILT was the difference between grouping students for interventions based on the causes of their struggles rather than the symptoms. This realization, however, only came after the school had identified essential outcomes, unwrapped these outcomes into learning targets, and learned how to assess targets more discretely instead of assessing entire standards. The evolution that led the school to provide highly diagnostic interventions was a result of constant reflection and asking the right questions, as guided by the ILT.

The staff of Gilbert Elementary in Yakima, Washington, got an abrupt wake-up call when our district notified us that we qualified for various school improvement grants based on student performance on state assessments. This was the first time we had qualified for such a grant, which meant our students were not as successful as we had perceived. We looked deeply at our data and saw our current reality: our students had not made growth in mathematics and reading for several years. The focus of the district at that time was on reading, so we also chose to focus on reading as we set off to raise achievement for all students.

The Gilbert staff decided that the professional learning community process was the structure we wanted to implement for student success, so we used the grant monies to jumpstart our PLC journey. We felt confident that we understood our curriculum well enough to look at the interventions needed for our students to experience success. As we met and began our planning, however, we quickly realized that what we were planning was actually remediation. While planning long-term instruction, we were looking at students who were significantly below grade level. It became apparent that we needed to focus our own learning on understanding the purpose and structure of interventions before we could move forward. We found that interventions were more immediate and focused on current skills for the students, so we regrouped to start again.

Our Instructional Leadership Team began to plan professional development that included gathering and assigning research books and articles to read, share, and discuss. The purpose of the reading was to build a common vocabulary and to jumpstart deeper conversations. From our reading came guided conversations to help answer the following questions.

- What truly are interventions?
- By whom and when are they delivered?
- What content makes a difference for the learning of all students?

As our staff went through internal learning, we also were sending teams to PLC institutes and summits. We learned that the critical foundation for interventions was to determine first what essential outcomes our students needed to learn and then how we were going to deliver a strong core curriculum with differentiation for all of our students in all classrooms.

This led us to create a dual focus of adult learning in our school: (1) understanding the entire PLC journey as a school and (2) determining the essential outcomes for students as teacher teams. The ILT took the lead in planning and facilitating both learning tracks. They helped each grade-level team work through a series of steps that intersected with other groups and teams at specific points along the way.

Through the leadership of the ILT, the staff spent substantial time working with the state standards. We determined the core of what needed to be taught (essential learnings), the priority weight of each standard, and the answer to the first critical question, What do we expect students to learn? After grade-level teams answered these questions, the teacher teams unpacked the essential standards and aligned the standards horizontally across grade levels and then vertically through the school. They also rewrote the standards in student-friendly language and posted them in classrooms to refer to throughout lessons.

The result of our learning was the realization that we still were not ready to plan interventions on a system level. We needed to gather evidence using a variety of assessments, multiple data points on a time line, rubrics, and viable data. The teacher teams had to work on the answers to the second critical PLC question (DuFour, DuFour, Eaker, & Many, 2010), How do we know they are learning it? Teacher teams studied and created common assessments, pretests, posttests, and different ways to assess student performance. A balanced assessment system began to develop at each grade level as teachers worked through action research on the effectiveness of the various assessments. Our data began to be more specific, and we knew more about each individual student. See figure 7.1 for an example of how we tracked these data.

Teacher: _____ Date: _____		
Assessment Results	**Student Numbers or Names**	**Intervention (Who and What)**
Above Grade Level		
At Grade Level		
Below Grade Level		

Figure 7.1: Sample assessment and intervention chart.

*Visit **go.solution-tree.com/rtiatwork** for a reproducible version of this figure.*

The deeper knowledge of each student caused the teachers to continue their struggle with how to best meet the needs of each student. To answer critical questions three and four (How do we respond when they do not learn? and How do we respond when they have already learned?), they asked a pattern of questions: "What needed to happen in the classroom and grade level if a student already knew or quickly understood a concept? What would happen if the student was so very close to that full knowledge and understanding of a concept and just needed a little extra help? What would happen if the student was going to need more support to understand the concept? How do we keep all students learning and moving along the reading competency continuum when there are many differing levels in a classroom?"

It was obvious that the continued goal was to do whatever it took to ensure that all students were successful. A critical component within each lesson was the planning of differentiation for student learning. As grade-level teams strove to answer guiding questions from the ILT about student data, they grew in their own understanding of the importance of analyzing data for each student in order to drive instruction. They then began to understand why interventions were important and discovered ways to provide these interventions for the students. Our learning had progressed from not really knowing what a student needed to learn to knowing specifics about each student. Only then were we able to plan interventions that met students' needs and more accurately measured their progress. It was not a program we could buy but a way of knowing the standards, content skills, and knowledge needed and of developing assessments that gave us the data most useful for both teachers and students (see figure 7.2).

Use this reflection tool when examining assessments with your grade-level team. Grade level: _____ Date: _____
Overall as a grade level, what are your students doing well? Why?
Overall as a grade level, where do your students need to improve? Why?
What are you going to do to meet this need?
How does this relate to your grade-level action plan? (SMART goal and big ideas)

Figure 7.2: Reflection tool for assessment results.

*Visit **go.solution-tree.com/rtiatwork** for a reproducible version of this figure.*

Our Research

The ILT again took the staff through various types of learning about curriculum and instruction on our PLC journey. We started with the *What Works* series from Robert Marzano. The entire staff took the overview online PLC course, and each year we sent different teacher teams to various PLC conferences until all faculty members had attended. This input told us *what* we were to look for in a curriculum, instruction, and assessment tool as well as *why*.

Various teachers gave us information from areas of their strengths or interests. We shared brain research along with positive accountability we learned from Roger Connors and Tom Smith (2009). The work of Kerry Patterson, Joseph Grenny, Ron McMillan, and Al Switzler (2002) on crucial conversations helped our teachers know how to talk with each other in a positive way, even when they had differing opinions.

The ILT read Mike Schmoker's (2011) book *Focus* and Michael Fullan's (2001) book *Leading in a Culture of Change* and looked at a variety of instructional frameworks and assessment books. Each team shared the information learned with the whole faculty. We then discussed the issues and emphasized the importance of adult learning within a school.

All of our reading led us to understand the importance of evidence. We gathered and analyzed data, which drove our decisions and celebrations. The research we studied continued to challenge us to know more about our students and to develop a guaranteed and viable curriculum. Student achievement grew as adult learning grew.

Our Barriers

Lest you think this was a smooth transition, I need to share with you our reality. This was a change from teaching in isolation to teaching as a team and as a school. We needed to build trust in each others' methods and in delivery of consistent content across the grade levels, which was a major cultural change. We had to take part in many conversations within the structure of our agreed-on mission, vision, and values. Norms kept us focused, and we needed to learn how to change the culture while honoring the people in the system.

Becoming a professional learning community was not an idea that the school district as a whole supported. We had to adhere to the mandated criteria from the school district and find ways to make excellent educational decisions for our students, while also fulfilling the district, state, and federal requirements for our budget and time. As Richard DuFour and Michael Fullan (2013) remind us, "People must be willing to look in the mirror for solutions, rather than out of the window while waiting for others in the system to save them" (p. 11). We had to look in the mirror at what we were doing for our students rather than looking out the window at the barriers that could stop us from best meeting our students' needs. This was a concept our school discussed often—we never wanted adult issues to stop the learning of students.

Time was another issue that we had to transform from a barrier to a tool. How were we supposed to use our time when we were mandated a specific number of minutes for reading and mathematics in our school? How could we best use the schedule without sacrificing our commitment to science, social studies, and the fine arts? We had to challenge our traditional way of looking at an elementary schedule and then plan out small steps rather than one big, bold step.

School scheduling traditions—when we had our planning time, who was our classroom support person, who had most seniority, how we had always done it—were the most important issues to address. The teacher's union negotiated agreement also had high impact on the number of minutes for prep and how we could use the minutes. To change the schedule and move from individuals to teams took negotiation and conversation about our prioritization of student learning.

The schedule was determined to be our first and biggest barrier of implementing strong interventions for our students. We began by letting teachers find time within their own personal schedule to meet individual student needs. When individual teachers had identified and implemented time within their own classrooms, they brought their ideas to their team.

Our Development

We compiled a large bank of improvement ideas from the individual teachers— what had worked, what had not, and why or why not. The literacy coach in our school also developed a bank of choices that would work with our curriculum for individual and team reference. These ideas began the conversation regarding when we could have interventions.

From the bank of ideas created, each team began to design when it could meet student needs as a team. We had learned the concept of "tight and loose" from our PLC trainings. The ILT began to develop and implement the concept of non-negotiables or the *what* that people and teams were held accountable for (tight). The "tight" criteria from the ILT were that each grade-level team needed to design interventions based on the data teachers had gathered from their common assessments. The "loose" criteria were what the teams had the freedom to determine, or *how* they would accomplish or implement the non-negotiables. The teachers were tasked to work together to implement their team ideas. The ILT also held each team accountable for the results of its interventions. How did the team know if the interventions worked or did not work? The teams analyzed the resulting data with coaches and administrators in teacher team meetings. The grade-level representative brought these data to the bimonthly ILT meetings. This put the responsibility on each grade-level team to experiment with what worked within that grade level. The teacher teams thus brought their successful ideas to enhance possible schedule changes for effective interventions throughout the entire system.

There were many discussions about the need for interventions to be a fluid system to avoid a tracking system or a permanent life sentence for each student. We determined that Tier 2 and Tier 3 interventions were to meet the needs of a student in specific concepts so they could move forward with confidence in this content area. This philosophy had to be understood throughout the whole school in order to provide a strong intervention system.

Each grade-level team started by identifying thirty minutes in its schedule (within the school day but outside of its reading block) as reading intervention time. From there, the teachers brought their schedules to the leadership team, who worked to have as many adults as possible available to assist the teachers during that time. This allowed the groups to be small and specific.

Each grade-level team determined the organization of the intervention time. The team had to decide how to best meet students' needs. The team also shared with the ILT the data and any evidence showing the impact of intervention time on students.

Our teacher teams started the PLC learning process by meeting twice a month. During their collaboration time, they focused on student learning and results. It became very clear to each team that meeting two hours a month did not accomplish what it wanted and needed to do for the students. So the teams adjusted their own schedules to meet once a week in formal, collaborative team meetings. The ILT was informed of the team schedules in order to attend and provide support in identifying students and resources needed. The team time gave the teachers a chance to develop curriculum, instruction, and assessment decisions together.

Since the intervention time had developed out of the common assessments teachers gave at each grade level, it was critical that the teacher teams clearly defined their guaranteed and viable curriculum (Marzano, 2010). Deciding which essential standards all students should achieve to mastery was a strong foundation the teachers could confidently build on. The work the teams had done to identify and unpack the essential standards guided not only the identification process but also the focus of the interventions.

The earlier discussions about remediation versus interventions laid a foundation for what needed to be done during intervention time. The students needed specific, targeted, differentiated instruction for a defined period of time, resulting in mastery of the identified skill. Teachers began to see the interconnectedness of what was happening in our building and how it was impacting student success. This was an energizing point for our teachers. Their work was moving them forward and was not just a hoop to jump through or a flavor-of-the-month exercise.

To determine student needs, the data had to show the specific knowledge or skills the student had not yet mastered. For example, it was not enough for our teachers to know that a student was below basic level in reading. We needed to determine specific needs, such as decoding, fluency, or second-language issues as the cause of the student's struggle. Each intervention group was specific to the student needs. For example, our district developed a worksheet to help our teachers use the data from their quarterly benchmark assessments. This worksheet helped the teachers quickly see if they had accomplished their grade-level goals for the quarter as well as develop a more specific "hot list" of students. This student list was developed from a few predetermined, research-based, specific, proven criteria that resulted in greater student success. See figure 7.3 for a sample worksheet to organize these data.

School or District:_____ Grade:_____ Date:_____

_____ Spring achievement goal percentage of students at benchmark

-     _____ Current (Winter) achievement percentage of students at benchmark

=   _____ percent increase needed

_____ Total number of students in grade level
✕ (multiplied by the goal percentage)

= _____ Goal number of benchmark students

- _____ Current number of benchmark students

= _____ Minimum additional number of students needed

Potential "hot list" students: Selection criteria will vary. In general, higher strategic students are likely candidates, but both word per minute and accuracy percentage are significant. (Note: This initial list may include a larger number but will be revised through the year, guided by careful tracking of individual progress with both rate and accuracy.)

Student	Rate Score	Accuracy Percentage	Intervention Needs

Figure 7.3: Analysis worksheet.

*Visit **go.solution-tree.com/rtiatwork** for a reproducible version of this figure.*

Interestingly, teachers found that the last thirty minutes of the school day were not the most effective for intervention groups. Students were not in prime form to learn, and teachers did not have the energy to teach their best. When the teachers did not see the results they wanted during late-in-the-day intervention time, they began to experiment with their own schedules, looking for a more productive time. A few teams began to take the first thirty to forty-five minutes of the day to run intervention groups. This became a grade-level-wide, all-student participation time during which individual student needs were met. These small groups were flexible and fluid. Students worked on the skills they needed to strengthen or expanded their skills to deeper levels of learning. Their successful results were shared with other teams, who followed suit. The early morning Tier 2 interventions that offered support for individuals and small groups of students who needed specific skill work, seemed to ease the students into deep thinking as the day began, while allowing more effective learning with Tier 1 support to continue throughout the day.

Another scheduling issue teams raised at leadership team meetings was that we saw a need to have reading instruction (or mathematics instruction) occur at the same time across a grade level's schedule. This allowed students to be instructed at their grade level and supported at their instructional level without missing core content in other subject areas. Our students began to "walk to read"—moving to various classrooms and teachers to receive reading instruction—which grew into the teachers working together so the students could receive differentiated instruction at their appropriate level. All teachers taught all students. In this way, we cultivated grade-level relationships, and the very culture of the building began to change. We were focused on learning and the results of that learning for each and every student no matter what it took.

Our Responsibility

Our PLC journey taught us that teachers working in teams, making important instructional decisions, learning together, and implementing what they designed were critical pieces of student success. Teachers were enjoying the journey and working hard for each student. Consequently, our ILT was able to hand many of the school instructional decisions completely over to the grade-level teams and then guide the intersections needed for the whole school.

Each grade-level teacher team determined (using its data) what each student needed—for example, help with initial sounds, vocabulary, or second-language patterns—and how they would best meet that need. The teacher teams looked at the data, determined the student groups, planned the learning activities, and decided who would be teaching each group. They also recommended strategies for each student group and determined what evidence they would accept that indicated mastery and effective strategies. See figure 7.4 for an example of recording lesson designs with instructional strategies.

Name: _____   Grade: _____

Topic or Unit of Study: _____

Instructional Structure: _____ Small group   _____ Whole group

_____ Partner activity   _____ Individual instruction

What do students need to know or be able to do (grade-level essential standards) for this lesson?

List two or three essential questions that will focus student learning on the big ideas related to this topic or unit of study.

List the assessment or product you will include to help determine the students' understanding of the big ideas in this unit.

List the major instructional strategies that you will use in your teaching lesson.

List the resources you will use.

Figure 7.4: Lesson design with instructional strategies.

*Visit **go.solution-tree.com/rtiatwork** for a reproducible version of this figure.*

The ILT took on the responsibility of supporting teacher teams in as many ways as it could. It provided additional adults during intervention time to support the students. We read and discussed Kati Haycock's (2009) work on the caliber of teachers, and this influenced the decision that the strongest teacher in any specific content would teach the weakest students in that content or skill. We recruited many adults within the school and community (parents, grandparents, retired people, professionals with high content knowledge, visual and performing artists) to aid the grade levels by helping plan and implement the curriculum for the students who needed extensions rather than interventions.

Because of the conversations, research, and personal success, teachers were able and willing to make excellent educational decisions. They also realized that with these decisions came the responsibility to prove that they were truly making a difference for each student.

Our Monitoring Process

Once again, the ILT took the direction for how we as a school were going to monitor our progress. We looked at the data. We listened to the teachers. We were part of our students' education. We began satiating our hunger for more information on our students, and we celebrated each student's success. The culture was deepening into one of learning success for all students.

Our system had district benchmark assessments, unit assessments, standardized state and program assessments, and common formative assessments, and from these assessments, we gathered different types of data that gave us a complete picture of our students. Austin Buffum, Mike Mattos, and Chris Weber (2012) call this *convergent assessment.*

Within their teams, teachers had to determine what constituted mastery of a standard and which pieces of evidence they would use to determine if their teaching and interventions were effective. With that ownership came several adult learning issues—areas in which the teachers needed to expand their own knowledge or perspective. As they looked at the assessments and the results as a team, they began to understand how to identify whether learning was taking place and at what mastery level students were learning. They also had to look closely at the standards and state assessment to ensure that the level of instruction and assessments given matched the level of rigor the students would encounter on the high-stakes assessments. Teams used Benjamin Bloom's (1956) Taxonomy of Learning Domains to determine each standard's level of rigor.

Another way that teacher teams monitored their own work was through vertical alignment. The teachers calibrated their own perspectives and data decisions based on the input of other grade levels looking at the same assessment and rubrics. This was done once a quarter so that teachers were always aware of how they fed into another grade level and if their standard of grading was in accordance with what we were expecting throughout the school. Once we identified trends within our data that spanned across the school (such as mathematics measurement or nonfiction text-based answers to questions), all grade levels came together to plan how to best meet student needs and create consistent learning.

Student results were posted in the common hallways for parents and students alike to review and celebrate. Privacy was honored, but learning was celebrated. In fact, we celebrated all students when they showed improvement, since it was vitally important for the students to see their own academic growth in comparison to the standard and not to other students. It was very motivating for students and teachers to see each student approach or surpass the mastery level of the grade-level standards.

The ILT also reviewed data once a quarter to determine how to best support the staff with instruction and interventions. The administrative team (made up of an administrator and coaches) reviewed all of the data for trends across grade levels and teacher teams, support needs of the staff, and celebrations of team successes. We turned monitoring student growth and classroom performance levels from negative ideas into positive actions that caused us excitement and joy at seeing exactly what our students and staff were accomplishing.

Our Changes

After experiencing interventions they had created, changes they had made in the schedule, and more planning and implementation, teachers were able to come together as a whole school to create a formal pyramid of interventions that identified what we as a system were doing or committed to doing for our students.

Teacher teams could also begin to discuss other ways that students could experience interventions or extensions. We identified other teachers, student tutors, online teaching, computer programs, and so on as possible tools. The administration also brought other non-teaching staff (such as custodians, cooks, or office staff) on board to use their strengths to help extend the learning or intervene with individual students. For example, one custodian would read with some of our students, while another custodian helped students with mathematics problems. All adults in the building were seen as educators to help our students succeed. Identifying what each student needed to know and providing that knowledge in different ways became our first priority. It didn't matter what the student's barrier was. Each person in our building was committed to do whatever it took (DuFour, DuFour, Eaker, & Karhanek, 2004) for that student to experience success. Everyone was considered a learning guide in one form or another.

To continue helping our teachers, we developed a comprehensive list of available intervention curriculums to use with students. We also organized extensions from the reading curriculum to use. We included our special education teachers within the pyramid response to intervention system as well.

Our schedules, curriculum, instructional strategies, and assessments were always under team review. If we were not getting the results we wanted, we discussed possibilities, planned responses, and implemented next steps. Response to student needs went from being a once-a-quarter or once-a-year discussion to being the regular ebb and flow of our school (see figure 7.5).

School: _____

Grade: _____ Date:_____

Area of Focus	Instructional Data	Who Delivers	Time line	Resources Needed	Measure of Effectiveness

Teacher Signatures:

_____

_____

_____

_____

Figure 7.5: Grade-level action plan.

*Visit **go.solution-tree.com/rtiatwork** for a reproducible version of this figure.*

Our Extensions

This whole process led us to better understand the fourth critical PLC question (DuFour et al., 2010), How do we respond when they have already learned? This question became a driving force behind our next major learning as a staff. When students take a pretest on prerequisite skills and knowledge directly aligned to essential standards before initial instruction begins, teachers can prepare strategies in advance to help scaffold instruction for those students lacking in the academic vocabulary, skills, and knowledge needed for mastery of those same standards. They were also allotted time, with guidance, to pursue topics of their own interest in order to apply the standard or concept.

To say that extensions came easier than interventions would be misleading. Extensions were an area in which our teacher teams struggled. How to successfully extend one student's learning while meeting the needs of other students within the class continued to be an area with less research and fewer strong answers. One of the best answers for our teams was to implement the schoolwide "walk to read" schedule so that students could be closer to their instructional level during core instruction with extensions built into the lesson.

During our intervention time, we placed the students who needed extensions in well-planned groups. Students were assigned to the extension groups as soon as they provided evidence of mastery. We recruited community members, building staff, and district staff to expand the learning of the standards. For instance, community members presented real-life scenarios to the students to expand their learning as well as to provide context and relevance for our students.

This work on real-life issues (lunch choices, playground equipment, dress codes, animal cruelty, and so on) that required them to understand the complexity of the problem and develop solutions also motivated all of our students to learn the standards as soon as possible in order to apply that learning to issues they were interested in. They were motivated to participate in proposing solutions to both school and community issues. This continued our implementation of the agreed-on philosophy that groups were fluid and open to all students.

Our Results

Once our teacher teams understood and implemented the core curriculum and assessments, we began to see strong results with our students. We were motivated to continue this upward trajectory, but then we heard about the infamous implementation dip we should expect to experience as we progressed in our own personal learning as well as in the student learning. We also needed to look at our system of interventions as long term and recognize that it would take at least three years for all of our learning to be a part of our culture. Within this implementation, there would be gains and losses. Accepting these times as learning times was a major foundation for our growth. We often had to remind each other that learning would not happen in a linear fashion. We were on a journey.

Not everything teachers tried worked, but by reading other people's stories, looking at the available research, and studying various strategies that were showing results with students, they overcame each obstacle. They came to understand that their own learning was a critical piece of the whole puzzle in meeting student needs.

As the teachers implemented interventions in their classroom, shared the ideas with their grade-level teams, and continued to have conversations with the whole staff, they began to see results. Doing action research on what they thought would work and then looking deeply at the results drove the teachers to make stronger decisions for each student. The ILT had to continually focus on what their teams knew, what they needed to know more about, what resources they needed, and each team's results. Using that information, the ILT members became resources in helping all teachers improve instructional skills and strategies for the benefit of student achievement. The differentiated learning expanded beyond a focus on the students to include each teacher's expertise.

We studied 21st century skills and determined that our teachers needed to give pretests, come together as teams, analyze the results, plan differentiation within the classroom and grade level, and *then* teach. As the adult and student learning took place within the school, we realized that our learning had changed our focus from teaching to learning for *all* students.

This was not an easy journey. But as with all journeys, there were highs and lows. What we did discover was that this journey was so very worth it. We experienced success with our students, and we experienced success as educators. Realizing how far we had come in our journey motivated us to continue refining what we knew about our students and ourselves in order to offer an excellent education for all of the students who came to our school.

References and Resources

Bloom, B. (1956). *Bloom's taxonomy of learning domains*. Boston: Allyn & Bacon.

Buffum, A., Mattos, M., & Weber, C. (2012). *Simplifying response to intervention: Four essential guiding principles*. Bloomington, IN: Solution Tree Press.

Connors, R., & Smith, T. (2009). *How did that happen?: Holding people accountable for results the positive, principled way*. New York: Penguin.

DuFour, R., DuFour, R., Eaker, R., & Karhanek, G. (2004). *Whatever it takes: How professional learning communities respond when kids don't learn*. Bloomington, IN: Solution Tree Press.

DuFour, R., DuFour, R., Eaker, R., & Many, T. W. (2010). *Learning by doing: A handbook for professional learning communities at work* (2nd ed.). Bloomington, IN: Solution Tree Press.

DuFour, R., & Eaker, R. (1998). *Professional learning communities at work: Best practices for enhancing student achievement*. Bloomington, IN: Solution Tree Press.

DuFour, R., & Eaker, R. (2002). *Getting started: Reculturing schools to become professional learning communities*. Bloomington, IN: Solution Tree Press.

DuFour, R., & Fullan, M. (2013). *Cultures built to last: Systemic PLCs at work*. Bloomington, IN: Solution Tree Press.

Fullan, M. (2001). *Leading in a culture of change*. San Francisco: Jossey-Bass.

Fullan, M. (2007). *The new meaning of educational change* (4th ed.). New York: Teachers College Press.

Haycock, K. (2009). *Access to strong teachers*. Washington, DC: The Education Trust.

Kotter, J. (1996). *Leading change*. Boston: Harvard Business School Press.

Marzano, R. J. (2010). *Formative assessment & standards-based grading*. Bloomington, IN: Marzano Research Laboratory.

Marzano, R. J., Pickering, D. J., & Pollock, J. E. (2001). *Classroom instruction that works: Research-based strategies for increasing student achievement*. Alexandria, VA: Association for Supervision and Curriculum Development.

McKenna, M. C., & Stahl, A. D. (2009). *Assessment for reading instruction* (2nd ed.). New York: Guilford Press.

National Research Council. (2000). *How people learn: Brain, mind, experience, and school* (Expanded ed.). Washington, DC: National Academies Press.

Patterson, K., Grenny, J., McMillan, R., & Switzler, A. (2002). *Crucial conversations: Tools for talking when stakes are high*. New York: McGraw-Hill.

Roger, C., & Smith, T. (2009). *How did that happen?: Holding people accountable for results the positive, principled way*. New York: Portfolio.

Schmoker, M. (2011). *Focus: Elevating the essentials to radically improve student learning*. Alexandria, VA: Association for Supervision and Curriculum Development.

Sousa, D. A. (Ed.). (2010). *Mind, brain, and education: Neuroscience implications for the classroom*. Bloomington, IN: Solution Tree Press.

 **Maria Nielsen** has served as a teacher and administrator at every level of K–12 education for thirty years. She began her career as an elementary teacher then moved to the middle school level as a teacher and administrator. She then served as the assistant principal at North Cache 8–9 Center in Richmond, Utah, before moving to Mountain Crest High School in Hyrum, Utah, as an administrator. She is currently the principal at Millville Elementary, a low-income, Title I school in Northern Utah.

With a passion for positive school culture, collaboration, and student learning, Maria empowered the staff at Millville Elementary with the skills and tools necessary to receive state and national recognition as a model professional learning community. Millville has received numerous awards from the Utah State Office of Education as a high-achieving, high-progress Reward School.

Maria was named the 2007 Utah Behavior Initiatives Principal of the Year, and in 2010, received the distinguished Huntsman Award for Excellence in Education. Her work has been published in *Impact Journal* and on All Things PLC (www.allthingsplc.info).

For more on Maria's work, follow @MariaNielsenPLC on Twitter.

To book Maria Nielsen for professional development, contact pd@solution-tree.com.

8

Making Time at Tier 2

Maria Nielsen

> **Editors' Note**
>
> This chapter, focusing on Tier 2 interventions, presents a profoundly important idea in the second paragraph that could easily be overlooked: Tier 2 interventions should provide additional time and support to those students who did not master the specific learning targets prioritized by teachers as part of Tier 1 instruction. While this might seem obvious, we have seen hundreds of schools whose Tier 2 interventions are not even remotely connected to what the school had determined as essential for all students to learn at Tier 1.
>
> The chapter also shares multiple examples of the reason why Millville Elementary's Tier 2 interventions are so successful—they are highly targeted by multiple assessments. This includes the weekly progress monitoring and, even more importantly, weekly feedback to students. Millville's formula for success is this: small groups + targeted interventions = increased student achievement.

The goal is simple. We want all of our students to have the skills necessary to move from grade to grade and ultimately be successful in life. Actually accomplishing this, however, is not simple. It requires a team of dedicated teachers and administrators with a plan of action to provide skill-specific interventions when students are struggling. We have found, through data analysis, that when students are divided into small groups for targeted interventions, student achievement increases significantly. This chapter will help you create time in your daily schedule for response to intervention and build a road map of success for your students. It is my hope that by reading about our obstacles and successes at Millville Elementary in Northern Utah, you will be able to move your school forward to meet the needs of each of your students.

The purpose of Tier 2 interventions is to ensure that students who do not understand the learning targets taught during Tier 1 receive additional support to master the concepts and skills. At Millville, Tier 2 instruction for reading and mathematics takes place during the school day, five days a week for thirty to forty-five minutes, depending on the grade level. Tier 2 groups are designed for skill-specific targeted interventions and extensions. We utilize a push-in model in which paraprofessionals go to the classrooms to work with groups of five to six students. All students in the grade level are involved and move quickly between classrooms. The classroom teachers, as well as highly qualified paraprofessionals, teach skill-specific groups. Teachers review Tier 2 common assessment data weekly to ensure that students are mastering the identified learning targets. Students are taught and retested until they reach mastery, and they do not miss new instruction to receive this support. Those students who do not require remediation are involved in rigorous extension activities.

It hasn't always been this way at Millville. It began with a conference in Scottsdale, Arizona, where Richard DuFour and Rebecca DuFour created a vision and gave a compelling reason to start the journey. The message was clear: "This process works in thousands of schools! It will work in yours too."

Did it magically just come together? No, it took hard work, stepping back, crawling forward, and being truly dedicated. We had to decide what was worth fighting for. We had to believe, really believe, instead of just writing it down on paper, that all students could learn at high levels. With steady energy, we moved from focusing on percentages of students passing to a focus on individual student mastery of essential standards during Tier 2, and we immediately started seeing results! Individual students were worth fighting for, and we championed their success.

A Compelling Reason

Prior to our work with RTI, we were an excellent Title I school that celebrated scores on state end-of-level tests at 80 percent proficient. We were satisfied with our level of student learning, and then it happened: we landed in program improvement and had to take a good, hard look at our educational practices and procedures. We came to the realization, as Richard DuFour often states, that we had settled rather than soared. We knew the students who weren't performing on grade level, but we blamed their lack of success on their demographics, their economic status, and their parents.

We knew that we needed to change or tighten up some of the things we were doing at Millville in regard to student learning; however, there were a few obstacles we needed to overcome first.

- Clarifying essential standards

- Finding time to collaborate

- Changing the master schedule so that grade-level teachers had a common planning time

- Aligning daily class schedules on each grade level to allow for movement of students from class to class during Tier 2

- Scheduling time for skill-specific Tier 2 reading and mathematics interventions and extensions

- Developing common assessments to identify students in need of additional support for skill-specific interventions

- Having our paraprofessionals and classroom teachers communicate concerning Tier 2 group data

- Digging into the data without getting bogged down

With a clear vision of where we wanted to go we mapped out a plan and jumped right in.

Clarifying Essential Standards

Kim Bailey, Chris Jakicic, and Jeanne Spiller (2014) write, "In the unwrapping process, teams huddle around a standard and dig deeply into what's written and not written to reveal specific learning targets" (p. 60). First, we had to get clear on the first critical PLC question (DuFour, DuFour, Eaker, & Many, 2010), What do we expect students to learn? This work was the foundation for Tier 1 instruction and subsequently Tier 2 intervention. In order to kick-start the process, we hired substitutes while the teachers met for a day to begin unwrapping and powering the standards (see figure 8.1, page 168). The remainder of this work took place during daily common planning times and on Fridays when all teachers met together. Rather than relying on a program to teach targets, we identified essential standards aligned with core standards.

Students go home early on Friday afternoon or attend the afterschool program, allowing time for teacher teams to meet and collaborate. This time is acquired by increasing school hours twenty minutes longer Monday through Thursday. To use this time wisely, we had to change our practice of using Friday team times for faculty meetings, committee meetings, and individual planning time to collaborative PLC meetings. Now, every Friday at Millville, all teachers meet in the media center in their grade-level teams. Meeting in a common area gives teams access to other grade-level teams for vertical alignment as well as opportunity for collaboration with administrators and specialty teachers such as resource, ESL, and reading facilitators.

Standard: RL.5.2—Determine a theme of a story, drama, or poem from details in the text, including how characters in a story or drama respond to challenges or how the speaker in a poem reflects upon a topic; summarize the text.		
Learning Target	**Instruction**	**Assessment**
Target: Determine a theme of a story, drama, or poem from details in the text, including how characters in a story or drama respond to challenges and how a speaker in a poem reflects upon a topic.	**Mini-Unit:** Review components of theme related to details of the text. Demonstrate how details convey theme/central idea. Guided practice in small or large groups	**Selected Response:** Theme identification in multiple choice **Short Constructed Response:** Identify theme/central idea and the details in the text that convey it.
Target: Summarize the text.	Include theme/central idea in summary and details. Review summary writing strategies. Review the difference between personal opinions and judgments. Use a model to demonstrate connection of theme and summary.	Assess with a writing prompt. Use a summary writing rubric.
Vocabulary: *theme, summary*		

Source: Adapted from NGA & CCSSO, 2010, p. 12.

Figure 8.1: Unpacking template.

*Visit **go.solution-tree.com/rtiatwork** for a reproducible version of this figure.*

Finding Time to Collaborate

This gave us the time we needed to define a guaranteed and viable curriculum, plan assessment and instruction, and look at student data to place students in skill-specific groups on a weekly basis. In his book *What Works in Schools*, Robert Marzano (2003) tells us that to *guarantee* a curriculum means that from class to class and school to school, all students in a grade level are guaranteed the same essential standards. *Viable* means that students are able to learn the concepts in the scheduled amount of time.

PLC meeting time is protected against housekeeping tasks, and teachers focus exclusively on the four critical questions (DuFour et al., 2010).

1. What do we expect students to learn?

2. How do we know they are learning it?

3.   How do we respond when they do not learn?

4.   How do we respond when they have already learned?

Providing time during the contractual day for grade-level teams to meet is essential for the work of collaborative teams. It sends the message that working together to plan solid Tier 1 instruction and Tier 2 interventions and extensions based on Tier 1 essential knowledge is critical to student success.

Creating Common Planning Times

In addition to team collaboration time on Friday, we changed the master schedule to ensure that all grade-level teachers had a common planning time during the regular school day (see figure 8.2). While a master schedule change sounds simple for an elementary school, it took a considerable amount of time to fit all of the puzzle pieces together. Special consideration had to be made for special services—such as special education, speech and language services, and ESL—to work with students.

		Monday				Tuesday		
	PE	MUS	ART	COMP	PE	MUS	ART	COMP
10:00–10:40	1M		1P/K		1P/K	1M		
10:40–11:20	2T	2L	2C		2C	2T	2L	
1:20–2:00	3D	3M	3K		3K	3D	3M	
2:00–2:40	4L	4JE	4J		4J	4L	4JE	
2:40–3:20	5X		5A		5A	5X		

		Wednesday				Thursday		
	PE	MUS	ART	COMP	PE	MUS	ART	COMP
10:00–10:40	1P/K		1M				1M	1P/K
10:40–11:20	2C	2L	2T		2L		2T	2C
1:20–2:00	3K	3M	3D		3M		3D	3K
2:00–2:40	4J	4JE	4L		4JE		4L	4J
2:40–3:20	5A		5X				5X	5A

(Master Schedule for Specials Instruction)

Figure 8.2: Common planning times.

Common planning times also required a shift in thinking. Teachers originally saw this time as their negotiated chance to prepare, and that meeting together as a team took away from their individual planning time. Soon, however, teachers discovered the benefits of co-laboring together as a professional learning community. This was accomplished by helping grade-level teams design units of study together, collect common assessment data, and drill down to individual students to provide skill-specific interventions. When teachers saw an increase in student learning through their team's efforts, they embraced working together on their common planning time as a benefit to themselves as teachers and, more importantly, to their students.

Aligning Daily Schedules by Grade Level

Next, grade-level teachers collaborated to align their daily classroom schedules (see figure 8.3). Alignment was essential in order to provide common blocks of time for reading and mathematics intervention and extension during the regular school day.

Time	Activity	Length
9:00–9:15	Self-Start	15 min.
9:15–10:00	Mathematics	45 min.
10:00–10:50	Tier 1 Reading	50 min.
10:50–11:35	Tier 2 Reading	45 min.
11:35–11:50	Tier 1 Grammar and English	15 min.
11:50–12:00	Tier 1 Spelling	10 min.
12:00–12:15	Tier 1 Vocabulary	15 min.
12:15–12:50	Lunch	35 min.
12:50–1:20	Tier 2 Mathematics	30 min.
1:20–2:00	Grade–Level Common Planning Time Students attend Art, Music, PE, or Computer Lab	40 min.
2:00–2:15	Recess	15 min.
2:15–2:20	Tier 1 Model Mathematics	5 min.
2:20–2:35	Tier 1 Sentence Editing	15 min.
2:35–3:15	Tier 1 Writing	40 min.
3:15–3:25	Wrap-Up and Clean-Up	10 min.

Figure 8.3: Sample third-grade schedule.

This was an interesting process as teachers took a thorough look at how they were spending their instructional time each day with students. It required some negotiation for teachers to cut out, expand, or refine what they were doing each minute of the day to better meet the needs of the students across their grade level.

Carving Out Time for Interventions and Extensions

The following year, grade-level teams were given a challenge to schedule time during the day to provide skill-specific interventions in reading and mathematics. Teams were given a time frame of a week and a half to come up with a schedule. Before we aligned classroom schedules and scheduled RTI times during the day, teachers were trying to provide interventions before school, after school, during their lunch, and on their planning time. Before- and afterschool tutoring and homework help was also offered through a federal grant, but not all students could or would attend. In *Simplifying Response to Intervention*, Austin Buffum, Mike Mattos, and Chris Weber (2012) tell us that the best time to provide interventions is during the regular school day. As you think about how to structure intervention in your school, here are a few examples from Millville grade-level teams.

Kindergarten was the first team to come up with a plan. (It is important to note that kindergarten in Utah is only two and a half hours a day.) Julie and Jen came to the office one afternoon with determination on their faces. After looking closely at their schedules, they had come to the conclusion that Julie, who was only teaching in the morning, would stay two days a week and teach all-day kindergarten with the most at-risk students. (We did find some grant funds to pay her aide wages for those two afternoons.) Julie said:

> I decided that I would volunteer two days a week and teach another section of students in the afternoon. Selected students would be placed in a morning kindergarten class then remain for the rest of the day when the other students went home for skill-specific intervention. Last year, our students came into our school with some of the lowest DIBELs scores in the district but ended the year with some of the highest scores in the district. The success of the students involved in the all-day program was directly linked to the kindergarten curriculum that we created each time we looked at the data. (J. Allgood, personal communication, April 2014)

The third-grade team decided to provide interventions once a week on Friday during what teachers called Math Camp. It has now evolved from weekly interventions to daily interventions. One teacher said:

> We found Math Camp to be so successful that we wanted to implement daily interventions to meet the needs of the kids more efficiently. In the beginning, we did Math Camp with only two teachers. At first it was hard to find time to plan, and it would have been nice to have another adult's help. The next year, we added another teacher to our team and were able to move some aide time around to make the groups smaller. (J. Knighton, personal communication, April 2014)

Angela, a fourth-grade teacher, was the most vocal about her concerns when asked to schedule time for skill-specific interventions. She openly questioned the rationale for intervention time outside of the prescribed programs and said that it was impossible with the district time guidelines to carve out any RTI time during the day. Here is her story in her own words:

Our solution was this . . . in the morning, we were spending about twenty-five to thirty minutes on a rather intense Self-Start that reviewed math and language arts skills. We then had about sixty minutes for writing time. We decided that we could shorten our Self-Start, make it more efficient, and sacrifice fifteen minutes of writing to benefit our kids in the long run.

Our plan was approved, and two aides were assigned to fourth grade so that we were able to divide our sixty-eight students into six smaller groups. The first two years, we alternated weeks focusing on math skills one week and reading skills the next week; now reading and math each have their own RTI times each day. We used our weekly Tier 1 data to make the groups. They were homogenously grouped according to similar skills they lacked. My colleague and I taught the two lowest groups, and we put the other groups with the aides.

Putting the groups together and getting specific activities for each group to do were very taxing, but the results were amazing, immediately! A side benefit was that we knew each student in the fourth grade better than ever. Instead of having individual classes of thirty-four, we had a combined class of sixty-eight, and we were familiar with their strengths and weaknesses. The extra time was worth it!

In the beginning, it was a huge time sacrifice. We felt it for the first couple of months, but the blow gradually decreased. Now, I can't even tell you what we gave up in our schedule, it just works. Maybe the benefits are so great that we just don't notice what could possibly be missing. Our fourth graders passed their end-of-level tests above 90 percent in both language arts and math. We were excited to continue this the next year.

Another benefit that we have discovered over the years is that this also provides a valuable opportunity for our high-level students to be truly challenged during this time.

After two years, we thought the time commitment in preparation would decrease. It hasn't really. Each year, different students have had different challenges. The core has changed. We are a little more efficient in putting students in groups, because we know exactly what we are looking for. We have a big magnet board and each child's name on a magnet in a different color, according to their home teacher that we move each week. The benefits are better than ever, and I wouldn't change it for anything! I consider it one of my biggest successes in the seventeen years I have been teaching. . . . I can finally meet individual needs in a timely manner and see their success. More importantly, *they* can see their success, which gives them the reassurance they can do anything . . . and they do. (A. Justesen, personal communication, April 2014)

Developing a Student Identification Process and Common Assessments

We administered long-cycle assessments such as Dynamic Indicators of Basic Early Literacy Skills (DIBELS), Scholastic Reading Inventory, or CORE Phonics three times a year to monitor student progress in phonemic awareness, reading fluency, and comprehension (see figure 8.4). One of their functions is initial placement of all students in Tier 2 at the beginning of the school year as a proactive approach to RTI. All assessments are tied to the essential knowledge students learn during Tier 1 instruction. We followed Mike Mattos's advice that the best intervention is prevention.

Reading Assessment	Reading Component	Assessment Schedule	Tier (if applicable)
DIBELS Benchmark Assessment	Fluency	September, December, April	Benchmark
DIBELS Progress Monitoring	Fluency	Bimonthly (intensive and strategic)	Benchmark
Scholastic Reading Inventory	Vocabulary, Comprehension	September, December, April	Benchmark
Daze (a comprehension component of DIBELS)	Comprehension	September, December, April	Benchmark
Reading Street	Comprehension, Vocabulary, Phonics, Writing Conventions	Weekly	Tier 1
Daily Language Workout (DLW)	Vocabulary, Comprehension	Biweekly	Tier 1
Write Tools	Vocabulary, Comprehension	Ongoing—rubric based	Tier 1
Corrective Reading	Phonics, Vocabulary, Comprehension, Fluency, Phonemic Awareness	Every five lessons	Tier 2
Reading Mastery In-Program Test	Comprehension, Vocabulary	Every five lessons	Tier 2
Elements of Vocabulary	Vocabulary, Comprehension	Weekly	Tier 2
Reading Success	Comprehension	Every five lessons	Tier 2
Language!	Vocabulary, Comprehension, Phonemic Awareness, Phonics, Fluency	Every ten lessons	Tier 2
Wilson	Vocabulary, Phonemic Awareness, Phonics, Fluency	Every six lessons	Tier 2

Figure 8.4: Sample third-grade assessment administration guide.

On a more frequent basis, teams identified students in Tier 1 reading and mathematics weekly for Tier 2 skill-specific interventions based on agreed-on common formative assessments. Grade-level teams created or agreed on common formative assessments to assess student learning during Tier 1. It is through these assessments that teachers identify students in need of additional support in order to master essential standards before the end-of-unit assessment.

Traditionally, end-of-unit assessments have been summative, where a final grade is entered in the computer and teachers move on to a new unit of study without further intervention for students. Our end-of-unit assessments were used in a formative manner with students receiving additional intervention during Tier 2. Students were given multiple opportunities for success, and grades were changed in the computer to reflect mastery of the essential standards.

Here is a simplified example. Capitalization and punctuation are expected for mastery in a unit of study. A few students, even though they have been receiving intervention during the unit of study, have not mastered this skill by the end-of-unit assessment. These students would continue working on mastery of capitalization and punctuation during Tier 2 time. During Tier 1 time, they will begin a new unit of study with their class on writing a simple paragraph.

Common assessments have the following characteristics.

- They focus on student learning.
- Teams create and agree on them.
- Teams collaboratively analyze their results and take action.
- They provide immediate feedback for students and teachers.
- With them, students have multiple opportunities for success.

Common formative assessments are at the heart of interventions and extensions for all students.

Digging Into the Data Without Getting Bogged Down

Collecting and analyzing data without getting bogged down in the process was a daunting task. We found that we were spending so much time compiling data from Tier 1 common formative assessments to inform Tier 2 interventions that by the time we got around to analyzing the data and taking action, we had already moved on to the next unit of study. This required teams to develop a fast, simple way to look at data.

We collected data in a variety of ways, depending on the grade level. Some grades preferred an item-analysis sheet (see figure 8.5) on which teachers marked the problems missed. Other grade-level teams created Excel sheets to organize and sort student data.

Class: 3-M 2013–2014

Instructor: McKell

Class Average: 16 (80 percent)

Date: December 19, 2013

Title: R.S. 3-1 Weekly Reading Test

Student	Vocabulary							Word Analysis								Comprehension				
	1	2	3	4	5	6	7	8	9	10	11	12	13	14	15	16	17	18	19	20
Jordyn											X			X						X
Brynli																X	X	X	X	X
Makendie													X		X		X		X	
Adam																		X	X	X
Lorna													X					X		X
Brennan													X			X	X		X	X
Savanna			X								X		X	X	X	X	X	X		
Michael																X		X		
Karli														X		X	X			X
Noah											X					X				
Kaysen			X		X	X							X	X	X					X
DeWayne													X			X		X		X
Courtnee																X	X	X	X	X
Braxton	X					X			X					X		X			X	X
Grace														X		X	X			X
Alexis											X			X	X	X	X		X	X
Kamrie														X	X	X				X
Allie													X			X		X		X
# missed	1		2		1	2			1		4		7	8	5	12	8	8	7	14

Figure 8.5: Sample item-analysis sheet.

Grade levels also utilized GradeCam (www.gradecam.com) to collect data and create reports (see figure 8.6). The most important consideration is that the data can be collected quickly to inform student learning.

Next, teacher teams analyzed data and divided students into groups based on targeted skills rather than test percentages. A data-analysis protocol (see figure 8.7, page 178) ensured consistency when looking at data. Teacher teams looked at student strengths and areas of growth according to learning targets. Analyzing data also fostered conversations about how to best teach the identified student learning targets.

After comparing common formative assessment data across the grade level, teams completed a data-analysis sheet (see figure 8.8, page 178) and placed students in skill-specific intervention or extension groups.

Once teams analyzed the data and prepared students to be regrouped, we decided which teacher or paraprofessional would teach each group. The outcome of the intervention was then noted on the team data sheet.

Teacher Determination Process

We identified staff members to teach small-group instruction based on their expertise in each skill area, which we determined by looking at item-analysis data on common formative assessments. Highly trained paraprofessionals also taught small-group instruction. The classroom teachers taught the most at-risk learners.

In the beginning, transparency when looking at common assessment data was an issue. Teachers did not feel comfortable with their team members looking at their student scores on common assessments. Teachers were worried about appearing inadequate to the other team members. It took time to build trust, but soon teachers were eager for feedback from their colleagues on best teaching practices, as well as how to best meet the needs of their students.

For example, one of our teachers, who was moving to a different grade level, felt uncomfortable about her first team meeting. Shawna had been a fifth-grade teacher for nine years when she was asked to move to the third grade due to a shift in student population. When it came time to administer the first common assessment of the year, she was discouraged when she looked at how low her students had scored on the test. She said, "I was nervous that I would feel uncomfortable in the meeting. I was so relieved when my team told me that we would figure it out. They helped me with instructional strategies, and I was grateful for the help" (S. Dean, personal communication, April 2014).

So how does the school know if the interventions are working?

Student	Score	Percentage
Jordyn	17/20	85
Brynli	15/20	75
Makendie	16/20	80
Adam	17/20	85
Lorna	17/20	85
Brennan	15/20	75
Logan	-/20	-
Savanna	12/20	60
Michael	19/20	95
Lailani	-/20	-
Karli	16/20	80
Noah	18/20	90
Kaysen	13/20	65
DeWayne	16/20	80
Colton	-/20	-
Courtnee	15/20	75
Braxton	13/20	75
Grace	16/20	80
Alyssa	-/20	-
Alexis	13/20	65
Kamrie	16/20	80
Allie	16/20	80

100–90 percent
Michael
Noah
89–80 percent
Jordyn
Makendie
Adam
Lorna
Karli
DeWayne
Grace
Kamrie
Allie

79 percent →↓
Brynli
Brennan
Savanna
Kaysen
Courtnee
Braxton
Alexis

Hard test! Quite pleased with results. Vocabulary and contractions both close to 100 percent. Comprehension skill: Drawing conclusions is low, but students are getting better.

Figure 8.6: Sample GradeCam score sheet.

Questions	Responses
What worked well?	Vocabulary and contractions are close to 100 percent.
Where do our students struggle the most?	Comprehension Skills: Drawing Conclusions
Item analysis: Which problems did students most frequently miss? Why?	14, 16, 17, 18, 19, 20—Which are all comprehension Students are having difficulty justifying their answers through the text.
How can we improve the assessment?	Question 20 was tricky. Besides being text dependent, it required background knowledge in bird migration. Change question 20 to be text dependent.
What teaching strategies can we share for interventions and extensions?	Intervention: Small-group practice with task cards. Each card has a scenario for which students are asked to draw conclusions from what they read. Extension: Students will read a complex passage where the conclusion is not clear. Students will come to their own conclusion. They will be required to cite evidence from the passage to support their conclusions.
Who are our at-risk students? How will we group for interventions?	Brynli, Brennan, Savanna, Kaysen, Courtnee, Braxton, Alexis

Figure 8.7: Data-analysis protocol.

*Visit **go.solution-tree.com/rtiatwork** for a reproducible version of this figure.*

First-Grade Mathematics Test Scores: Common formative assessment 2B					
Teacher	**Number of Students Who Took Assessment**	**Overall Average Score**	**Number of Students Proficient**	**Number of Students Not Proficient**	**Names of Students Needing Additional Intervention**
Kendrick	24	92 percent	19	5	Erick, Landon, Maya, Daxton, and Chase—all retaught and passed
Miner	18	92 percent	17	1	Amber—needs additional intervention
Jarrett	23	92 percent	21	2	Griffin and Tayla were retaught and passed
Total	65	92 percent	57	8	

Figure 8.8: Sample grade-level team data-analysis sheet.

The Monitoring Process

Monitoring progress has to be a priority when developing and implementing RTI. In our school, data are received from the paraprofessionals each Thursday on a weekly feedback form (see figure 8.9), which bridges the communication gap between the paraprofessional and the classroom teacher. On average, there are six aides per grade level assigned to help during Tier 2. The aides are on a tight schedule and often do not have time to communicate with the classroom teacher before moving to the next grade level. Thus, it became evident that we needed a way to track student data in Tier 2 groups and provide classroom teachers with timely feedback in regard to their students.

Student	Teacher	Skill or Program	Lesson Number	Practice	Test	Correct Words per Minute	Errors	Pass Y/N	Comments
Ashlee	4J	Comprehension	23	62%	NA	126	0		Reads well but struggles with practice questions
Jacob	4L	Comprehension	23	84%	NA	96	2		A bit distracted, but okay
Brynn	4T	Comprehension	23	92%	NA	128	1		Doing well

Figure 8.9: Sample weekly feedback form for Tier 2.

Teachers can now quickly see how their students were doing in reading groups they were not personally teaching. The weekly feedback form shows a running record of student achievement data as well as any anecdotal notes the paraprofessional may have for the teacher regarding a student's progress and behavior. The forms are put in the teacher's box by Thursday morning each week in order for the teacher to use this information during PLC collaboration time on Friday. One aide fills out the sheet, which usually has several different grade-level groups on the same sheet, depending on which groups the aide is teaching.

Despite interventions, some students may still not have mastered the requisite skills. In these cases, we return to the drawing board.

The Move to Mastery

If a student is still in need of intervention, the team meets again to share ideas for further interventions. Students are once again placed in a skill-specific intervention group and may also be placed in an at-risk Tier 3 intervention group. Tier 3 at Millville is special education; however, we serve some at-risk students with our resource students for skill-specific interventions, even though they don't currently qualify for special education services.

After students work with special education teachers as an at-risk student, they are referred to the Student Assistance Team for consideration for special education services. The Student Assistance Team includes the resource teacher, speech language pathologist, reading facilitator, district psychologist, classroom teacher, administrator, and other specialists as needed, such as the district audiologist or occupational therapist. It may be interesting to note that resource students are still taught on grade level. They have extra support in the classroom during Tier 1, skill-specific small-group instruction during Tier 2, and extra skill-specific intervention by the resource teacher during Tier 3. Importantly, students are taught Tier 1 skills related to their current class rather than resource programs, which are typically two years behind their peers.

A spiral review of a learning target is also implemented by the classroom teacher during Tier 1 to ensure long-term retention of essential knowledge, meaning that targets identified as essential are reviewed throughout the school year rather than one isolated unit of study.

When students have mastered Tier 1 standards, we identify targets for extension groups that more deeply explore the materials.

The Extension Process

Students who have reached mastery are taught in an extension group during Tier 2. Essential knowledge from Tier 1 is explored at a more rigorous, complex level. This is accomplished by using informational text, writing, and problem solving, as well as other grade-level content, such as science and social studies. Teachers guide students to synthesize and create using the skills and concepts learned during Tier 1.

The Journey

According to Bob Eaker, this is messy business! Often, the journey requires that we start and stop, wade through things, and trudge forward.

In the beginning, teachers felt that collaborating was just one more thing to do. It became important to connect the *why* with the *how*. We developed team meeting learning logs, norms, protocols, and tools to help bring clarity to the work. This boosted confidence as teachers discovered the simplicity of the process. It is important to note that a simple process does not mean the work is easy. However, successful teams soon discovered what Daniel Pink (2005) refers to as *being in the flow*, and seemingly difficult work turned into a positive challenge.

In order to focus on student learning, we implemented the following structural PLC practices.

- **Grade-level common planning time:** We changed the master schedule to ensure that all teachers in a grade level had a common planning time for collaboration during the school day.

- **Schedule adjustment:** Grade-level teams aligned their daily schedule to allow students to move from class to class during Tier 2.

- **Whole-staff PLC meeting times:** We scheduled weekly PLC meetings for an hour and a half during contract time. Grade-level teams, the principal, the reading facilitator, the resource teacher, and the ESL teacher met in the media center each Friday and were actively involved in the PLC process.

In addition, collaborative teams have developed the following.

- Student learning based on a pyramid of interventions (Tier 1, Tier 2, and Tier 3)

- Norms that guide team member interaction

- Essential learning outcomes for each subject

- Shared best practices for continuous improvement

- SMART (strategic and specific, measurable, attainable, results-oriented, time-bound) goals based on data analysis and aligned with school goals

- Common formative assessments to frequently monitor student learning and teaching

- Timely, directive, and specific interventions and extensions during the school day

Implementing RTI practices has transformed Millville into a student-centered, data-driven school that celebrates student success. Previously, teachers worked in isolated classrooms with little or no collaboration. Curriculum was void of curriculum maps, essential standards, and common formative assessments. The positive impact of RTI practices is visible in the school as teachers collaborate, share best practices, review student learning, and work together to ensure the success of every student at

Millville. This growth was accomplished through the development of a guaranteed and viable curriculum, common assessments, common pacing guides, common interventions and extensions, and collective ownership of all students across a grade level. As a result, our end-of-level scores have soared above 90 percent in all areas of the curriculum. We now talk about mastery student by student and target by target rather than percentages and have found that providing students with skill-specific interventions is well worth the journey.

References and Resources

Bailey, K., Jakicic, C., & Spiller, J. (2014). *Collaborating for success with the Common Core: A toolkit for professional learning communities*. Bloomington, IN: Solution Tree Press.

Buffum, A., Mattos, M., & Weber, C. (2012). *Simplifying response to intervention: Four essential guiding principles*. Bloomington, IN: Solution Tree Press.

DuFour, R., DuFour R., Eaker, R., & Many, T. W. (2010). *Learning by doing: A handbook for professional learning communities at work* (2nd ed.). Bloomington, IN: Solution Tree Press.

Marzano, R. (2003). *What works in schools: Translating research into action*. Alexandria, VA: Association for Supervision and Curriculum Development.

National Governors Association Center for Best Practices & Council of Chief State School Officers. (2010). *Common Core State Standards for English language arts and literacy in history/social studies, science, and technical subjects*. Washington, DC: Authors. Accessed at www.corestandards.org/assets/CCSSI_ELA%20Standards.pdf on May 27, 2014.

Pink, D. (2005). *Drive: The surprising truth about what motivates us*. New York: Riverhead Books.

 **Paul Goldberg** is the assistant superintendent for district improvement for Schaumburg School District 54 in Illinois. Previously, he was principal of John Muir Literacy Academy, a Title I school with a population that is over 80 percent minority students, in the same district. John Muir Literacy Academy is a suburban school with more than five hundred students in early childhood through sixth grade. John Muir Literacy Academy was recently on the state watch-list for not making adequate yearly progress and had 69 percent of students meeting state standards in 2005. By 2012, approximately 90 percent of its students were proficient on state assessments in reading and mathematics. Muir has achieved some of the highest student learning growth in the United States in both mathematics and reading, performing near the 99th percentile nationwide.

Paul is formerly the principal of Robert Frost Junior High, where he helped lead the school to a National Blue Ribbon Award. He has also worked as an elementary school teacher. Paul has been selected as the North Cook County Principal of the Year and was nominated for Illinois Principal of the Year in 2014.

For more on Paul's work, follow @paulgoldberg00 on Twitter.

To book Paul Goldberg for professional development, contact pd@solution-tree .com.

9

Accelerating Learning With an Aligned Curriculum

Paul Goldberg

Editors' Note

The curriculum-aligned acceleration model presented in this chapter reinforces the idea that Tier 2 interventions should be closely aligned to Tier 1 core instruction. However, as the author points out, it is important that this is not interpreted to mean that students would be taught the same thing, the same way, twice. One of the ways that the John Muir Literacy Academy ensures this does not happen is by reducing student-teacher ratios for struggling students by flooding or pushing in additional staff during Tier 2 intervention time. Along with reduced student-teacher ratios, the school uses multiple data points to help diagnose causes and symptoms of students who need additional support.

Another important aspect of this chapter is the emphasis throughout on extending student learning. Scaffolded and supported learning groups represent the floor of expectations for all students to master, but they do not limit teachers in providing extension to groups who have already mastered the standard. The school guards against a tracking mechanism by fluidly and frequently regrouping students based on multiple data points.

The staff and community of John Muir Literacy Academy in Illinois set forward to intervene and extend for all students by ensuring instructional standards in both Tier 1 and Tier 2 in reading and mathematics were aligned. Our goal was to ensure proficiency and growth on all of our standards for all students at the end of each year. Richard DuFour, Rebecca DuFour, and Robert Eaker (2008) explain the outcomes we hoped to achieve:

> Teachers work collaboratively to ensure students have access to the same knowledge and skills, regardless of the teacher to whom they are assigned.

> Teachers use frequent common formative assessments as part of the school's process to monitor student learning, and they use the results to inform and improve their classroom practice. And, very importantly, each school has created a plan to respond to students who are not learning with action taken *during the school day in a timely, directive, and systematic way.* (p. 254)

In a curriculum-aligned acceleration model (Allington, 2009; Myers, 2012), students are accelerated in literacy (reading, writing, and so on) and mathematics. All students get what they need—extra time and support. Typically, for thirty to forty-five minutes a day, ideally five days per week for both literacy and mathematics, new instruction stops while a grade level (or two) is flooded with additional teaching support. In our situation, we have as many specialists join as we do grade-level teachers. We place students who are struggling and performing below grade level in small groups with a teacher whose expertise matches their needs. Students who are at or above grade level are taught in extension classes. In both cases, instruction aligns with the curriculum, and trained professionals teach all students grade-level standards.

Curriculum-aligned acceleration requires that we teach the same skill and strategy in both Tier 1 and Tier 2, and it asks that we follow a balanced instructional model to meet the needs of all students. By *balanced* we mean a combination of large-group modeling and checking for understanding with small-group differentiated instruction. Our instructional strategy may change, but our focus on the same standard in Tier 1 and Tier 2 remains consistent. Students in both intervention and extension groups receive targeted instruction at their level while teachers maintain curricular coherence across initial instruction and the students' second dose of instruction. By *targeted* we mean instruction zeroing in on and supporting a student's deficit area or area for growth.

For example, if third-grade students are comparing and contrasting the theme of different stories during Tier 1 instruction, the same skill or strategy is the focus of Tier 2 instruction. Similarly, if first graders are solving problems using subtraction during Tier 1 instruction, the same standard exists in Tier 2 instruction. The only changes that typically occur are the instructional strategy, the resources, and the level of extension for each group or class. Struggling students continue to focus on the grade-level standard while proficient students receive extended learning on the standard.

We knew we needed to accelerate learning for all students and needed a structure that was urgent, timely, directive, targeted, and systematic. In 2010, about half of Muir's students were performing below grade level, and a quarter were performing substantially below grade level based on Northwest Evaluation Association's Measures of Academic Progress (MAP) assessments. We expected that our acceleration program would advance learning for all students, and it has made a substantial difference in both mathematics and reading (see figure 9.1). In mathematics, in the fall of 2010, 47 percent of our students were performing at grade level (Tier 1), and by spring of 2013, 80 percent were performing at grade level (Tier 1). We also reduced the percentage of students performing well below grade level (Tier 3) from 26 percent to 3 percent. In reading, in the fall of 2010, 54 percent of our students were performing at grade level (Tier 1), and by spring of 2013, 78 percent were performing at grade level (Tier 1). Similar to mathematics, in reading we reduced the percentage of students performing well below grade level from 24 percent to 5 percent.

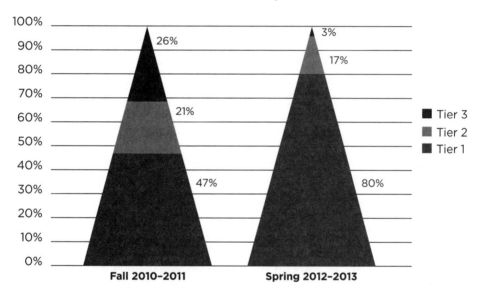

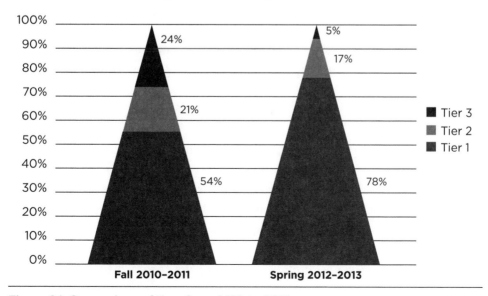

Figure 9.1: Comparison of tiers from 2010 to 2013.

There is substantial evidence that intervention should align with initial instruction. There is also evidence that a lack of alignment between initial instruction and intervention has proven problematic for students. We relied heavily on Richard Allington's (2009) research as we considered the best approach for our students and our school. In order to determine how to design our intervention lessons, we aligned instruction with what occurred during initial instruction. As Allington (2009) states, "Intervention lesson design should take its cues from the classroom" (p. 89). We asked our teachers to ensure, as they collaboratively planned, that the skills and strategies being taught during initial instruction, regardless of the levels of our students, be taught during intervention as well.

Allington (2009) refers to the coordination between Tier 1 and Tier 2 as *curricular coordination*. He writes, "Curricular coordination occurs when the two curricula appear to support similar philosophies of reading and similar strategy use" (p. 90). It may seem obvious, but why would we ask our readers who are struggling the most to adapt to different reading philosophies? For some reason, many schools lack the structure necessary to provide struggling students with an instructional model that is coordinated across each layer of intervention. In fact, "The vastly dominant instructional model [is] one that create[s] curricular and strategy conflicts for struggling readers" (Allington, 2009, p. 91). Shouldn't we coordinate our philosophies and strategies to streamline learning for our students?

We approach literacy instruction with the goal of coordinating our curriculum and strategy so students accelerate on each objective from Tier 1 to Tier 2 instruction. This method also aligns with how we approach mathematics intervention. Mathematics intervention "needs to provide the student with an opportunity for action on the specific learning target gaps as the gaps occur" (Kanold, 2012, p. 124). When we notice a gap during initial mathematics instruction, we immediately intervene during our mathematics acceleration block. This intervention often occurs the same day or no later than the next day. Mastery of the standard during initial instruction and, when needed, during the acceleration block is always our goal.

How We Got Here

As we moved to a curriculum-aligned acceleration model, we faced the challenge of nearly half of our students performing below grade level. Our data indicated about a quarter of our students required a third round of intensive support beyond Tier 2. How were we going to meet the needs of 300 students needing Tier 2 support and 150 students needing Tier 3 intervention? We didn't have fifty available teachers (six per group) to support small groups in Tier 2, and we certainly didn't have seventy-five teachers (two per group) to support pairs of students needing a Tier 3 intervention.

Our school leadership team, made up of our administration, teacher leaders, support staff, and a parent began with a couple hypotheses. According to our data, our initial instruction needed improvement so more students' needs would be met. We speculated that staff development in this area needed to occur. We also felt it would be wise to initially only focus on one content area, since too many goals might have led us astray or to do nothing well. We chose literacy. This isn't to say that mathematics or any other content area is less important, but we recognized that the ability to read and write helps students be successful across all content areas.

We began by strengthening staff development and then worked on scheduling and learning how to fluidly group students.

Strengthening Staff Development

If we were going to ensure the success of all students, as our mission requires, we needed to first build the capacity of our staff. Through the support of building and district administration as well as our instructional coaches, we provided customized staff development, differentiated to primary, middle elementary, and upper elementary staff in all areas of balanced literacy—shared reading, guided reading, word work, writing, and independent reading structures. We designed these frequent small-group sessions to build the capacity of the staff so we were consistent in instructing our students.

We also knew that a key to our success would be collaboration around a guaranteed and viable curriculum:

> A guaranteed and viable curriculum is, for the most part, a composite of opportunity to learn and time. Although this school-level factor has the most impact on student achievement, it probably is the hardest to implement, especially within the context of the current standards movement. Schools must identify essential versus supplementary content and ensure that the essential content is sequenced appropriately and can be adequately addressed in the instructional time available. Schools must also ensure that teachers cover the essential content and protect the instructional time available. (Marzano, 2003, p. 34)

Our teacher teams needed planning tools that would help guide team discussions around the curriculum we expected our students to attain. For this to happen, teams required time to share and discuss best practices. By enabling every teacher who supports a particular grade to be able to plan with his or her team while students attend specials—physical education, art, music, and library media—our teams had the time they needed. Our school leadership team worked together to create a planning document. After all, "an elementary school has a far better chance of creating interventions that respond to 6 coordinated teams (one per grade level) instead of 24 independent kingdoms" (DuFour et al., 2008, p. 256). To achieve this coordinated planning document, we set out to accomplish the following goals.

- Guide team discussions about the instructional practices that will work within our structures.

- Ensure curricular coherence during Tier 1 and Tier 2 instruction.

- Allow for reflection and collective inquiry.

- Encourage autonomy to make instructional decisions within a tight structure and schedule.

The team planning guides allowed our teams to focus on the following five questions in the area of literacy. These five questions essentially steer all team planning.

1. What do we expect all students to know and be able to do during the literacy block?

2. What texts and instructional tools will we use to guide this learning?

3. What instructional strategies will we use to help our students learn?

4. What academic language will we use to teach our objectives?

5. How will we intervene and extend for all students?

With our teams working together to answer these questions, we enabled all students to receive the learning they need in both Tier 1 and Tier 2 instruction. Without this coherence, our curriculum-aligned acceleration model would not work. By setting up appropriate parameters for our teams, we were able to provide solid initial instruction followed by Tier 2 instruction that gave students the extension and support they needed.

There is a difference between using curriculum-aligned acceleration and doing the same thing twice and expecting a different result. Austin Buffum, Mike Mattos, and Chris Weber (2012) remind us how careful we must be in actually intervening and extending for our students:

> When it comes to interventions, giving at-risk kids more of what is not working is rarely the answer. Common sense would tell us this, yet many schools continue to build their system of interventions with practices that don't work, have never worked, and have no promise of getting better results next year. (p. 130)

A teacher might continually teach the same letter blends for weeks in a row, in the same manner, to the same students, and see no progress. During mathematics, a teacher might model how to carry the ones to the tens place in an addition problem over and over despite not seeing progress. In a curriculum-aligned acceleration model, however, a teacher would have data substantiating that a student didn't learn the first time he or she were taught during initial instruction, and the teacher would take a different approach. Let's say, for example, that students during initial instruction were learning to estimate in a second-grade class. During initial instruction, the teacher may use real-life story problems and model how to estimate using two- and three-digit numbers. Students would then practice on their own using different story problems. During Tier 2, the acceleration teacher may use manipulatives or base ten blocks in addition to the story problems and scaffold the support for the students. As the students get stronger she may meticulously pull the manipulatives away until the students demonstrate mastery without support.

Scheduling

As we analyzed research to construct our acceleration blocks, we needed both an instructional model and an approach to maximize our time that aligned with best practice. We needed to provide students the opportunity and time to learn. Robert Marzano (2003) notes that the "opportunity to learn (OTL) has the strongest relationship with student achievement of all school-level factors identified" (p. 22). Certain students need more time, more support, and more intensity to learn. As Allington (2012) notes, "There is good research evidence that such added instruction can foster reading development, but, again, the most powerful extended time interventions provide more intensive, expert instruction during the added time" (p. 176).

We used this information to construct smaller groups that our most qualified teachers taught to help our struggling students. This allowed our students a greater level of intensity, more repetition, and expert instruction. Douglas Fisher, Nancy Frey, and Carol Rothenberg (2011) guided other structural considerations for us, and we ensured our acceleration block for our struggling students met these criteria.

- Increased frequency and duration of interventions

- Small-group instruction

- Additional instructional time outside of the regular mathematics (and reading) class

- Intensive development of language proficiency to develop content knowledge

Each of these elements was carefully considered as we devised our plan to help all students learn at high levels.

We began by creating a forty-minute literacy acceleration block per day. We accomplished this mostly by reducing a lengthy literacy block and by being efficient with the time we had available. We also avoided lengthening the day, taking away specials (art, music, physical education, library media), removing recess, or relying on before- or afterschool time. While we shortened some instructional blocks to accomplish these acceleration blocks, student learning growth increased exponentially each year.

Once we defined our Tier 1 and Tier 2 literacy blocks to help students learn at high levels, with 20 percent more students performing at grade level in just one year, we began implementing a thirty-minute mathematics acceleration block per day for each grade in a very similar manner. Mathematics instruction during initial instruction was also balanced. We provided staff development to meet the needs of the various ages and levels of our students, and collaborative conversations focused on mathematics. As with literacy, intervention and extension in mathematics follow our curriculum-aligned acceleration model. In table 9.1 you can see approximately how many minutes we allocated each day for the major blocks within our schedule. At no point did the school day get longer; we simply made the time we needed to help all students learn at accelerated levels.

Table 9.1: Reallocation of Time

	Before Acceleration	With Literacy Acceleration	With Literacy and Mathematics Acceleration
Literacy Block	165 min.	135 min.	110 min.
Mathematics Block	60 min.	60 min.	60 min.
Lunch and Recess	45 min.	45 min.	45 min.
Science and Social Studies Block	60 min.	45 min.	45 min.
Specials	60 min.*	60 min.*	60 min.*
Literacy Acceleration Block		45 min.	40 min.
Mathematics Acceleration Block			30 min.
Total	390 min.	390 min.	390 min.

* Average—Four days per week (more science and social studies occur on days without specials)

There certainly are a multitude of ways to use the time available to embed a literacy and mathematics acceleration block. Our approach isn't the only way—it may not be the best way—but our student learning gains demonstrate that it is at least a *good* way.

For the most part, the top priority in scheduling our reading and mathematics intervention teachers and our special education and EL teachers is our intervention and literacy and mathematics blocks. This enables us to flood the grade with maximum support for classroom teachers. Figure 9.2 is a sample schedule for one grade level. Our kindergarten and early childhood programs are half days and, for the most part, have half the time for each block. What isn't evident from looking at the schedule is that each classroom in every grade follows the same schedule. Every classroom in a grade level has literacy, mathematics, lunch and recess, science and social studies, specials, and literacy and mathematics acceleration at the same time. This allows for support to flood each block and reduce student-teacher ratios so we can best differentiate to intervene for struggling students and extend for proficient students. Also, our specials block allows our classroom teachers in a given grade and the teachers who support that grade to collaborate. During this time, teams plan for instruction, analyze data to group students, and reflect on how we can meet all students' needs.

8:35–9:35: Mathematics—Tier 1, Initial Instruction

9:35–10:05: Mathematics Acceleration Block

10:05–10:45: Literacy Acceleration Block

10:45–11:35: Literacy—Tier 1, Initial Instruction

11:35–12:35: Specials for Students, Common Planning Time for Teachers

12:35- 1:20: Lunch and Recess

1:20–2:15: Literacy—Tier 1, Initial Instruction

2:15–3:00: Science and Social Studies Block

Figure 9.2: Sample grade-level schedule.

We learned from our mistakes in making our schedule, but our primary objective was to ensure that our schedule always mirrors our school goals and mission. Now, we begin by coordinating schedules across grades, staggering the planning times and acceleration blocks so overlap across grade levels is minimal, and scheduling our top priorities first. We then ensure the correct people are supporting each grade. Teachers who support multiple grade levels will often have a finite amount of time and obviously cannot be in two places at once.

We always find a few challenges that need to be overcome. For instance, the Tier 1 literacy block, due to its length, often occurs at separate parts of the day. Greater priorities, like having acceleration blocks, trump this minor challenge. Maximizing science and social studies time remains a priority and an area we hope to expand. Additional science and social studies time occurs during the specials block on days when we do not have specials. We also incorporate science instruction into our library time. Lunch and recess are often the last thing we schedule. We make sure the students have the allotted time at an appropriate time, but we don't allow this to drive our schedule. Our priorities remain clear and occur in the following order.

1. Maximize collaborative plan time.

2. Ensure sufficient literacy and mathematics acceleration time.

3. Block off initial instruction blocks in mathematics and literacy.

4. Establish appropriate science and social studies blocks.

5. Make sure every grade has an appropriate lunch and recess.

This way, we use every minute, and students never miss initial instruction in mathematics or literacy or an acceleration block, regardless of disability, language need, band lessons, and so on.

All student needs are serviced within this schedule, whether they be IEP, EL, special needs, or gifted accommodations. Curriculum alignment, coordination, intervention, and extension occur throughout every block for our students. After all, as Allington (2012) points out, why wouldn't we? He writes, "If current programs seem fragmented, with little coordination between, for example, special education reading lessons and classroom reading lessons, then how difficult will it be to ensure a coherent instructional plan?" (Allington, 2012, p. 25).

Fluidly Grouping Students

At Muir, teacher teams use a combination of common formative assessments, nationally normed assessments, running records, and anecdotal notes to identify students and work with school administrators to place these students in the appropriate acceleration groups. As Buffum, Mattos, and Weber (2009) indicate, this process is critical:

> Clearly, an extremely effective student identification and placement procedure is essential to a pyramid response to intervention. If a school does not accurately identify every student in need of intervention, determine why each student is struggling, and place each student in the proper intervention, then all the school's efforts to design effective interventions will be rendered virtually useless. (p. 94)

Teachers collaborate around the feedback and data of those who work with a student in initial instruction, acceleration, and all other levels of support. For reading, the teachers typically use data from common formative assessments and anecdotal notes from guided and independent reading to identify an appropriate level for each student. These data help teachers identify a Fountas & Pinnell Benchmark Assessment System (BAS) text-gradient level for each student, and then based on the levels of the students in a particular grade, groupings are made to match student need to teacher strengths. These levels were

> created and refined as a teaching and assessment tool over the last twenty years, represent twenty-six points on a gradient of reading difficulty. Each point on that gradient from easiest at level A to the most challenging at level Z,

represents a small but significant increase in difficulty over the previous level. (Fountas & Pinnell, 2008, p. 2)

Groupings are fluid and meant to be changed whenever students demonstrate they are ready to be challenged or need additional support. The team mostly executes this process, with input from the principal. Given how critical this process is, we always use multiple data points to ascertain whether a student is proficient and belongs in extension or is struggling and belongs in intervention. Data points we consider are a student's NWEA MAP score, common formative assessment data, and the student's BAS text-gradient level. By considering the results of these data points, we often have considerable information to determine whether a student needs extension or intervention.

Students are initially grouped based on our universal screener—NWEA's MAP test. We use multiple past assessments to get a general idea of a student's level. Students below the 40th percentile nationally are placed in small groups, and students above the 40th percentile are typically placed in regular class size groupings. Throughout the year, common formative assessment data, teacher informal data collection, and additional MAP tests enable us to adjust groupings as students make progress. This process typically occurs at each grade level once a month, but it does occur as needed if a student is wrongly placed based on more current learning data.

High Expectations

With our schedule in place, we vary how students are supported and targeted within each small-group intervention and with each extension class. Intervention and extension are always provided by teachers with appropriate pedagogical skill, which usually includes our classroom, special education, EL, and reading and mathematics intervention teachers.

In literacy acceleration, the students receive a balance of shared reading, guided reading, word work, and writing most days. The level of instruction varies from group to group, depending on student need. For example, teachers often embed word work into each part of instruction but can be explicitly taught if necessary. As students become older and ideally more proficient readers, the type of word work changes from blending sounds to determining the meaning of words in context. Teams target comprehension skills based on the grade-level standard and provide scaffolded support dependent on student need. Allington (2009) describes how coordinated intervention services can help students and specifically how intervention teachers should design lessons:

These lessons are linked to the work the students did in the classroom earlier that day. So the lesson might involve reteaching a strategy that the struggling readers did not acquire from the classroom lesson, or, if they acquired the strategy it might involve extended work on using the strategy. (p. 103)

He goes on to say, "The point is that this intervention model provides basically seamless coordinated reading instruction. Struggling readers get both added lessons and opportunities to read and help to maintain their progress in the differentiated classroom reading program" (p. 103).

In mathematics acceleration, we target student need in a similar fashion while making sure that students master the grade-level standard in the unit's allotted time. We recognize that some students need additional time for numeracy development, so this time is built into the instructional block. Numeracy development is often taught explicitly to younger or struggling students, while in higher or older groups, numeracy development is frequently embedded into the application of a particular skill. Figure 9.3 demonstrates how our leveled groups during mathematics acceleration all receive targeted yet differentiated support.

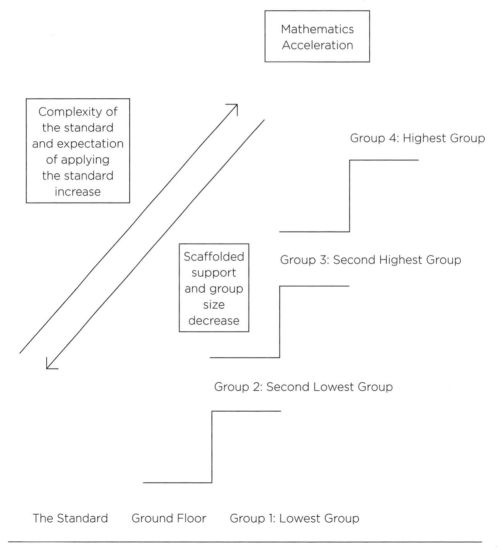

Figure 9.3: Mathematics acceleration staircase.

Notice how no student group is working below the ground floor of our staircase; we expect every student to learn the grade-level standard. This does not prohibit teachers from teaching prerequisite skills, but it does prevent them from using a large block of instructional time on a remedial skill.

Timothy Kanold (2012) illustrates the need for high expectations in mathematics:

> The data should not be used to place a student into lower-level mathematics experiences, which would perpetuate limited access to higher-level mathematics. In a PLC, the idea is to give the student a box to stand on so he or she can make it over the bar of expectations for the grade level or course. The solution should not be to lower the bar for that student. (p. 117)

Curriculum-aligned acceleration is not remediation, because our goal throughout the process is to expose the student to the grade-level standard and help him or her master it. Our expectation is that every student learns the grade-level curriculum. We know some students will need greater support, guided reading at their instructional level, use of manipulatives, or smaller group sizes, but we also know that if we don't continue our focus on the grade-level standard, the gap continues to widen.

How We Assess

Our teachers use valid data points from common formative assessments, informal assessments, and nationally normed assessments to track student progress. Common formative assessments are created by the grade-level team and support staff prior to each instructional unit and are delivered every one to four weeks in each subject. The teachers align the common formative assessment to the Common Core State Standards for each grade level. In literacy, our teachers take informal running records and anecdotal notes on each student each week. In mathematics, our teachers take informal anecdotal notes on student progress daily. Such note taking often occurs at the end of whole-group instruction to check for understanding and then again throughout guided mathematics. On a more formal basis, our students take NWEA's MAP assessment three times a year in reading and mathematics, which enables our teachers to monitor student proficiency and growth relative to millions of U.S. students who take these nationally normed assessments. We also take the state assessment. We monitor the aforementioned data at the student, group, grade, and schoolwide level.

At the conclusion of every month, and more frequently when needed, teams reflect on student achievement and regroup students using our literacy and mathematics tracking tools in conjunction with the BAS text-gradient level (see figure 9.4, pages 198–199, and figure 9.5, page 202). These documents monitor individual and team progress toward getting every student to grade level and to his or her targeted growth

The highlighted line moves at each part of the year in each grade. The goal is for students to be at or beyond the highlighted line.

Last Name	First Name	Classroom Teacher	Acceleration Teacher	Guided Reading Level	Kindergarten Beginning of Kindergarten	Winter of Kindergarten	End of Kindergarten	First Grade Winter	End of First / Fall of Second			
					A	B	C	D	E	F	G	H	I

Second Grade			Third Grade			Fourth Grade			Fifth Grade			Sixth Grade				
Winter			End of Second / Fall of Third	Winter	Spring	End of Third / Fall of Fourth	Winter	Spring	End of Fourth / Fall of Fifth	Winter	Spring	End of Fifth / Fall of Sixth	Winter	Spring	End	
J	K	L	M	N	O	P	Q	R	S	T	U	V	W	X	Y	Z

Figure 9.4: Literacy tracking tool.

goal for the year. This information not only identifies reading and mathematics levels but also helps us group students; select texts, resources, and manipulatives; plan instruction; and identify students for intervention. The process of completing our tracking tools and monitoring student progress helps us evaluate the effectiveness of the interventions and instructional strategies our teachers use. These documents enable us to monitor the progress of students as they, ideally, move at an accelerated rate toward grade level.

If a student is not making appropriate progress (based on multiple data points) while his or her group is, the teachers working with the student begin a problem-solving process to identify a more specific systematic plan. This may result in changes to instructional strategies and, when necessary, further interventions. When groups are not making progress, the collaborative team and instructional coach provide support to ensure teachers implement instructional efforts with fidelity.

Students whose data indicate they are making appropriate growth are fluidly moved to higher groups to further accelerate their progress.

Teams track grade-level progress against our three whole-school SMART goals.

1. Student learning growth will be at the 99th percentile nationwide.

2. All students will read and perform mathematics at grade level by third grade.

3. The gap for all subgroups will be closed.

When we achieve these goals, we celebrate. When progress is slow, reflection occurs at the team level with all necessary supports. In the past, support has included guidance from our instructional coaches or administrators, job-embedded staff development, and more frequent data and problem-solving meetings. Adaptations to our model have occurred throughout each year as we constantly seek better results for our students.

U.S. schools cannot be satisfied that nearly half of our high flyers (students above the 90th percentile) are losing that status over time (Xiang, Dahlin, Cronin, Theaker, & Durant, 2011). In the case of our students performing at and above grade level, we have instituted an extension instructional model to allow for authentic written responses to reading and high-cognitive-demand tasks in mathematics.

Solid Extensions

Once students demonstrate mastery, they are fluidly moved into extensions of the content. During literacy extension, students receive demonstration of the same skill or strategy at an extended level, followed by collaborative engagement and independent application. The students work independently on their authentic writing assignments or independent reading text, or they work with their teacher to promote critical thinking. As Gretchen Owocki (2013) writes:

> This layout makes it possible to implement an approach of demonstrating various techniques and strategies for writing, giving students opportunities to write and try out the strategies in a supportive environment, and ultimately encouraging a gradual takeover of responsibility and control by the students. (p. xix)

On a typical day during a literacy extension lesson, students receive whole-group instruction for about ten minutes while the teacher models high-level thinking skills in a text at or above the student's reading level. This is followed by students reading or writing independently, while others work with the teacher for a guided reading lesson or a coaching session on the skill and strategy at hand. The guided reading lesson during acceleration is typically only for students performing just at grade level so we can maintain and improve their status within the extension class.

In mathematics, our teachers typically begin an extension acceleration lesson by briefly modeling the extended skill or task for the day. The students are expected to solve and create new problems, work with manipulatives, or do inquiry-based activities. As James Bellanca, Robin Fogarty, Brian Pete, and Rebecca Stinson (2013) note, "The Common Core standards signal a shift from ways of learning and teaching that call for students to *recall* information to ways that spotlight how they *apply* that information to achieve a deeper learning" (p. 2). Our extension acceleration teachers require our students to apply their learning at deeper levels. Instead of only solving a story problem, these students may write story problems connected to a real-world skill and then allow group members to solve the problem using multiple strategies. Teachers typically guide small groups to higher levels of learning and provide specific feedback to individual students. No matter the student's level, curricular alignment remains a tight expectation while teachers appropriately differentiate and accelerate instruction and activities to meet student needs.

Solutions for Acceleration

With curriculum-aligned acceleration blocks, we identified and conquered many challenges. To recap, following are the challenges along with the solutions we used to overcome them.

- **Literacy intervention:** We initially used common formative assessments as the main data point to enter students into an intervention. The only problem was that, at the time, we had half the school majorly struggling on most assessments. We learned that initial instruction was just as important as intervention

Name	Classroom Teacher	Acceleration Teacher	Fall National Percentile	Winter National Percentile	Spring National Percentile	Common Formative Assessment	Common Formative Assessment	Common Formative Assessment
Performing Well Below Standards (Based on Multiple Data Points)								
Performing Below Standards (Based on Multiple Data Points)								
Performing at Standards (Based on Multiple Data Points)								
Performing Above Standards (Based on Multiple Data Points)								
Performing Well Above Standards (Based on Multiple Data Points)								

Figure 9.5: Mathematics tracking tool.

instruction. After all, no intervention structure in the world is strong enough to meet the needs of half of a school. Common assessments were not the problem. We needed to improve our initial instruction.

- **Literacy extension:** We learned that an instructional structure for this block was necessary. Just because these students were doing well didn't mean we should just have teachers pass out books and teach an unidentified curriculum. These students deserved just as much structure, just as much purpose behind what they learned, and the chance to make just as much growth. The model we found most successful was curriculum-aligned acceleration, so we set up a model in which students experience authentic writing opportunities and coaching with specific feedback in the student's deficit area.

- **Mathematics intervention:** It did not take long for us to figure out that asking sixth graders substantially below grade level to master grade-level mathematics skills was going to be difficult. We were fortunate in knowing that our structure of high expectations worked in literacy and our teachers were confident it would also work in mathematics. Allington (2012) explains how high expectations and the belief in every student are critical—

  > If we are ever to create schools where all children are developing reading proficiency normally, we will need schools where every teacher believes that is possible and is committed to providing the types of individual instruction that some students need. (p. 41)

  It certainly wasn't hard for us to make this connection to mathematics. We set up small-group targeted instruction with appropriate supports like manipulatives to help our students access the grade-level curriculum. Our teachers learned quickly that by raising the bar, our students could and would learn, and while some basic numeracy skills remain a challenge for some students, they are no longer falling further behind in every other area of mathematics. In fact, as a result of moving beyond memorizing rudimentary tasks, the gap has started to close.

- **Mathematics extension:** Designing authentic learning experiences and high-cognitive-demand tasks connected to a skill or strategy taught during initial instruction is hard work. Worksheets won't cut it. We've learned to make our students think, defend, apply, perform inquiry-based activities, critique, create, and design in mathematics. This was something we were used to doing in reading, but we know it is good for students in mathematics too, and we expect this level of rigor of our students.

Curriculum-aligned acceleration has proven to support the needs of nearly every student at Muir. Due to a coordinated effort at each tier to ensure students learn the agreed-on standards, our results have soared. We are now helping students grow at unforeseen levels. "College and career ready" is not just a catchy federal slogan at Muir, it is a path we are committed to getting all of our students on.

References and Resources

Allington, R. L. (2009). *What really matters in response to intervention: Research-based designs*. Boston: Pearson Education.

Allington, R. L. (2012). *What really matters for struggling readers: Designing research-based programs* (3rd ed.). Boston: Pearson Education.

Bellanca, J. A., Fogarty, R. J., Pete, B. M., & Stinson, R. L. (2013). *School leader's guide to the Common Core: Achieving results through rigor and relevance*. Bloomington, IN: Solution Tree Press.

Borman, G., Wong, K., Hedges, L., & D'Agostino, J. (2003). *Coordinating categorical and regular programs: Effects on Title I students' educational opportunities and outcomes*. Mahwah, NJ: Erlbaum.

Buffum, A., Mattos, M., & Weber, C. (2009). *Pyramid response to intervention: RTI, professional learning communities, and how to respond when kids don't learn*. Bloomington, IN: Solution Tree Press.

Buffum, A., Mattos, M., & Weber, C. (2012). *Simplifying response to intervention: Four essential guiding principles*. Bloomington, IN: Solution Tree Press.

DuFour, R., DuFour, R., & Eaker, R. (2008). *Revisiting professional learning communities at work: New insights for improving schools*. Bloomington, IN: Solution Tree Press.

Fisher, D., Frey, N., & Rothenberg, C. (2011). *Implementing RTI with English learners*. Bloomington, IN: Solution Tree Press.

Fountas, I. C., & Pinnell, G. (2008). *Fountas & Pinnell Benchmark Assessment System*. Portsmouth, NH: Heinemann.

Kanold, T. D. (Ed.). (2012). *Common Core mathematics in a PLC at work, leader's guide*. Bloomington, IN: Solution Tree Press.

Marzano, R. J. (2003). *What works in schools: Translating research into action*. Alexandria, VA: Association for Supervision and Curriculum Development.

Myers, N. J. (2012). *Getting district results: A case study in implementing PLCs at work*. Bloomington, IN: Solution Tree Press.

Owocki, G. (2013). *The Common Core writing book, K–5: Lessons for a range of tasks, purposes, and audiences.* Portsmouth, NH: Heinemann.

Xiang, Y., Dahlin, M., Cronin, J., Theaker, R., & Durant, S. (2011). *Do high flyers maintain their altitude? Performance trends of top students.* Washington, DC: Thomas B. Fordham Institute. Accessed at http://edexcellencemedia.net/publications/2011/20110920_HighFlyers /Do_High_Flyers_Maintain_Their_Altitude_FINAL.pdf on July 24, 2014.

 **Paula Rogers** serves as the deputy superintendent of Hallsville Independent School District, a rural school district in East Texas with 4,700 students and a free and reduced lunch population of over 40 percent. She is also cofounder of the website Tools for Great Teachers (www.toolsforgreatteachers .com). In her role as deputy superintendent, she has had the opportunity to lead the implementation of PLC and PRTI practices in her district. She has seen the powerful results of building a team that embraces the collective responsibility of providing an educational experience that fully prepares students for life beyond high school. Being a part of this team of educators and seeing the results in student achievement are the most rewarding experiences of her educational career.

For more on Paula's work, visit www.toolsforgreatteachers.com or follow @ToolsTeachers on Twitter.

To book Paula Rogers for professional development, contact pd@solution-tree.com.

Ensuring *All* Really Means *All*

Paula Rogers

Editors' Note

Readers should not be thrown off by references in this chapter to resources many schools may not have—behavior assistants, social workers, and so on. Instead, readers should try to understand the thinking and reasoning behind the processes explained in the chapter and then ask themselves and their colleagues, "How can we approximate the ideas presented here despite the fact that we don't have all of the same resources? How could we approximate this with what we do have?" While doing so, don't overlook the staff members who teach Tier 1 behavioral expectations to students, model the expectations, and give students opportunities to practice with feedback. In Hallsville, this group of staff includes librarians and counselors. Who could help teachers do this in your school?

Taking this further, schools should take care not to focus so intently on Tier 3 behavioral interventions that they fail to provide a strong instructional component around Tiers 1 and 2. Without a strong prevention approach at Tiers 1 and 2, schools will soon be overwhelmed in dealing with too many students referred for Tier 3 interventions.

Prior to the implementation of the systematic processes present in a professional learning community, Hallsville Independent School District in East Texas was a school district with great teachers committed to their students, but there was not a system to support and coordinate their efforts. We could not guarantee a viable curriculum to every student. We are honored that as a result of our efforts, we were included in a U.S. Department of Education study of effective RTI practices, recognized districtwide through All Things PLC, and featured in the video series *Pyramid Response to Intervention: Four Essential Guiding Principles* (Buffum, Mattos, & Weber, 2011).

One way schools can demonstrate their belief that all students can learn at high levels is by establishing schoolwide Positive Behavior Intervention and Supports (PBIS) that include explicit instruction in Tiers 1 and 2 and the support necessary for individual students at Tier 3. Schoolwide PBIS create a safe and respectful school culture with support for individual students.

Initially in Hallsville, our data showed that we had too many students whose behavior was causing them to spend significant amounts of time out of class. Some of the out-of-class placements were due to minor disruptions, while others were due to aggressive behavior and serious outbursts in class. Our goal was to design a behavior support program that met the wide spectrum of students' needs while maintaining their placement in their academic setting. It was imperative that we maintained a safe learning environment for all students. This required a tiered system of behavior support.

Hallsville is committed to the implementation of PLC and PRTI practices. The academic and behavior pyramid of interventions and the processes we use to determine student needs are a part of one seamless support system in place for every student. Research indicates that aligning academic and behavioral supports into a multitiered system is best practice (University of Southern Florida [USF], 2011). Our district has been very purposeful in creating one overall academic and behavioral system with a data review process that supports and monitors 100 percent of our students. The PRTI system is how we work and what we do; we do not have an intervention system that works separately from other processes.

Defining Schoolwide Behavioral Support

Every tier of our PBIS framework includes instruction in behavioral expectations and social skills. As a part of the overall pyramid of interventions, Tier 1 behavior instruction is for all students, Tier 2 is designed for small groups of students, and Tier 3 is individualized. At Tiers 2 and 3, a significant component is providing students with strategies to help them manage their own behaviors. According to the U.S. Department of Education's Institute of Education Sciences (IES; 2012), strong evidence exists for direct teaching of appropriate social skills. Tier 3 strategies are very individualized, and parents, teachers, and support personnel must have frequent communication and be clear on the goals that have been agreed to for the student. Frequent communication with families is critical.

A schoolwide behavior system should be seen as a core component of Tier 1 instruction. The importance of explicitly teaching behavior expectations at Tier 1 cannot be overemphasized. Students need to clearly understand expectations, consequences, and the vocabulary associated with those expectations and consequences and have appropriate behavior modeled for them in each major area of the school. The U.S. Department of Education's Office of Special Education Programs (OSEP; 2010) outlines the following six characteristics of schoolwide PBIS.

1. Preventive

2. Instructionally oriented

3. Culturally responsive

4. Functional

5. Systematically implemented

6. Evidence based

According to Teaching Tolerance, a Southern Poverty Law Center (2008) study, schools that implement schoolwide PBIS see a reduction in office referrals, improved attendance, improved academic engagement, and a reduction in dropout rates.

Tier 2 of a schoolwide behavior program should include support for 15 percent of students (OSEP, 2010). It will typically include supplemental support in the form of small-group instruction. Tier 2 behavior support might include social skills instruction, anger management strategies, mentoring groups, or counseling for group issues, such as students dealing with divorce or grief. Tier 2 may also include areas such as organizational skills or homework groups for intentional nonlearners. Some students at Tier 2 may have frequently monitored goal-setting and behavior-tracking sheets with accompanying reward systems.

Tier 3 highly individualizes behavior support for students who are identified through a systematic review of data gathered from behavior tracking sheets, discipline records, a functional behavioral analysis, and a battery of assessments that a school psychologist or other licensed professional administers. Tier 3 intervention is designed for students with high-risk behavior (OSEP, 2010). At this level, students will have the support of a trained professional on a daily basis, with frequent monitoring of behavior during the day.

Incorporating PBIS at Hallsville

A foundation of support has been available to all students in all grades in Hallsville for several years. As a part of the district implementation of PRTI practices, a research-based behavior program that includes the six characteristics outlined in the *Implementation Blueprint and Self-Assessment* (OSEP, 2010) is in place. In its early stages in our district, this program was a response to students with behavioral challenges that were so significant that the students were being frequently removed from class. As the district evolved in its commitment to PRTI practices, the program has been implemented in a comprehensive approach at all tiers. The district is committed to teaching appropriate behavior and providing the necessary support for students who need it in the same manner that we would provide academic support.

While schools are typically comfortable with PRTI academic interventions, implementing comprehensive behavioral supports is often a challenge. Implementing schoolwide PBIS is a positive step for a district or campus but must be approached very systematically with training and implementation stages. Training should be ongoing and targeted for each tier of service. Research has shown that ongoing training and on-site support have a positive impact on the implementation and success of schoolwide PBIS frameworks (Reinke, Herman, & Stormont, 2013).

We approached Tier 1 training by initially providing comprehensive training to campus leaders, teachers, and support staff. Each year, campuses provide training to new staff members, and revisit the schoolwide rules and classroom systems that support those rules with all staff. We dedicate the first few days of each school year to teaching schoolwide behavioral expectations. Teachers, counselors, librarians, and other instructors take groups of students into every area of the building and model the expectations for that area as well as have the students practice the appropriate behavior by demonstrating it. The walls display posters with icons for all rules throughout the building as visual reminders of expectations. Implementing a schoolwide behavior program in a comprehensive manner can be a challenge because it requires training, preparation, and a significant commitment of time. However, we have found that when a schoolwide behavior program is done consistently and correctly, the rewards are great, and teachers feel that the time spent is worthwhile. Because Tier 1 is designed to be preventive, the reduction in behavior issues significantly reduces the amount of time staff spend on discipline as the year progresses (Newcomer, 2009).

At Tiers 2 and 3, it is equally important to provide training, consultation, and support to the classroom teachers of the students with significant behavioral challenges. They have to be experts in classroom management while being able to individualize their system for some students. We offer ongoing training at all grade levels in classwide discipline management and strategies that teachers can use to effectively implement behavior intervention plans. The training topics cover issues such as defiance, anger management, disruptive behavior, and aggression. The district also provides crisis prevention training to those who serve students at Tiers 2 and 3. It is imperative that teachers feel confident and fully prepared to handle the outbursts or aggressive behavior of individual students if and when they occur. They have to be able to have a well-managed learning environment, answer questions from concerned parents, and meet the needs of the individual student.

Implementing the level of support and individualized interventions necessary at Tier 3 is often the most problematic (Bambara, Goh, Kern, & Caskie, 2012). Students needing behavior support at Tier 3 often present complex challenges that require intense time and training and may or may not have identified disabilities. Most schools have limited resources and find it difficult to provide the services necessary to meet the needs of students who require this level of support. In Hallsville, Tier 3 support in behavior includes the following.

- A licensed social worker who acts as a case manager or program coordinator

- An individualized behavior plan and reward system

- A morning check-in with the behavior assistant or other identified professional

- An end-of-the-day check-in with a review of behavior

- The behavior assistant or other identified professional periodically monitoring during the day

- Frequent home and school communication (three to five times per week)

- In-class support as needed

- The use of a redirection or a calm-down area—an area of the school that a student can elect to go to or be removed to for short periods of time to allow him or her to gain control of his or her behavior in a quiet and private area

- Social skills instruction

- Counseling

- Training and ongoing support for all staff working with the students

Tier 3 services are recognized as such because of the data used for identification, individualized planning, and frequent progress monitoring. The students in the program have a team of professionals, including the program coordinator, principal, teacher, and behavior assistant who monitor progress and adjust the program as necessary every three weeks, if not more frequently. If a student needs academic intervention in addition to behavior support, then the school offers it as it would to any other student based on the student's academic data. All team members take great care to ensure that academic support is available as needed so that academic gaps are not created due to the student's behavior. In fact, at Tier 3, the student's core academic instruction and setting are not changed. Our program is designed to teach appropriate behavior while maintaining the student in the home classroom learning grade-level curriculum with his or her peers. It is important to recognize that even though students in Tier 3 in our school may need a place that they can remove themselves to or be removed to in order to calm down, the ultimate goal is for them to learn strategies to have appropriate behavior. In keeping with this goal, calm-down areas have the look and feel of small academic environments.

The collective responsibility and collective commitment of a school are most evident when implementing programs designed for students with the most difficult academic and behavioral challenges. The leadership of a school must be prepared and remain committed to every student for a program such as this to be successful. As stated in *Revisiting Professional Learning Communities at Work* (DuFour, DuFour, & Eaker, 2008), "It is impossible for a school or district to develop the capacity to function as a professional learning community without undergoing profound cultural shifts" (p. 91). This culture will never be more evident or tested than when implementing Tier 3 behavior support.

Our experience has shown that administrative staff must provide the necessary training in the area of group and individual behavior-management strategies, as well as show their support by frequently communicating with staff members regarding any issues that arise. It is critical for administrators to be prepared to handle questions that occur when a student displays aggressive behaviors or verbal outbursts in class. If teachers and administrators are prepared and these events are well-managed, parents and staff members move forward and feel comfortable with the systems in place. The ongoing support that teachers need from administrators when serving students with high-risk behaviors is critical to reducing their burnout and fatigue.

In addition to training and support for classroom teachers, we have found that focused training and consultation for the behavior assistants who work directly with students is important. This training is designed to address the specific needs of the students with the greatest behavioral challenges. As with all staff development, in order for it to be effective, the training must be tailored to meet the needs of the staff and the goals of the program. In our district, providing this support several times per year through an outside consultant has been very important for the success of our students. The training we provide typically includes strategies in de-escalation, implementation of reward systems, and specific social skills strategies to teach the students. It frequently involves case studies of individual students and a group review of the strategies that are working, as well as those that have not been successful. This allows the behavior program staff to learn from each other and replicate effective practices.

At Tiers 2 and 3, we individualize behavior assistant schedules (figure 10.1, page 214) and change them based on student needs. Some of the students in our behavior program have a daily or periodic check-in, check-out procedure (Weber, 2013). Check-in, check-out consists of a behavior assistant going to the student's classroom and doing an informal observation of the student as well as checking with the teacher. A short conference with the student about his or her daily goals may also occur, which provides an opportunity to gather informal data as well as have a positive contact with the student.

Students' schedules and levels of need often change several times during the year. A student may be in a crisis and need a high level of support and then, after a period of time, learn the necessary skills to manage his or her behavior, thus causing the level of support to change. We serve students in the behavior program in our district just like students with academic interventions; they can move between tiers of service based on their data.

Teaching PBIS Strategies

In Hallsville, students in Tiers 2 and 3 of the behavior program are taught goal setting, how to monitor their own progress, and the four strategies for anger control. The anger control strategies are:

1. Stop and Think

    • Picture a stop sign and freeze!

2. The Turtle Technique (Joseph & Strain, 2010)

    • Get your hands and feet still.

    • Take three deep breaths and relax.

    • Think of a plan to solve the problem or walk away.

3. The 3Bs (McConnell & Ryser, 2005)

    • Be quiet.

    • Back away.

    • Breathe deeply three times.

4. Relax

    • Picture a relaxing scene.

    • Take three deep breaths.

Students are taught how to use these strategies when they are angry or upset. When a student uses one of these strategies they complete a form that allows them

Name: Maria, John   **Campus:** Hallsville Elementary   **Dates:** August 26, 2013 to August 30, 2013

Service Codes:
- + = Redirection (reward time, happy visit)
- − = Redirection (behavioral problem, time-out)
- BA = Behavior assistant
- T = Teacher contact or conference
- C = Classroom assistance and observation
- P = Paperwork and reports
- M = Monitor (brief check-in)

Time	S	Monday Students	S	Monday Teacher	S	Tuesday Students	S	Tuesday Teacher	S	Wednesday Students	S	Wednesday Teacher	S	Thursday Students	S	Thursday Teacher	S	Friday Students	S	Friday Teacher
8:00	C	Elijah	C	Smith BA Maria	C	Pat	−	Jones BA John	C	Henry and Kathy	−	Rodriguez, Erickson BA Maria and John	C	BJ	C	Roberts BA John	M	Jane, Matt, Juan, Sam		Turner, Martin, Anderson, Blackmon BA Maria and John
8:30	C	BJ, Mia, Danny	C	Roberts BA John Anderson, Franklin BA Maria	C	BJ	T C	Roberts BA John	C	Jada, BJ, Matt	T C	Blackmon, Roberts BA Maria and John	C	Jada	C	Blackmon BA John	P	Redirection—Social Skills Class		BA Maria
9:00	C	"	C	"	C	"	T C	"	C	BJ, Jada, Jane		Roberts	C	"	C	"	C	BJ		Roberts BA John
9:30	C	"	C	"	P	George	M	Hawkins BA Maria and John		Kenneth, Marc, Bob	M	Smith, Roberts BA Maria and John	C	BJ	T	Roberts BA John	T	Danny		Anderson BA Maria
10:00	C	George, Jake, Andy	M	Hawkins BA Maria and John	M	Redirection—Social Skills Class	M T	BA Maria	C	BJ, Henry	M T	Roberts BA Maria and John	C	BJ	C	Roberts BA John	C	BJ		Roberts BA John
10:30	C	Elijah, BJ, Rod, Jada, Evan, Gabe	M	Turner, Roberts, Anderson, Blackmon BA Maria and John	M	Jada, Elijah, Mia	−M	Gym BA John	C	Jane, Mia	−M	Turner, Nelson, Blackmon BA Maria	C	BJ, Elijah, Mia, Matt, Jada	C	Turner, Nelson, Blackmon BA John	C	BJ		Roberts BA John
11:00	C	BJ, Elijah Cafeteria Monitor		Roberts BA John Turner BA Maria	M	BJ, Elijah Cafeteria Monitor	M	Roberts BA John Turner BA Maria	C	BJ, Elijah Cafeteria Monitor	M	Roberts BA John Turner BA Maria	C	BJ, Elijah Cafeteria Monitor	C	Roberts BA John Turner BA Maria	M	BJ, Elijah Cafeteria Monitor		Roberts BA John Turner BA Maria
11:30	C	Elijah		Smith BA Maria	M	Elijah	M	Smith BA Maria	C	Elijah	M	Smith BA Maria	C	Elijah	C	Smith BA Maria	P	Redirection—Social Skills Class		BA Maria

Figure 10.1: Sample morning behavior assistant schedule.

to reflect on their choices and identify other possible solutions to use in the future. If they become angry and do not use one of these strategies then re-teaching occurs. This allows for instruction in problem solving. See figure 10.2 for a safe place form with anger control strategies.

Name: *Hannah K.*   Date: *September 3, 2014*

1. What was the problem? *I got mad because Mike called me a name. I called him a bad name.*

2. What did you do to calm down? *I did the 3Bs. I stopped talking, walked away, and did deep breathing.*

3. Circle the one you did.

Stop and Think   The Turtle Technique   The 3Bs   Relax

Think: "It's OK to be mad. It's not OK to be mean."

4. What are some solutions? *I could ask Mike to stop, or I could ignore him.*

5. What solution are you going to use? *Ask him to stop.*

Figure 10.2: Safe place form.

*Visit **go.solution-tree.com/rtiatwork** for a reproducible version of this figure.*

Learning to monitor and adjust your behavior consistent with expectations is a very high-level skill. The behavior tracking sheet (figure 10.3, page 216) is used to help students self-evaluate their own behavior throughout the day based on a target set by their teacher. This tool should always be linked to student goal setting and adult feedback during a conference or one-to-one meeting. Frequent feedback is critical for a student to learn how to adjust his behavior and meet his goal.

Social skills are explicitly taught at Tier 2 and Tier 3 by using social stories and lessons on specific issues, such as handling disappointment, accepting responsibility, and accepting *no* for an answer.

Scheduling Timely Identification and Interventions

The timely identification process for Tier 2 and Tier 3 interventions in elementary schools is critical. As a part of the PRTI process in our district, each campus has three

	3 = Great 2 = OK 1 = Oops!

What did my social story say?

Name of student: *Brian*

	Personal Space	Work / On Task	Nice Words	Quiet Mouth	Raise Your Hand, and Wait to Be Called On
Time: 8:00–9:00 *Ms. Jones* Teacher or Adult	3	2	3	2	2
Time: 9:00–10:00 *Ms. Jones* Teacher or Adult	3	1	3	1	1
Time: 10:00–11:00 *Mr. Rice* Teacher or Adult	2	2	1	1	1
Time: 11:00–12:00 *Ms. Carpenter* Teacher or Adult	2	2	2	2	2 *Yay! Back on track!*
Time: 12:00–1:00 *Ms. Morris* Teacher or Adult	2	3	3	2	2
Time: 1:00–2:00 *Ms. Jones* Teacher or Adult	2	2	2	2	3

Brian: Great job getting back on track with Ms. Carpenter!

Figure 10.3: Behavior tracking sheet.

*Visit **go.solution-tree.com/rtiatwork** for a reproducible version of this figure and others used for behavior tracking.*

types of teams with regular meetings, protocols, and purposes. All campuses have collaborative teacher teams, a campus leadership or data review team, and a student intervention team (SIT). Collaborative teacher teams review data on their students and assign and provide academic and behavior support within Tier 1. Behavior support in Tier 1 may include re-teaching expectations or setting individualized goals in order for a student to be successful with the classwide behavior system. The campus leadership or data review teams review data on every student on campus every three to four weeks. They monitor the progress of students and assign or change interventions at Tier 2. The SIT team includes teachers, administrators, counselors, and staff members providing academic or behavior interventions. This team is responsible for reviewing the data of students assigned to Tier 3 interventions in a comprehensive fashion (see figure 10.4, page 218). All teams monitor the progress of students using a data matrix. If a student is referred for a formal evaluation beyond Tier 3, it is done by the SIT team.

We have found it important for teams to have an efficient and easy-to-use problem-solving model. We use a four-step problem-solving model that includes (1) identifying the problem and possible causes, (2) learning together about best practices and brainstorming solutions, (3) developing a plan of action, and (4) determining how and when to monitor progress. This problem-solving model allows teams to be efficient with their time and target interventions for the specific need of the student. Visit **go.solution-tree.com/rtiatwork** to download a reproducible version of this model.

As a part of problem solving for students with behavioral challenges, we consider the types of behavior the student is displaying, the frequency, times of day, and locations in the school where they occur when deciding the type and level of support the student needs. A student who is having difficulty with transitions from one class to the next or in unstructured areas of the school may need a simple adjustment to his passing periods or seating area in the cafeteria. A student who becomes agitated after a period of time in class may need to be taught strategies to calm him- or herself. Others may need an area of the school that they can remove themselves to so that they can work in a quieter area. If a student's behavior is unpredictable or aggressive, he may need someone in the classroom with him so he can be removed if necessary while he is learning appropriate behavior. Just as there is not a one-size-fits-all approach to academic interventions, behavior interventions should be individualized to meet each student's needs.

(3 to 5 percent of total student population estimated to need individualized support monitored by the SIT team)

Who: Responsibilities

Teacher of Student	Ensure progress-monitoring data include RTI classroom documentation form, common assessments, intervention reports, grades, attendance, and so on.
Interventionist and Campus Support	Provide a summary of progress-monitoring reports to include attendance in intervention, progress in intervention, and any other pertinent data.
Campus Administrator	Assign person to enter data for RTI meetings into system. Lead meetings utilizing the problem-solving process.
Counselor, Behavior Specialist, Campus Licensed Specialist in School Psychology, or Diagnostician	Review all assessment information, and make suggestions.
Parent	Invite but do not require.

What: To develop a plan for students making little or no progress in Tiers 2 and 3 interventions

When: Every fourth week following RTI meetings

Where: Campus level

How: Data set used—

- Tiers 2 and 3 intervention reports
- Progress-monitoring reports
- Additional assessments

Figure 10.4: SIT meeting process.

*Visit **go.solution-tree.com/rtiatwork** for a reproducible version of this figure.*

In our district, we have one elementary-age student who initially had very aggressive and disruptive behavior. He required 1:1 assistance and frequent class removals. Over time, he has learned techniques to manage his own behavior and will sometimes remove himself to a calm-down area if needed. He utilizes a visual schedule designed to provide him structure and the ability to predict changes in his routine. His schedule is a folder with icons that communicates the order of his school day. As he completes a scheduled activity, he removes the icon and stores it in his folder for the next day. This increases his level of independence and reduces his anxiety (see figure 10.5). His teachers regularly monitor his progress and adjust his level of intervention based on his needs.

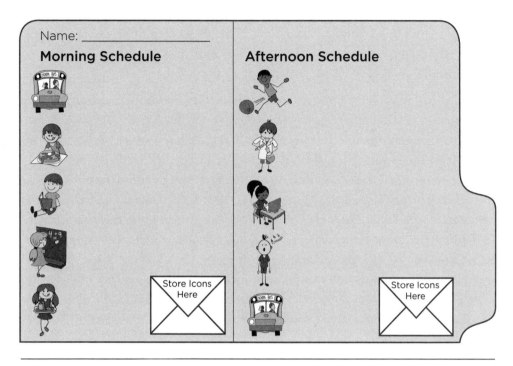

Figure 10.5: Sample visual schedule.

He is a successful student, and his case is one of many success stories. His principal, teachers, and support staff remain committed to his success and the safety and needs of his classmates. As a young student who is learning strategies to manage his own behavior, we know there will continue to be times when we'll have to adjust his services. He is learning, and learning takes time.

Many students in this program served as elementary students have continued to need support through high school, and some have not. Those who have continued to need support beyond elementary school have learned much more appropriate social and academic behaviors, are successful in their academic programs, and do not require support as intense as when they were first identified as elementary students. For example, one student who is now in high school needed 1:1 assistance and frequent class removal to calm down as an elementary student. This student displayed oppositional and explosive behavior. In high school, this student does not require 1:1 assistance, classroom check-ins, or class removal but receives counseling and periodic contact from a case manager or teacher for the primary purpose of having a familiar face to go to if a problem arises. The student has learned the age-appropriate skill of accessing assistance from a trusted person when needed. The goal with all students needing interventions of any type is for them to learn the skills necessary to be successful in life beyond high school. It is not uncommon for any teenager to need a familiar face in a large comprehensive high school. The fact that this student needs this personal contact is not unusual, and learning to access help when needed is a high-level skill that will help in all areas of life. Regardless of the level of support necessary, academic and behavior interventions must be prescriptive and adjusted systematically.

In order to provide the support necessary for students in a flexible manner, frequent collaboration and coordination are necessary. In our district, we accomplish program coordination through the services of a licensed clinical social worker (LCSW) whose skills and talents are invaluable. She works directly with licensed specialists in school psychology (LSSPs), administrators, teachers, teams, and parents to be sure that students receive the level of intervention they need. Due to the frequency of her contact with all stakeholders, she is quickly able to communicate with campus leadership and adjust staff members' schedules to meet students' changing needs. In addition to program coordination, she provides direct service to students. This support could be provided by a campus counselor, LSSP, or school psychologist. No matter who coordinates these services, they must have the vision and commitment necessary to communicate and coordinate a highly specialized program.

In Hallsville, campus leadership teams conduct data-review meetings every three weeks for all students in grades K–12. If students are receiving support at Tier 2, this process is used to review progress and adjust support as needed. A SIT team thoroughly reviews every student receiving a Tier 3 intervention. The data collected on students in the behavior program in both Tiers 2 and 3 include academic data, attendance, classroom observations, time on task, number of class removals, progress toward goals, parent and teacher conferences, discipline referrals, and any other formal or informal data available.

Student data are reviewed weekly by behavior program staff. These staff members will immediately call the program coordinator and schedule a SIT meeting if they see a change in a student's behavior or if a student is not making progress. This process is consistent with Austin Buffum, Mike Mattos, and Chris Weber's (2009) recommendations that "an SST [student study team] should schedule frequent, short, formative assessments that inform its decisions about future work with each student" (p. 129).

We have found that it is just as critical to have systems in place to revise a student's program in a timely manner as it is to have a timely identification system. Our experience shows that monitoring student progress and making necessary adjustments accordingly are critical to student success. Students being successful should not have to continue to receive the same intensity of intervention, and those not showing progress should not have to wait long periods of time for their intervention to be reviewed and changed.

Through the PRTI process that our district has in place and the ongoing monitoring the behavior program staff provide, our students can and do have their programs adjusted as needed. Because our campuses have schoolwide teams with roles and responsibilities clearly outlined, they are able to function very systematically and efficiently. Each campus has collaborative teacher teams, a leadership/data-review team, and an intervention team (Buffum et al., 2012). The intervention team is responsible for assigning interventions, monitoring student progress, and adjusting services as needed for students receiving Tier 3 interventions.

In the same manner that students can have the intensity of their program increased in our program, they can also receive a lower level of support if they are making progress on their behavior goals. If a student has been receiving 1:1 assistance or scheduled monitoring in their classroom, we can reduce this level of service to allow them greater opportunity to display appropriate behavior independently. If students are aware and are participating in reaching their behavior goals, this is very rewarding. In our district, we do this very deliberately with support being phased out so that staff can determine if students need support in some environments but not others.

Building a Strong Future

The most important role we have in any school is to ensure a safe environment. Well-implemented schoolwide PBIS does this. However, schools should take caution when trying to partially implement this type of system without all necessary levels of instruction and support at all tiers of the behavioral pyramid. Just as an academic pyramid of interventions will not be successful without strong Tier 1 instruction, implementing a behavior model at only Tier 3 will not either. Without a strong Tier 1 program, too many students will be referred for intervention, and those receiving Tiers 2 and 3 interventions will not be able to have services reduced and be successful at Tier 1.

During the implementation of a tiered schoolwide PBIS program, administrators should realize that it will take time for each phase of implementation to be successful, and until full implementation occurs, the urge to have a reactive approach will persist. This has happened on several occasions in our school. Each time, it has been critical for administrators to provide the support needed to deal with individual situations while maintaining a commitment and focus on the long-term plan.

During the years that our program has been in place, we have faced the challenges of limited budgets, concerned staff, students with serious aggressive behavior, students with mental health issues, and students whose behavior was something we had never experienced before. We addressed each of these cases in the same manner. We always look at the data and try to fully understand the problem, brainstorm solutions, put an action plan in place, and then monitor and adjust that plan as needed. We have never underestimated the need for training and consultation for staff. In many cases, a program such as ours is a student's only chance at being successful in school and in life. We know that it works. We believe in each other, we believe in our students, and we never give up!

References and Resources

Bambara, L., Goh, A., Kern, L., & Caskie, G. (2012). Perceived barriers and enablers to implementing individualized positive behavior interventions and supports in school settings. *Journal of Positive Behavior Interventions, 14*(4), 228–240.

Buffum, A., Mattos, M., & Weber, C. (2009). *Pyramid response to intervention: RTI, professional learning communities, and how to respond when kids don't learn.* Bloomington, IN: Solution Tree Press.

Buffum, A., Mattos , M., & Weber, C. (2011). *Pyramid response to intervention: Four essential guiding principles* [Video series]. Bloomington, IN: Solution Tree Press.

Buffum, A., Mattos, M., & Weber, C. (2012). *Simplifying response to intervention: Four essential guiding principles.* Bloomington, IN: Solution Tree Press.

DuFour, R., DuFour, R., & Eaker, R. (2008). *Revisiting professional learning communities at work: New insights for improving schools.* Bloomington, IN: Solution Tree Press.

Hierck, T., Coleman, C., & Weber, C. (2011). *Pyramid of behavior interventions: Seven keys to a positive learning environment.* Bloomington, IN: Solution Tree Press.

Institute of Education Sciences. (2012). *Reducing behavior problems in the elementary school classroom.* Washington, DC: U.S. Department of Education.

Joseph, G. E., & Strain, P. S. (2010). *Helping young children control anger and handle disappointment.* Accessed at http://csefel.vanderbilt.edu/modules/module2/handout7.pdf on October 13, 2013.

McConnell, K., & Rogers, P. (2012). *Response to intervention and collaboration: RTI problem solving process.* Accessed at www.toolsforgreatteachers.com/rti-problem-solving-process on October 5, 2013.

McConnell, K., & Ryser, G. R. (2005). *Practical ideas that really work for students with ADHD: Preschool through grade 4* (2nd ed.). Austin, TX: Pro-Ed.

McConnell, K., Ryser, G. R., & Patton, J. R. (2010a). *Practical ideas that really work for students with disruptive, defiant, or difficult behaviors: Grade 5 through grade 12* (2nd ed.). Austin, TX: Pro-Ed.

McConnell, K., Ryser, G. R., & Patton, J. R. (2010b). *Practical ideas that really work for students with disruptive, defiant, or difficult behaviors: Preschool through grade 4*. Austin, TX: Pro-Ed.

Newcomer, L. (2009, March). *Universal positive behavior support for the classroom*. Accessed at www.pbis.org/pbis_newsletter/volume_4/issue4.aspx on October 14, 2013.

Office of Special Education Programs. (2010). *Implementation blueprint and self-assessment: Positive behavioral interventions and supports*. Washington, DC: U.S. Department of Education.

Reinke, W., Herman, K., & Stormont, M. (2013). Classroom-level positive behavior supports in schools implementing SW-PBIS: Identifying areas for enhancement. *Journal of Positive Behavior Interventions, 15*(1), 39–50.

Southern Poverty Law Center. (2008). The building blocks of positive behavior. *Teaching Tolerance, 34*. Accessed at www.tolerance.org/magazine/number-34-fall-2008/feature/building-blocks-positive-behavior on October 13, 2013.

Strauss, V. (2013, September 19). *Study: Impact of unaddressed mental health issues on students is severe*. Accessed at www.washingtonpost.com/blogs/answer-sheet/wp/2013/09/19/study-impact-of-unaddressed-mental-health-issues-on-students-is-severe/ on October 7, 2013.

University of South Florida. (2011). *Implementing a multi-tiered system of support for behavior: A practical guide*. Tampa, FL: Author.

Weber, C. (2013). *RTI in the early grades: Intervention strategies for mathematics, literacy, behavior, and fine-motor challenges*. Bloomington, IN: Solution Tree Press.

 **Chris Weber, EdD,** is an expert in behavior, mathematics, and response to intervention who consults and presents internationally to audiences on important topics in education. As a principal and district office leader in California and Chicago, Chris and his colleagues developed RTI systems that have led to high levels of learning at schools across the United States. In addition to writing and consulting, he continues to work with teachers and students every day as director of instruction for Distinctive Schools in Chicago and at some of the highest performing urban schools. He is also a former high school, middle school, and elementary school teacher and administrator.

Chris feels fortunate enough to partner with dedicated and gifted educators in building and sustaining RTI-inspired systems of behavioral supports. He has had the honor of supporting several K–8 buildings within Chicago Public Schools. One of these in particular, CICS West Belden (K–8), has transformed its school culture, students' behaviors, and academic outcomes with the leadership and dedication of a bright, hardworking staff. Chris has been in service to his community and country his entire life. A graduate of the U.S. Air Force Academy, he flew C-141s during his military career.

To learn more about Chris's work, visit www.chriswebereducation.com or follow @Chi_educate on Twitter.

To book Chris Weber for professional development, contact pd@solution-tree .com.

Creating Consistency and Collective Responsibility

Chris Weber

Editors' Note

Results govern and inform professional learning communities. This chapter suggests a number of tools that schools can use to gather information that will better inform their behavioral interventions. In our book, *Simplifying Response to Intervention* (Buffum, Mattos, & Weber 2012), we write about the importance of making a diagnostic assessment of the exact causes of student struggles, rather than merely identifying students for help based on broadly defined symptoms. Misbehavior is indeed a broadly defined symptom and not a well-diagnosed cause of poor behavior—so what tools could your school utilize to better determine why a student is misbehaving? What tools could be used to monitor the progress of students receiving behavioral interventions? Another important point for schools to consider is the question West Belden Elementary School staff pose: What will success look like when addressing misbehavior? As the author suggests, it will often involve compromise and not just one party prevailing over the other. Stephen Covey (2000) suggests that we begin with the end in mind and encourages schools to engage in this conversation.

We don't always associate extension with behavioral interventions, but West Belden asks students not requiring behavioral interventions to focus more deeply on their academic behaviors—those needed for postsecondary success. Have you considered adding academic behaviors to the social behaviors your school teaches and monitors?

West Belden Elementary School is a K–8 school within the city of Chicago that serves 750 students. The student population is diverse, reflecting the neighborhood and city in which it is located.

- Over 65 percent of students qualify for free and reduced price lunch.

- Over 53 percent of students are designated as English learners.

- Fifty-three percent of students are Latino, 23 percent are African American, and 14 percent are Caucasian.

Behavioral RTI rests on a sense of collective responsibility for improving students' behaviors. At West Belden, all staff members have assumed responsibility for all students' behaviors. Eighth-grade teachers take responsibility for correcting kindergarteners' behavior, and kindergarten teachers take responsibility for positively reinforcing the desired behaviors of eighth-grade students. Collective responsibility also requires that staff members commit to teaching behaviors as part of the school's responsibility. West Belden has clearly defined common expectations for positive behaviors and has committed to explicitly teaching, modeling, and positively reinforcing these behaviors when they are exhibited—the school has built a Tier 1 system of support.

However, we can predict that some students will need more than Tier 1. Some students will require more time, intervention, and alternative behavioral strategies to exhibit the behaviors we expect, behaviors that will lead to college and career success. Through collaborative diagnoses, targeted supports, and frequent, student-involved progress monitoring, West Belden has met the behavioral needs of an increasingly greater percentage of students. In this chapter, I will share West Belden's specific evidence of success and the resources used to achieve improved student outcomes.

The Purpose

In order to get where we want to go, we first have to define our goals. West Belden recognized that a combination of essential factors was critical to improving student behaviors to achieve high levels of student learning and more respectful and engaged students.

- A firm belief in the responsibility of the adults on campus to teach, model, and reinforce the types of behaviors that lead to more positive learning environments, higher levels of learning, and all students graduating with the executive and self-regulatory skills necessary to be successful in Chicago high schools, in college, and in skilled careers

- A commitment to achieving these goals through cooperation, collaboration, compromise, and consistency

- A recognition that three of the most powerful influences on improved behaviors are (1) an explicit and obvious focus of adult-student relationships; (2) adults explicitly and metacognitively modeling the very same behaviors they desire from students; and (3) classrooms boasting well-designed, high-quality instruction and clear routines, procedures, and expectations

The staff realized that a scholarly tone was too often missing from classrooms and that a lack of clear and consistent Tier 1 expectations and timely and systematic supports was leading to noncompliant and disruptive behaviors that interrupted all students' learning. They also agreed that procedures for supporting students who required more time and alternative strategies to meet behavioral expectations needed to fit seamlessly into the day and be linked to academics. The realities of limited staff resources necessitated clearly defined roles; in the absence of clear procedures for supporting students with behavioral needs, adults were becoming overwhelmed and did not sustain well-intentioned efforts.

The school's staff were and are committed to higher levels of learning for all students. The missing element in the school's prior efforts was a commitment to collective responsibility for improving student behavior. *Collective responsibility* means that all staff members consistently expect, model, teach, reinforce, and reteach the same behaviors, routines, procedures, and policies. As staff recognized that sustained behavioral improvements would only be possible if every staff member accepted collective responsibility for each and every student's behavior, they reached the tipping point.

The Research

West Belden drew on the time-tested work of several researchers and practitioners. In the area of professional learning communities, staff referenced the work of Richard DuFour, Rebecca DuFour, Robert Eaker, and Tom Many (2010). To ensure that professional development was impactful and connected to practice, the work of Bruce Joyce and Beverly Showers (2002) provided critical insights. In the field of response to intervention, my work and writing with Austin Buffum and Mike Mattos (Buffum et al., 2009, 2012) helped shape the cultures and structures required to transform from *I*-centered to *we*-centered schools—from success for many to success for all.

In addition to resources and research-based practices and tools cited within this chapter, the principles of Whole Brain Teaching (Biffle, 2014) guided West Belden's work, which involve active, engaged instruction in multiple modalities. A clear understanding of these principles and consistent use of these practices resulted in more widespread successes.

The Obstacles

The journey wasn't always smooth—especially at the start. The challenges that staff faced were based as much on cultural beliefs as on the structural features of the school. For instance, staff felt helpless to counter the poverty and perceived lack of parent involvement of students, and there was a sense that the solution was a demerit-based punishment system of behavioral management. Some staff members initially felt that explicitly teaching and reinforcing behaviors were not the responsibility of the school. They believed that lack of motivation, for example, represented unchangeable deficits within the student, and poor attendance reflected features of the family that the school had no influence over.

The school also lamented a lack of time to plan, teach, assess, and reinforce behaviors. Staff stress and limited time stemmed in part from the overwhelming amount of academic content that the staff felt they needed to cover. A lack of actual evidence regarding student behavior also negatively impacted the staff's abilities to build consensus to inform their efforts. Staff initially struggled to monitor and sustain the adult practices necessary to support Tier 2 behavioral RTI, and teachers doubted their abilities and qualifications to diagnose and target behavioral needs. Some staff members felt they lacked the resources to adequately meet students' needs and that a purchased social-skills program would lead to better student behavior. A few teachers simply felt that there was already too much for staff to do.

To overcome these obstacles, the school leadership team addressed the *why* behind behavioral RTI in order to build greater consensus around the staff's responsibility and capacity for improving all students' behavior. The leadership team accepted that the key to improving student behavior was changing the behavior of adults on campus. To address the very real reality of a lack of time, teachers committed to prioritizing the academic content that they would ensure all students mastered, and they partnered with administrators to create Start Doing, Keep Doing, Stop Doing lists to help teachers focus on students and their needs (see figure 11.1).

Administrators took the lead on schoolwide behaviors, ensuring consistency across all classrooms and other school locations, spearheading professional development on clearly defining desired behaviors and behavioral strategies, and taking the lead on diagnosing behavioral needs and prescribing targeted supports. To ensure

Start Doing	Keep Doing	Stop Doing
• Teaching behaviors • Modeling behaviors • Precorrecting when misbehaviors are likely to occur • De-escalating misbehaviors	• Positively reinforcing appropriate behaviors • Progress monitoring with check-in, check-out	• Inappropriately sending students to the office • Only responding to behavior with negative reinforcement • Isolated classroom management systems • Referring minor infractions to the counselor

Figure 11.1: Sample Start Doing, Keep Doing, Stop Doing lists.

consistency across classrooms, leadership team members visited classrooms daily to provide judgment-free feedback on the agreed-on procedures and routines, including how students participate, how students work collaboratively, and how student binders are organized. The staff also engaged in monthly professional development sessions where they learned about collaborative inquiries into Tier 1 behavioral supports and shared formative evidence of changing student behaviors and successes in supporting students. Lastly, the staff agreed that there did, in fact, exist a sufficient quantity of research and free resources in the area of behavior but that, as in many areas of education, a knowing-doing gap existed.

The best-first behavioral instruction had been inadequate in terms of both quantity and quality. So, the staff researched (Hierck, Coleman, & Weber, 2011; Hulac, Terrell, Vining, & Bernstein, 2010; Martens & Kelly, 1993; Sprick, Borgmeier, & Nolet, 2002; Walker & Walker, 1991) and defined the social and academic behaviors that all students should exhibit (table 11.1, page 230).

Recognizing that a more focused list of essential behaviors would be necessary for mastery and consistency to be achieved, the school adopted PRIDE (positivity, responsibility, integrity, dependability, and engagement) as its set of common expectations.

- Positivity
    - Use kind words.
    - Encourage myself and others using statements that support a growth mindset.
    - I can; you can; we can.
    - Never give up.

Table 11.1: Desired and Undesired Social and Academic Behaviors

Social Behaviors	
Desired Behaviors	**Undesired Behaviors**
Cooperation	Disruption
Social respect	Defiance
Physical respect	Aggression
Verbal respect	Inappropriate language
Attention	Inattention
Self-control	Impulsivity
Attendance	Absences
Honesty	Lying, cheating, or stealing
Empathy	Harassment or bullying
Academic Behaviors	
Desired Behaviors	**Undesired Behaviors**
Metacognitive practices	Rote learning
Growth mindset and positive self-concept	Fixed mindset or negative self-talk
Engagement and motivation	Apathy
Self-monitoring and internal locus of control	External loci of control
Strategy creation and use	Passive learning
Volition and perseverance	Giving up
Resiliency	Emotional crises

- Responsibility
    - Bring daily materials.
    - Follow directions the first time given.
    - Follow uniform requirements.
- Integrity
    - Accept responsibility for actions.
    - Put forth full effort in all activities throughout the day.
    - Exemplify PRIDE at all times.
- Dependability
    - Be where you are assigned to be.

- Attend school all day every day.
- Engagement
  - Respond to attention getters as directed.
  - Physically and verbally participate.

To operationalize PRIDE, the staff collectively committed to promoting well-defined, clearly communicated, consistently applied (within and between classrooms), explicitly modeled, and positively reinforced expectations for student behavior. To begin implementing PRIDE, the staff adjusted the schedule to better meet student academic and behavioral needs.

The Schedule

Behaviors are best taught, reinforced, and remediated within the context of authentic school environments; thus, there are not necessarily daily schedule blocks during which the school provided behavioral Tier 1 instruction and supports. However, the school most definitely specifies when instruction and monitoring take place.

The staff committed to a three-pronged approach to consistent, schoolwide behavior instruction. First, the school sets aside one- and two-hour blocks of time within the first week of school, during which all staff members participate in explicitly describing behavioral expectations to all students. Half of the staff (including office staff, paraprofessional staff, and cafeteria staff) deliver minilessons to revolving groups of multigrade students, while the other half supervise these rotating groups. While the staff recognize that these minilessons take time from academic instruction in the class, they believe that behavioral instruction deserves the attention that academic instruction receives, and they believe that early instruction in expected behaviors would greatly increase the quality of later academic classroom instruction. Minilessons target specific components of PRIDE within certain environments of the school. Parents also participate in interactive informational sessions about PRIDE and the school's system of behavioral supports. The school wants to ensure that parents understand the expectations, procedures, and rationale behind expectations and procedures so they can actively support and reinforce PRIDE at home.

Second, the school explicitly reinforces PRIDE within classrooms during the first six weeks of school. While teachers also teach and assess content to students during the first month and a half of school, practicing behavioral expectations, routines, and procedures is the priority. Teachers and other staff have permission to, and are encouraged to, spend time ensuring that expectations are clearly understood. In the past, teachers felt pressure to begin covering curriculum at the expense of establishing routines, procedures, and community within the classroom. All staff members acknowledge that the remaining thirty-plus weeks of school are much more productive if they establish solid behavioral foundations up front.

The third prong of explicit behavior instruction is to embed the modeling and practicing of desired social and academic behaviors into instruction. Staff collaborate on how to reinforce behaviors during instruction—for example, prior to a mathematics lesson, within small-group instruction, or when studying for a test. In addition, staff make the inextricable link between academics and behaviors explicit for students.

Beyond providing a foundation of behavioral instruction for all students, West Belden also had to decide how to best identify students in need of behavioral help as well as how to determine the best course of corrective action.

The Identification and Determination Process

Some students need differentiated, individualized Tier 1 supports to be successful. These strategies include:

- Preferential seating

- Adapted, personalized, or more-frequent redirections

- Adapted, personalized, or more-frequent positive reinforcement

- Visual schedules

- Tactile and sensory supports

- Repeated or more detailed directions

- More detailed problem-solving steps

- Multimodal instructional strategies

- Preparation for transitions

When students are still not responding to differentiated Tier 1 behavioral instruction and supports, the staff provide more time and alternative strategies, just as they do when students have not mastered academic content. For behavior, Tier 2 support begins with the staff determining the causes of students' misbehavior, using the simplified functional behavioral analysis (FBA). This FBA is shorter and presented in clearer language. Figure 11.2 is an example of a simplified FBA.

A simplified FBA helps teachers understand what behavior they are attempting to help a student improve and why the student might be misbehaving in order to ensure that supplemental behavioral supports are successful. At West Belden, principals, deans, teachers on special assignment, social workers and counselors, and psychologists work with teacher teams to complete this simple analysis. The school

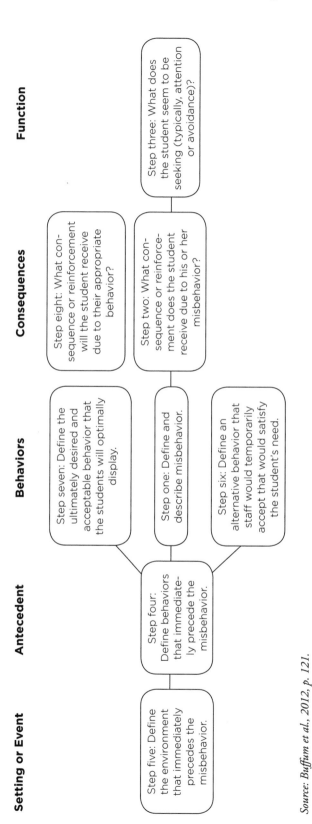

Source: Buffum et al., 2012, p. 121.

Figure 11.2: Simplified functional behavioral analysis.

has also developed more specific tools for determining the causes of inattention and apathy, two of the more common misbehaviors that they encounter. These simple diagnostic tools are intended to structure problem-solving conversations, through which staff determine the why behind student difficulties.

Students with significant deficits in foundational behavioral skills will experience difficulties if not adequately supported, so it is important to gather data regularly to clarify their needs. Therefore, West Belden administers the Student Risk Screening Scale (SRSS) and the Student Internalizing Behavior Screening Scale (SIBSS) three times a year—at six weeks into the school year (after staff have come to know students), midyear, and at the end of the year. Staff complete these screeners with all students. The school leadership team (principal, dean, and teachers on special assignment) also gathers information on students' academic and behavioral needs during biweekly meetings.

The SRSS and SIBSS are validated, normed, research-based screening tools that identify students likely to have significant deficits with foundational behavioral skills (see figure 11.3).

After they analyze results to the SRSS and SIBSS, staff prioritize students with significant needs. They also take other factors, such as academic and pre-existing social-emotional needs, into consideration when analyzing results. These prioritizations do not reflect prejudgments of students; on the contrary, the staff commit to providing proactive, positive supports for students if and when those supports are deemed necessary.

In determining the causes of the most frequent and severe misbehaviors, the school always considers academic deficits that may be contributing to frustration and to behavioral incidents. When there are academic antecedents to misbehaviors, academic interventions are provided in addition to behavioral interventions. To determine the most appropriate and targeted Tier 3 supports, staff complete a formal functional behavioral analysis or similarly detailed and diagnostic assessment. This formal analysis involves more comprehensive and diagnostic elements than the simplified FBA. These assessments require weeks of observations, data gathering, and discussions from a qualified staff member, typically a school psychologist. Yet the benefits of committing to a formal FBA can be enormous, as it informs the collaborative design of a targeted plan.

Importantly, the leadership team communicates the results of all FBAs and screenings with all staff members to share the team's reasoning and plan for supporting prioritized students and to discuss and address trends. As part of their explicit, consistent instruction, modeling, and reinforcing of PRIDE, the West Belden staff are committed to one set of classroom management procedures for all teachers, grade levels, courses, and environments across campus.

Teacher name:

Directions: To determine who may be at risk in the area of social behavior, please rate how often your students show each behavior using the following scales.

SRSS Scale	SIBSS Scale
0 = Never	9–21 = High risk
1 = Occasionally	4–8 = Moderate risk
2 = Sometimes	0–3 = Low risk
3 = Frequently	

Use the scales to rate each item for each student.

Student Name	SRSS Externalizing Behaviors							
	Steal	Lie, Cheat, or Sneak	Behavior Problem	Peer Rejection	Low Academic Achievement	Negative Attitude	Aggressive Behavior	Total

Student Name	SIBSS Internalizing Behaviors							
	Nervous or Fearful	Bullied	Spends Time Alone	Low Academic Achievement	Withdrawn	Sad or Unhappy	Complains About Being Sick or Hurt	Total

Source: Adapted from Buffum et al., 2012, p. 118.

Figure 11.3: SRSS and SIBSS chart.

As is the case at so many schools across North America, West Belden students rarely interact with a single adult during their school day. Thus, consistent expectations and procedures are an absolute necessity.

The Implementation of Tiers 1 and 2

As noted previously, misbehavior is a symptom; staff know that improving students' behaviors and building better habits require a diagnosis of the antecedents and functions of misbehavior. While multiple behaviors may require attention, teams know that to be successful in academic or behavioral interventions, they must target specific skills. After clearly targeting a behavior, staff choose a strategy proven to successfully help students improve that specific behavior. Teachers must understand and explicitly teach the strategy to the student. All staff must consistently and frequently reinforce it when students exhibit appropriate behaviors.

Consider a teacher who becomes frustrated by a disruptive student. A simplified FBA identifies the function of this misbehavior to be avoiding an assigned task, and further inquiry reveals that this disruption often occurs during tasks requiring reading, due to the student's difficulties with this skill. The specific behavior the teacher targets is self-advocating. She matches this behavior with the strategies of asking for assistance and using the techniques the student is receiving support for during Tier 3 reading intervention support. The teacher also assumes responsibility for ensuring that scaffolds are in place so the student can access written material. Knowing that the student may act out when frustrated by reading assignments, the teacher supplements these strategies by subtly presenting the student with a precorrection card that reminds the student, "You can do it! Be a clever reader!" just prior to the task. Ideally, teachers use these cards before misbehavior occurs—they serve as a reminder about how to behave during a situation a student has previously experienced difficulties in. They can also serve as a nonverbal reminder for students once a misbehavior has begun.

When the student uses these strategies, the teacher provides positive reinforcement. When the student disrupts, the teacher gives him clear choices, and if necessary, provides him with nonjudgmental, de-escalating consequences. After which, he receives reteaching and processes through the incident with a mentor, who coordinates and communicates the student's needs among the different staff members with whom the student works. Thus, all staff and the student monitor his success with self-advocating at regular intervals throughout the day.

The school's acceptance of collective responsibility for all students' behaviors includes a collective belief in every student's ability to behave well. When learning to implement behavioral interventions, a key question the staff addressed was, What does success look like when addressing misbehavior? West Belden agreed that success does not mean that the will of adults prevails; compromise may be needed. Success also does not mean that students who begin to misbehave are removed from the class; de-escalation of misbehaviors is practiced and valued. In addition, success does not mean that student misbehavior must inevitably lead to negative consequences; if teachers can apply precorrections in a timely manner, students can be taught to successfully regulate their own behaviors and can increasingly remain in the classroom and at school.

To successfully apply precorrections, the staff glean all they can from simplified FBAs. This allows teachers to utilize tools, such as precorrection cards, as nonverbal reminders to students throughout a lesson. To the maximum extent possible, teachers address behaviors within the classroom. For many students, removal from the classroom satisfies a need—often the need for avoiding an undesirable subject, lesson, or situation.

Administrative and leadership staff members recognize that there is often a direct correlation between the amount of time they spend in the office and the number of students in the office. Getting out of the office, walking the hallways, and visiting classrooms allow students to feel their presence and help prevent misbehaviors, sometimes unknowingly. Staff also use electronic communication such as text messaging to precorrect and de-escalate misbehavior. If a teacher notes that a more serious misbehavior may be likely to occur, he or she sends a text message discreetly to the leadership team members, who are likely already out of the office in the hallways and classrooms of the school. These leadership team members then visit the classroom in question, redirecting students or talking with them just outside of the classroom so that learning can continue successfully and uninterruptedly.

The staff have identified a few dozen research-based strategies, or Tier 2 behavioral interventions, that adults on campus use to help students improve their behavior. Among the most widely they use successfully are the following.

- **Behavior reflections (Hattie & Timperley, 2007):** When disruptions to learning occur, teachers guide students through a written, graphical, or oral report that addresses the following questions, which are shared with the student's check-in, check-out (CICO) mentor.

  - What did you do?

  - Why was that a bad thing to do?

  - What happened after you were disruptive?

  - What were you trying to accomplish?

  - How do you think your actions made people feel?

  - Next time you have that goal, how will you meet it without impacting others?

- **Self-talk scripts (Purkey, 2000):** The staff teach, model, and help students practice positive internal dialogue.

  - A teacher and a student create a script that defines thoughts, words, and actions that the student can follow in specific situations.

  - An adult and the student complete the first use of the script.

  - The student can follow the script verbatim during the first few uses.

  - The student fades explicit use of the script as behaviors improve.

  - Staff members check in with the student regularly to reinforce, remind, and reteach.

- **Cognitive restructuring (Taylor, 1996):** Staff members guide students through systematic reflections.

  - The student describes the situation and physical or emotional sensations.

  - The student describes why the situation occurred and considers others' perspectives.

  - A teacher challenges, extends, and corrects irrational perspectives, perhaps in a humorous but respectful way.

  - The student and teacher construct a more rational perspective.

  - The staff and student apply the new explanation, and practice a new response.

  - The student agrees to record when they use the new response.

  - Staff members check in regularly to reinforce, remind, and reteach.

- **Stop-walk-talk (Smith & Brain, 2000):** The staff teach students to respond to difficult situations, guiding students to do the following.

  - *Stop*—When students experience or witness aggression or bullying, they raise their hands to a stop signal and say, "Stop."

  - *Walk*—When students have tried stop, and the aggression or bullying continues, they walk away from the aggression or bullying. If a student is the witness, he or she walks away with the student experiencing the aggression or bullying.

  - *Talk*—When the students have walked away, they talk to an adult.

Importantly, all staff receive ongoing professional development in Tier 1 and 2 strategies. In fact, the school's commitment to regular, ongoing, collaborative professional development has been one of the most significant contributors to success and to improved student behaviors.

Staff members know that Tier 2 supports may not work immediately. The behavior they targeted may need to shift, or they may need to alter the strategy. Success, however, is viewed as inevitable—even if Tier 3 supports are required first.

The Implementation of Tier 3

When students are not responding to Tier 1 or 2 behavioral supports, or when the school identifies students with significant deficits through universal screening in the areas of foundational skills (such as behavior) at the beginning and end of the school year, they initiate Tier 3 interventions.

A formal FBA informs the collaborative design of a targeted behavior intervention plan (BIP) that a student's continuing difficulties have deemed necessary. A BIP provides the greatest degree of specificity regarding expectations, consequences, and procedures related to a student's behavioral needs. It typically includes the following elements.

- Staff clearly identify and describe targeted desired behaviors.

- Staff clearly identify and describe the opposite of each appropriate behavior, the misbehaviors that have not yet been successfully modified.

- Staff clearly identify and describe targeted desired behaviors, recording these elements on the agreed-upon form.

- Staff provide ongoing, targeted, and intensive supports that address the diagnosed needs and functions of misbehaviors.

- Academic deficits that emerge through diagnoses of needs are remediated with appropriate interventions. For example, if a student's significant behavioral needs are potentially exacerbated by significant reading difficulties, then reading interventions are provided.

- Teachers provide positive reinforcements when students display desired behaviors, and staff provide cumulative reinforcement when predefined thresholds associated with displaying desired behaviors are reached.

- Staff establish and consistently enforce clear and appropriate consequences for misbehaviors in a timely manner.

- Staff provide specific examples of corrective action that accompany consequences, including the following:
  - Reteaching
  - Reflection
  - Knowledge of impact
  - Restitution

See figure 11.4 for a sample BIP.

The school accepts that it can make a positive difference in supporting students with significant behavioral needs only when the staff collectively accept responsibility for diagnosing and intensively targeting the causes of misbehavior.

At West Belden, intensive Tier 3 behavioral interventions often include small-group supports as part of the BIP. Psychologists, social workers, and deans receive training in these behavior interventions. Targeted, research-based behavioral interventions exist for students who have been diagnosed with intensive needs. A few of the research-based, small-group behavioral interventions that West Belden utilizes include the following.

- **The Cognitive Behavioral Intervention for Trauma in Schools (Ngo et al., 2008):** The Cognitive Behavioral Intervention for Trauma in Schools (CBITS) program is a group and individual intervention designed to reduce symptoms of post-traumatic stress disorder, depression, and behavioral problems. The supports within CBITS have been shown to improve behavior, academic performance, attendance, and coping skills through cognitive-behavioral techniques for students who have experienced traumatic life events.

- **Coping Power Program (Lochman & Wells, 2002):** Based on the Anger Coping Program, the Coping Power Program promotes and supports social competence, self-regulation, and positive parental involvement by reducing students' aggressive behaviors and improving behavioral functioning at school, social information processing, internal locus of control, and the ability to resolve problems through cognitive-behavioral approaches.

At West Belden, the leadership team takes the lead with schoolwide behavior by diagnosing and determining Tier 3 supports. While all staff assume collective responsibility for student behavior, and while teacher teams are essential in this process, the buck stops with the principal and the leadership team when it comes to behavior.

If . . . (Misbehavior)	Positive Representations of Misbehavior	Initial Teaching of Expectations	Then (First) . . .	Then (Second) . . .	Then (Third) . . .	Adult the Student Reports to Upon Removal From Class	Positive Reinforcement When Thresholds Are Reached	Corrective Action When Removed From Class
Out of seat without permission	Stay in seat; request permission to leave seat.	Role-play scenarios.	Tally mark on board	Removal from class to time-out space for in-school suspension (ISS)		1) Assistant Principals, 2) Principal, 3) Secretary, 4) Attendance Clerk	Positive reinforcement tickets at end of period or half period if student does not display any of the identified behaviors	Reteaching, Reflection, Knowledge of impact, Restitution (apology)
Talking back • Lipsmack or tsking • Words	Quietly, immediately comply.	Role-play inappropriate and appropriate reactions to corrections.	Tally mark on board	Removal from class to time-out space (ISS)			Participation in End-of-Week activities when 1) no removals from class, AND 2) no classes with more than 1 'tic,' AND 3) Eagle Tickets recovered in 80% of classes each day	
Verbal outbursts • Obscene • Disruptive	Verbalize appropriately.	Frankly share inappropriate and appropriate utterances.	Removal from class to time-out space (ISS)					
Calling out of turn	Follow participation norms.	Role-play participation norms.	First tally mark on board	Second tally mark on board	Removal from class to time-out space (ISS)			

Figure 11.4: Sample behavior intervention plan.

Continued ↓

If . . . (Misbehavior)	Positive Representations of Misbehavior	Initial Teaching of Expectations	Then (First) . . .	Then (Second) . . .	Then (Third) . . .	Adult the Student Reports to Upon Removal From Class	Positive Reinforcement When Thresholds Are Reached	Corrective Action When Removed From Class
Disruptive noises • Tapping • Banging • Slamming	Quietly comply and participate.	Role-play norms of nondisruptive individual behaviors.	Tally mark on board	Removal from class to time-out space (ISS)		1) Assistant Principals, 2) Principal, 3) Secretary, 4) Attendance Clerk	Positive reinforcement tickets at end of period or half period if student does not display any of the identified behaviors	Reteaching, Reflection, Knowledge of impact, Restitution (apology)
Out of class without permission	Stay in class; request permission to leave class.	Role-play scenarios.	Removal from class to time-out space (ISS)					
Physical aggression	Respond appropriately to provocation and conflict.	Role-play scenarios.	Removal from class to time-out space (ISS)				Participation in End-of-Week activities when 1) no removals from class, AND 2) no classes with more than 1 'tic,' AND 3) Eagle Tickets recovered in 80% of classes each day	
Name calling	Verbalize appropriately.	Frankly share inappropriate and appropriate verbal interactions.	Tally mark on board	Removal from class to time-out space (ISS)				
Noncompliance or refusal	Quietly, immediately comply.	Role-play inappropriate and appropriate reactions to corrections.	Tally mark on board	Removal from class to time-out space (ISS)				
Special environments, such as the library and cafeteria	Quietly, immediately comply and follow norms.	Role-play norms in nonclass settings.	Removal from setting to time-out space (ISS)					

The Monitoring Process

To ensure that students are responding to Tiers 2 and 3 interventions, schools use the check-in, check-out (CICO) process to frequently monitor the effectiveness of the strategy and the improvement of the behavior. CICO is a research-based monitoring process (Campbell & Anderson, 2011) that capitalizes on the power of adult mentoring. Once the RTI team determines target behaviors and selects strategies that match these targeted behaviors, the leadership team chooses a mentor to support the student and the student's teachers in monitoring success. The only criterion for a mentor is that this on-campus adult is willing to have a positive relationship with the student. The staff member checks in before school and after school, reviews the student's CICO sheet, guides the student through self-reflection, and helps the student set short-term and long-term goals. While schools can use CICO as a strategy and intervention, they can also use the tool to monitor behavioral progress. When utilizing CICO to monitor an identified strategy for a targeted behavior, the mentor and student decide how many points will be earned and a target date by when the goal will be met (see figure 11.5, page 244).

West Belden uses CICO to assess the effectiveness and focus of the behavioral strategy and to ensure that the student is responding to intervention.

The Extensions

Students not requiring remediation are expected to exhibit more authentically and academically engaged behaviors, which the Partnership for 21st Century Skills (Kay, 2014) defines as essential for postsecondary success, such as thinking creatively, innovating, reasoning effectively, using systems thinking, and making sound judgments and decisions.

1. Key cognitive strategies
2. Key content knowledge
3. Key learning skills and techniques
4. Key transition knowledge and skills

Key cognitive strategies are behaviors that allow students to learn, understand, retain, use, and apply (see table 11.2, page 245).

CICO Expectations
Teach target behavior to student, and explain plan.
Graph weekly data.
Make sure parent signs form and student returns it every day.
Ensure constant communication with the parent.

Check-in, check-out for
_____

Check-in, check-out with
_____

Check-in: "How was your afternoon? How many points did you earn yesterday? What was one thing that went well yesterday? What was one thing that could have gone better? What is your goal for today? Have a great day, and good luck on your mathematics test. See you after school."

Check-out: "Let's take a look at your sheet. I notice that Ms. Harris and you disagree about how well you did in reading? Can you tell me about that? What are you most proud of today? What could have gone better? How was your mathematics test? What are you doing after school? How many points did you earn today? What's your point goal for tomorrow?"

Date:

Specific and measureable goal

Today, I am working on:

This is how I did today:

3 = Great! (I was reminded to be on task at least one time.)

2 = Pretty good (I was reminded to be on task two or three times.)

1 = So-so (I was reminded to be on task more than three times.)

Students monitor, evaluate, and score their behavior first.	Times of the Day	Staying on Task	
		Student	Staff

Today I earned _____ points.
_____ points or more = _____

Figure 11.5: Monitoring through CICO with student.

Table 11.2: Key Cognitive Strategies

Problem Formulation	Hypothesize
	Strategize
Research	Identify
	Collect
Interpretation	Analyze
	Evaluate
Communication	Organize
	Construct
Precision and Accuracy	Monitor
	Confirm

Key content knowledge is necessary to understand academic disciplines (see table 11.3).

Table 11.3: Key Content Knowledge

Structure of Knowledge	Master: • Reading and writing • Mathematics • Science • Social studies • Art
Student Characteristics	Understand that: • Learning and intelligence can be changed through effort • Students control effort, and effort is related to motivation • Academic topics are most interesting when related to real-world contexts • Challenges are welcomed, not avoided • Students must engage and expend effort to master what is taught

Key learning skills and techniques are the self-management skills, attitudes, and habits necessary for students to learn and perform effectively and efficiently (see table 11.4, page 246).

Table 11.4: Key Learning Skills and Techniques

Ownership of Learning	Goal setting
	Persistence
	Self-awareness
	Motivation
	Help seeking
	Progress monitoring
	Self-efficacy
Learning Techniques	Technology proficiency
	Memorization and recall
	Collaborative learning
	Time management
	Test taking
	Note taking
	Strategic reading

Key transition knowledge and skills are the information and behaviors necessary to understand the norms, cultures, expectations, and processes for navigating postsecondary environments (see table 11.5).

These college and career readiness skills are embedded into classroom instruction. These attributes increasingly represent the way things are done at West Belden. Learning strategies and tasks to reinforce these behaviors, making them explicitly obvious to students, and sharing these characteristics with parents have become key priorities for the school.

Students' passive compliance and improved social behaviors are not enough. The staff understand that college and career readiness and unlimited possibilities for students will also require active engagement and the mastery of academic behaviors.

The Implementation Dip

West Belden experienced a few challenges after implementing the schoolwide behavior improvement process. Inconsistency of implementation, expectations, modeling, and reinforcement were the most common and impactful obstacles. West Belden staff overcame this obstacle through hard work and patient but persistent

Table 11.5: Key Transition Knowledge and Skills

Role and Identity	Role identity
	Role conflict
	Role models
Self-Advocacy	Resource acquisition
	Institutional advocacy
Postsecondary Awareness	Postsecondary aspirations
	Postsecondary norms and culture
Postsecondary Costs	Tuition awareness
	Financial aid awareness
Matriculation	Postsecondary eligibility
	Admissions procedures
	Program selection
Career Awareness	Career options
	Career requirements
	Career readiness

mutual support and accountability. Through monthly staffwide professional development, guided by the leadership team, and weekly teacher team collaborative meetings, guided by teachers on special assignment, consistent staff actions resulted in improvements in student behaviors. During team meetings, staff discuss the positive changes they can make to their practice to produce the desired positive changes in student behavior.

During the professional development sessions, the staff reviewed data that the leadership team gathered on the frequencies and natures of misbehavior to fashion timely, proactive, schoolwide responses. The staff also analyzed case studies—typically actual situations from the preceding weeks—and collaborated on effective, productive responses that reflected the school's collective agreements.

In addition to constant attention to consistency, the importance of clarity in purpose and policies and frequent, timely communication among all stakeholders were key to West Belden's success. The staff recognized that they were not entirely prepared to build and sustain a successful system of behavioral supports. The study and professional development staff members committed to and engaged in led to increased capacities for supporting the whole student.

Conclusion

West Belden's tiered model of behavioral supports achieved success as a result of practicing sound tenets of school and organizational success. Whether schools are addressing students' academic or behavioral needs, there are a few key principles necessary for success.

First, what we do all day, every day, in all classrooms, in all settings, matters most of all. Consistent Tier 1 behavioral practices will accomplish more than just decreasing the number of students in need of intervention; it also sets a positive, scholarly, purposeful tone for the entire school. To improve students' social and academic behaviors, we all must improve together, or we'll have a difficult time improving at all.

The next key principle is that leadership teams and dogged determination will ensure that staff and students follow through on well-intended initial commitments. While all staff members accept collective responsibility for student behavior, the principal and leadership team take the lead. The principal is the symbolic and practical leader on campus. When the principal's attention and focus are visibly and publicly known to be on behavior, then behaviors will get everyone's attention. When behavior is a schoolwide topic, behavioral expectations extend from classroom to classroom, teacher to teacher, from before school to after school, and from the cafeteria to the hallways. The principal and the leadership team must take the lead on behavior, supporting the whole staff in Tiers 1, 2, and 3 supports and ensuring that all efforts are being made so that success is inevitable.

Lastly, improved schoolwide social and academic behaviors require systems of coordination, communication, and support. Ensuring that all staff members are clear on who does what and when it gets done is fundamental. In addition, timely and efficient meetings and documentation procedures are essential to coordinating and communicating efforts. We are in a people profession—the most important profession in the world—but systematic structures are necessary to guide us in our work.

A system of positive behavioral supports that ensures all students learn at high levels is possible. Through collective commitments and the consistent application of research-based practices, West Belden has helped staff and students reach high levels of success.

References and Resources

Biffle, C. (2014). *Whole brain teaching*. Accessed at www.wholebrainteaching.com on July 25, 2014.

Bloom, B. S. (1968). Learning for mastery. *Evaluation Comment, 1*(2), 1–12.

Bloom, B. S. (1971). Mastery learning. In J. H. Block (Ed.), *Mastery learning: Theory and practice* (pp. 47–63). New York: Holt, Rinehart & Winston.

Boynton, M., & Boynton, C. (2005). *The educator's guide to preventing and solving discipline problems.* Alexandria, VA: Association for Supervision and Curriculum Development.

Braithwaite, R. (2001). *Managing aggression.* New York: Routledge.

Brock, S. E. (1998). Helping the student with ADHD in the classroom: Strategies for general education classroom settings. *School Psychology Quarterly, 16,* 142–157.

Buffum, A., Mattos, M., & Weber, C. (2009). *Pyramid response to intervention: RTI, professional learning communities, and how to respond when kids don't learn.* Bloomington, IN: Solution Tree Press.

Buffum, A., Mattos, M., & Weber, C. (2010). The why behind RTI. *Educational Leadership, 68*(2), 10–16.

Buffum, A., Mattos, M., & Weber, C. (2012). *Simplifying response to intervention: Four essential guiding principles.* Bloomington, IN: Solution Tree Press.

Burns, M. K., & VanDerHeyden, A. M. (2006). Using response to intervention to assess learning disabilities: Introduction to the special series. *Assessment for Effective Intervention, 32*(1), 3–5.

Cameron, J., Banko, K. M., & Pierce, W. D. (2001). Pervasive negative effects of rewards on intrinsic motivation: The myth continues. *Behavior Analyst, 24*(1), 1–44.

Cameron, J., & Pierce, W. D. (1994). Reinforcement, reward, and intrinsic motivation: A meta-analysis. *Review of Educational Research, 64*(3), 363–423.

Cameron, J., & Pierce, W. D. (2002). *Rewards and intrinsic motivation: Resolving the controversy.* Westport, CT: Bergin & Garvey.

Campbell, A., & Anderson, C. M. (2011). Check-in/check-out: A systematic evaluation and component analysis. *Journal of Applied Behavioral Analysis, 44*(2), 315–316.

Carnine, D. W. (1976). Effects of two teacher presentation rates on off-task behavior, answering correctly, and participation. *Journal of Applied Behavior Analysis, 9*(2), 199–206.

Compton, D. L., Fuchs, D., Fuchs, L. S., & Bryant, J. D. (2006). Selecting at-risk readers in first grade for early intervention: A two-year longitudinal study of decision rules and procedures. *Journal of Educational Psychology, 98*(2), 394–409.

Conley, D. T. (2010). *College and career ready: Helping all students succeed beyond high school.* San Francisco: Jossey-Bass.

Covey, S. R. (2000). *The 7 habits of highly effective people: Powerful lessons in personal change.* New York: Free Press.

DuFour, R., DuFour, R., Eaker, R., & Many, T. W. (2010). *Learning by doing: A handbook for professional learning communities at work* (2nd ed.). Bloomington, IN: Solution Tree Press.

DuPaul, G. J., & Ervin, R. A. (1996). Functional assessment of behaviors related to attention-deficit/hyperactivity disorder: Linking assessment to intervention design. *Behavior Therapy, 27,* 601–622.

DuPaul, G. J., & Stoner, G. (2003). *ADHD in the schools: Assessment and intervention strategies* (2nd ed.). New York: Guilford Press.

Fletcher, J. M., & Vaughn, S. (2009). Response to intervention: Preventing and remediating academic difficulties. *Child Development Perspectives, 3*(1), 30–37.

Ford, A. D., Olmi, D. J., Edwards, R. P., & Tingstrom, D. H. (2001). The sequential introduction of compliance training components with elementary-aged children in teachers. *School Psychology Quarterly, 16*(2), 142–157.

Fuchs, D., Fuchs, L. S., & Vaughn, S. (Eds.). (2008). *Response to intervention: A framework for reading educators.* Newark, DE: International Reading Association.

Fuchs, D., & Young, C. (2006). On the irrelevance of intelligence in predicting responsiveness to reading instruction. *Exceptional Children, 73*(1), 8–30.

Fuchs, L. S., & Deno, S. L. (1991). Paradigmatic distinctions between instructionally relevant measurement models. *Exceptional Children, 57*(6), 488–501.

Fuchs, L. S., & Fuchs, D. (2007). A model for implementing responsiveness to intervention. *Teaching Exceptional Children, 39*(5), 14–20.

Fuchs, L. S., & Fuchs, D. (2009). On the importance of a unified model of responsiveness-to-intervention. *Child Development Perspectives, 3*(1), 41–43.

Fuchs, L. S., Fuchs, D., Hosp, M., & Jenkins, J. R. (2001). Oral reading fluency as an indicator of reading competence: A theoretical, empirical, and historical analysis. *Scientific Studies of Reading, 5*(3), 239–256.

Gettinger, M. (1988). Methods of proactive classroom management. *School Psychology Review, 17*(2), 227–242.

Gettinger, M., & Seibert, J. K. (2002). Best practices in increasing academic learning time. In A. Thomas (Ed.), *Best practices in school psychology IV* (Vol. I., 4th ed., pp. 773–787). Bethesda, MD: National Association of School Psychologists.

Hattie, J., & Timperley, H. (2007). The power of feedback. *Review of Educational Research, 77*(1), 81–112.

Heward, W. L. (1994). Three "low-tech" strategies for increasing the frequency of active student response during group instruction. In R. Gardner III, D. M. Sainato, J. O. Cooper, T. E. Heron, W. L. Heward, J. Eshleman, et al. (Eds.), *Behavior analysis in education: Focus on measurably superior instruction* (pp. 283–320). Monterey, CA: Brooks.

Hierck, T., Coleman, C., & Weber, C. (2011). *Pyramid of behavior interventions: Seven keys to a positive learning environment.* Bloomington, IN: Solution Tree Press.

Hulac, D., Terrell, J., Vining, O., & Bernstein, J. (2010). *Behavioral interventions in schools: A response to intervention guidebook.* New York: Brunner-Routledge.

Jalongo, M. R. (1994). *Creating learning communities: The role of the teacher in the 21st century.* Bloomington, IN: Solution Tree Press.

Joyce, B., & Showers, B. (2002). *Student achievement through staff development* (3rd ed.). Alexandria, VA: Association for Supervision and Curriculum Development.

Kay, K. (2014). *Partnership for 21st century skills.* Accessed at www.p21.org on July 25, 2014.

Lanceley, F. J. (1999). *On-scene guide for crisis negotiators*. Boca Raton, FL: CRC Press.

Little, J. W. (1990). The persistence of privacy: Autonomy and initiative in teachers' professional relations. *Teachers College Record, 91*(4), 508–536.

Lochman, J. E., & Wells, K. C. (2002). Contextual social–cognitive mediators and child outcome: A test of the theoretical model in the Coping Power program. *Development and Psychopathology, 4*, 945–967.

Long, N. J., Morse, W. C., & Newman, R. G. (Eds.). (1980). *Conflict in the classroom: The education of emotionally disturbed children* (4th ed.). Belmont, CA: Wadsworth.

Louis, K. S., & Kruse, S. D. (1995). *Professionalism and community: Perspectives on reforming urban schools*. Thousand Oaks, CA: Corwin Press.

Maeroff, G. I. (1993). *Team building for school change: Equipping teachers for new roles*. New York: Teachers College Press.

Martens, B. K., & Kelly, S. Q. (1993). A behavioral analysis of effective teaching. *School Psychology Quarterly, 8*, 10–26.

Martens, B. K., & Meller, P. J. (1990). The application of behavioral principles to educational settings. In T. B. Gutkin & C. R. Reynolds (Eds.), *The handbook of school psychology* (2nd ed., pp. 612–634). New York: Wiley.

Marzano, R. J. (2003). *What works in schools: Translating research into action*. Alexandria, VA: Association for Supervision and Curriculum Development.

Mayer, G. R. (2000). *Classroom management: A California resource guide*. Los Angeles, CA: Los Angeles County Office of Education. Accessed at www.static.kern.org/gems/schcom /ClassroomManagement.pdf on April 20, 2014.

Mayer, G. R., & Ybarra, W. J. (2004). *Teaching alternative behaviors schoolwide: A resource guide to prevent discipline problems*. Los Angeles, CA: Los Angeles County Office of Education. Accessed at www.lacoe.edu/includes/tem plates/document_frame.cfm?toURL=/DocsForms /20031008084414_ TABS.pdf on December 12, 2013.

Ngo, V., Langley, A., Kataoka, S. H., Nadeem, E., Escudero, P., & Stein, B. D. (2008). Providing evidence based practice to ethnically diverse youth: Examples from the Cognitive Behavioral Intervention for Trauma in Schools (CBITS) program. *Journal of the American Academy of Child and Adolescent Psychiatry, 47*(8), 858–862.

O'Neil, J. (1995). On schools as learning organizations: A conversation with Peter Senge. *Educational Leadership, 52*(7), 20–23.

Popham, W. J. (2008). *Transformative assessment*. Alexandria, VA: Association for Supervision and Curriculum Development.

Powell, S., & Nelson, B. (1997). Effects of choosing academic assignments on a student with attention deficit hyperactivity disorder. *Journal of Applied Behavior Analysis, 30*(1), 185–186.

President's Commission on Excellence in Special Education. (2002). *A new era: Revitalizing special education for children and their families*. Washington, DC: Author.

Purkey, W. W. (2000). *What students say to themselves: Internal dialogue and school success.* Thousand Oaks, CA: Corwin Press.

Reeves, D. B. (2002). *The leader's guide to standards: A blueprint for educational equity and excellence.* San Francisco: Jossey-Bass.

Reeves, D. B. (Ed.). (2007). *Ahead of the curve: The power of assessment to transform teaching and learning.* Bloomington, IN: Solution Tree Press.

Scherer, T. (2001). How and why standards can improve student achievement: A conversation with Robert J. Marzano. *Educational Leadership, 59*(1), 14–18.

Senge, P. M. (1990). *The fifth discipline: The art and practice of the learning organization.* New York: Doubleday.

Shapiro, E. S., Zigmond, N., Wallace, T., & Marston, D. (Eds.). (2011). *Models for implementing response to intervention: Tools, outcomes, and implications.* New York: Guilford Press.

Shores, C. (2009). *A comprehensive RTI model: Integrating behavioral and academic interventions.* Thousand Oaks, CA: Corwin Press.

Smith, P. K., & Brain, P. (2000). Bullying in schools: Lessons from two decades of research. *Aggressive Behavior, 26*(1), 1–9.

Spears, J. D., & Oliver, J. P. (1996). *Rural school reform: Creating a community of learners.* Paper presented at the annual meeting of the American Educational Research Association, New York, NY.

Sprick, R. S., Borgmeier, C., & Nolet, V. (2002). Prevention and management of behavior problems in secondary schools. In M. A. Shinn, H. M. Walker, & G. Stoner (Eds.), *Interventions for academic and behavior problems II: Preventive and remedial approaches* (pp. 373–401). Bethesda, MD: National Association of School Psychologists.

Stiggins, R. (2004). New assessment beliefs for a new school mission. *Phi Delta Kappan, 86*(1), 22–27.

Sugai, G., & Horner, R. (2002). The evolution of discipline practices: School-wide positive behavior supports. *Child and Family Behavior Therapy, 24*(1–2), 23–50.

Taylor, S. (1996). Meta-analysis of cognitive-behavioral treatments for social phobia. *Journal of Behavior Therapy and Experimental Psychiatry, 27*, 1–9.

Thompson, G. J., & Jenkins, J. B. (1993). *Verbal judo: The gentle art of persuasion.* New York: William Morrow.

U.S. Department of Education. (2004). *Teaching children with attention deficit hyper-activity disorder: Instructional strategies and practices.* Accessed at www.ed.gov/teachers/needs/speced/adhd/adhd-resource-pt2.doc on March 31, 2014.

VanDerHeyden, A. M., & Burns, M. K. (2005). Using curriculum-based assessment and curriculum-based measurement to guide elementary mathematics instruction: Effect on individual and group accountability scores. *Assessment for Effective Intervention, 30*(3), 15–31.

VanDerHeyden, A. M., Witt, J. C., & Gilbertson, D. A. (2007). Multi-year evaluation of the effects of a response to intervention (RTI) model on identification of children for special education. *Journal of School Psychology, 45*(2), 225–256.

VanDerHeyden, A. M., Witt, J. C., & Naquin, G. (2003). Development and validation of a process for screening referrals to special education. *School Psychology Review, 32*(2), 204–227.

Walker, H. M. (1979). *The acting-out child: Coping with classroom disruption.* Longmont, CO: Sopris West.

Walker, H. M., Colvin, G., & Ramsey, E. (1995). *Antisocial behavior in school: Strategies and best practices.* Pacific Grove, CA: Brooks.

Walker, H. M., Horner, R. H., Sugai, G., Bullis, M., Sprague, J. R., Bricker, D., et al. (1996). Integrated approaches to preventing antisocial behavior patterns among school-age children and youth. *Journal of Emotional and Behavioral Disorders, 4*(4), 194–209.

Walker, H. M., & Walker, J. E. (1991). *Coping with noncompliance in the classroom: A positive approach for teachers.* Austin, TX: Pro-Ed.

Wignall, R. (1992). *Building a collaborative school culture: A case study of one woman in the principalship.* Paper presented at the European Conference on Educational Research, Enschede, the Netherlands.

Wiliam, D. (2011). *Embedded formative assessment.* Bloomington, IN: Solution Tree Press.

Regina Stephens Owens is director of enrichment for Coppell Independent School District in Coppell, Texas, where she is working to create an international mindset and using technology to partner with others around the world. An administrator since 2000, Regina participated in designing and opening the high-performing Virtual School and the Early College in Spring Independent School District. She is a highly sought-after educational consultant and coach serving and supporting school systems in the United States and Canada in utilizing the philosophy of professional learning communities.

While serving as academic dean of Marshall Independent School District in Marshall, Texas, she led a team of educators at the campus level to develop a professional learning community. The team's efforts evolved into a districtwide PLC initiative. She is most noted for understanding and leading the change process in transforming schools, and she leads that process in establishing effective systems and structures in the online environment.

A presenter, consultant, and educational coach, Regina shares what it takes to build a successful PLC and which assessment practices are most effective for sustaining this important work. Her passionate belief that a brilliant child exists inside every student fuels each presentation. With experience as a teacher, campus administrator, and district leader in rural and urban schools, Regina knows the unique challenges and opportunities educators who serve youth at risk face. She encourages students to partner and have a voice in their education while working to their strengths.

Regina earned a bachelor's degree in business administration and education from East Texas Baptist University and a master's degree in educational leadership from Stephen F. Austin State University in Texas.

To learn more about Regina's work, follow @Regina_Owens on Twitter.

To book Regina Stephens Owens for professional development, contact pd@solution-tree.com.

Personalizing Learning Through Online Interventions

Regina Stephens Owens

Editors' Note We conclude with this chapter on the Virtual School and the Early College to provide you with a vision of the future. Technology has forced retail businesses to reconsider meeting their customers' needs beyond brick-and-mortar buildings and in-person interactions. From banking to holiday shopping, customers expect access to online information, shopping, and virtual services, allowing individuals to meet their personal needs on their own time schedule. Failure to provide this level of service would be a death knell to most businesses. Education, in general, has been very slow to embrace and utilize technology, both as a way to provide information and services to our customers—our students and parents—and to allow students to use personal technology at school as a learning tool.

While Spring Independent School District created an entire learning environment around technology, complete transformation is not required to begin incorporating digital tools into the curriculum. The Virtual School's and the Early College's student inventory and personalized goal-setting process are powerful tools any school can use. With a smartphone, which most secondary students already possess, students have access to the world's largest library for research, an immediate feedback tool for formative assessment, a time-management tool to track assignments, and a social media tool to promote personalized communication and peer collaboration. There are also many powerful online intervention tools that can provide students with remediation and acceleration. Most schools restrict access to these tools in fear that a small handful of students might use these tools inappropriately. This is akin to prohibiting all adults to drive in fear that a few people might speed and crash. In reality, students' personal technology misuse is already happening, regardless of the school's policies. By offering students access to these tools, schools can extend time for interventions beyond the school day.

In the end, it will be difficult to prepare our students for the 21st century, when we expect them to learn in the 20th century while on campus. The Virtual School's and the Early College's programs provide a real-life example of what this might look like.

Across the United States, programs often heap help on our schools and our students to quickly move learning forward, to close the achievement gap, to get struggling learners caught up, to ensure scores increase, and to save campuses. Many educators struggle with the multitude of initiatives and the promise that an online component of a program or technology will save us. It is not our educational community, however, that needs to be saved—it is the strength of our democracy. That strength depends on all of us—who are committed to this country and care about the next generation of government officials, school board members, community members, school leaders, parents, and students—as we embrace the moral issue that all students must learn at high levels. It is high time we educational leaders transform our thinking and good intentions from that of a deficit model of working on the students, to one in which we work *with* learners to discover their strengths, voices, and potential.

With student input, we can provide a path to personalized learning that leaves the student ready to embrace all the United States has to offer and all the future holds, which is a right the Constitution affords each student. Technology and online interventions provide access to these opportunities; online interventions allow us to partner with the student in learning as the technology makes the learning tangible and transparent. The learner becomes knowledgeable of what she knows and needs to know, and she can experience learning via a variety of styles, allowing her to become aware of how she learns best. We must use digital resources to help students navigate not only the *what* but the *how* of learning. *Personalization*, as the National Education Technology Plan defines, involves using adaptive pacing, styling instruction to learning preferences, and tailoring content to learners' interests (Bienkowski, Feng, & Means, 2012). No longer can we have our students sit in front of a computer to simply pass an assessment or increase test scores. We must use the technology to refine both interventions and the way we respond when students are underachieving—an outcome that we, administrators and staff, have taken from theory to reality at Spring ISD in Houston, Texas. Spring ISD serves over 36,500 preK through twelfth-grade students in a diverse and growing urban district located in Houston. The district is working toward being recognized nationally as a leader among learning organizations and being known for exemplary student achievement; one step in that process was our creation of the Virtual School and the Early College.

Building the Virtual School and the Early College

We designed the Virtual School to provide students in the district with the opportunity to learn anytime, anywhere with flexible scheduling to meet their needs. The school serves students receiving general education, special needs, and gifted and talented services with the mission of providing an exemplary education, preparedness for postsecondary education and career choice, the use of emerging technologies, and individualized instruction that inspires while ensuring the development of 21st century skills.

The Early College, another innovative school, blends high school and college work with the mission that first-generation college goers will graduate with a high school diploma and an associate degree or sixty college credit hours toward a baccalaureate degree. The school provides dual credit at no cost to students, rigorous instruction and accelerated courses online, and academic and social support services to help students succeed. In addition, it increases college readiness by decreasing barriers to college access (Texas Education Agency, 2013).

The goal for students in both of these nontraditional learning environments is to offer exemplary learning and hold students to high expectations while providing the coaching, extra time, and support needed to ensure a guaranteed and viable curriculum in which all students have the opportunity and time required to learn. More specifically, the desired intervention outcomes include students:

- Mastering grade-level essentials and being prepared for the next course of study

- Learning how to learn and how to request assistance when they are not learning

- Being taught to know how they learn best, how to work to their strengths, and how to persist until their learning needs are met

- Participating in personalized accelerated instruction utilizing online interventions

To achieve these outcomes, we established a strong intervention framework.

Designing Belief-Driven Interventions

The evidence and research used to design both the Virtual School and Early College evolved from the vision, values, and beliefs of the district and schools, which include creating capacity and leadership at all levels and working in a continual improvement culture with clarity that the student is our customer who we must prepare for both college and career. With this reality in mind, we began the intervention process by ensuring our behavior mirrored our collective commitments. In these nontraditional settings, where students and parents expect to receive not only an exemplary academic education but experiences that prepare them socially, we wanted to provide extra time and support in a manner they had not experienced in the past. Thus, the intervention system was greatly impacted by the philosophy of Yvette Jackson (2011), author of *The Pedagogy of Confidence*, who demands educators work to the strength of the learners, knowing they are different and learn differently. In light of this, Jackson suggests we ask ourselves, "What are the operational practices that will generate high intellectual performances?" (p. 88). Simply put, what must we do to ensure our students are successful? In response to this research, we wanted students to be college ready, which is:

> the level of preparation a student needs in order to enroll and succeed—without remediation—in a credit bearing course at a postsecondary institution that offers a baccalaureate degree or transfer to a baccalaureate program, or in a high-quality certificate program that enables students to enter a career pathway with potential future advancement. (Conley, 2011, p. 4)

Thus, we designed our interventions to ensure students would attain the following college and career readiness skills.

- Critical thinking and problem solving

- Collaboration

- Agility and adaptability

- Initiative

- Effective oral and written communication

- The ability to access and analyze information

- Curiosity and imagination

We created an intervention experience that would give our students what they needed.

Before receiving interventions, students learn about their personality styles, are provided a multiple intelligence assessment and learning style survey, and participate in prescreening and goal-setting meetings. Grade-level committees conduct prescreening meetings for each student and determine a plan for additional time and support as well as how to best support that individual student. During these meetings, we collect as much information and data as possible to help us design support for the student's learning as indicated in the student prescreening interventions inventory (figure 12.1).

Student:	Grade:	Campus:	Date:
Courses:	Teachers:	Counselor:	
Multiple intelligences:			
Learning styles:			
Career or college pathway:			
Preplacement Concerns (Check all that apply.)			
Academic performance			
Standardized test			
Attendance			
Extracurricular activities			
Work			
Social and emotional issues			
Behavior			
Parental involvement			
Previous interventions			
Additional Support or Intervention Needed (Check all that apply.)			
Teacher watch			
Peer assistance			
Student contract			
Attendance management			
Daily student accountability			
Time-management support			
Required intervention			
Level of Support Required by Area of Need:			

Figure 12.1: Sample student prescreening interventions inventory.

After we conduct all prescreening meetings, we construct our master schedule for the learning needs of the students as opposed to allowing the schedule to dictate service and support. Students are scheduled in a manner that allows their needs to be met. For example, some students may take an accelerated course that would allow them to complete the course in a semester, while others may be scheduled in the course for a full year. Some students may be assigned mandatory interventions, while others are assigned student study groups face to face or online to provide sustained systemic support.

However, we expect *all* students to participate in a goal-setting meeting with a teacher advisor who reviews the student's multiple intelligence report that dictates the student's innate capabilities, learning styles inventory that dictates the way students learn best, and expectations of the learning environment and how to get assistance. That teacher then leads the student in writing goals for the upcoming six or nine weeks that include measurable outcomes. During the goal-setting meeting at the beginning of the year, whether online or face to face, it is important to have an agenda, goal-setting worksheet, and to obtain student signatures so they are involved in working to their strengths, are problem solving regarding their own learning, and are empowered to take initiative to get help when needed, to learn how to communicate verbally and in writing with adults, and to imagine how their lives will be as they start to exhibit the modeled behaviors in day-to-day learning. Student-led conferences occur in the late fall at the end of the first semester to allow the students to demonstrate their participation and ownership in their learning. During this conference, students lead the discussion and share with their parents their learning goals and progress toward meeting the goals. It is imperative that students own the language and understand what they must do to succeed, what additional support is needed, and what they need in order to create a plan for their success.

In *Systems Thinkers in Action*, Michael Fullan (2004) states, "The best system produces a culture in which it becomes easier to accomplish more by moving beyond dependence on the heroic or martyr-like efforts of a few" (p. 8). We agree that select individuals cannot maintain systemic efforts, and therefore we must agree that our students should be empowered to participate in their own learning, and we should select online programs with adaptive learning that would allow them to do so. In our school, we design the interventions and deliver them based on our core beliefs: we allow students to become participants in their learning. This practice, in our opinion, breeds hope.

Facing Challenges While Fueling Continuous Improvement

When a school offers interventions that include online and blended learning models with adaptive learning, there will be obstacles to overcome, such as system compatibility, access to the Internet, and use of analytics and reports. To clarify terminology, the percentage of time learning occurs in an online environment defines whether learning is *blended* or *virtual*. When instruction occurs 30 to 60 percent of the time online rather than in a brick-and-mortar building, it is considered blended. When instruction occurs more than 60 percent of the time online, it is considered virtual (Wicks, 2010). Both learning methods promise individualization; student control over time, place, and pace; and personalized learning experiences, as the research of Clayton Christensen and colleagues supports (Christensen, Horn, & Staker, 2013).

Adaptive learning is an educational method that uses computers as interactive teaching devices. Computers adapt the presentation of educational material according to students' learning needs, as their responses to questions and tasks indicate (Bienkowski et al., 2012). Realizing that we cannot achieve tailored learning on a large-scale basis using traditional approaches has partially driven our use of adaptive learning. Adaptive learning systems endeavor to transform the learner from passive recipient of information to a partner and collaborator in the educational process.

To address the concerns and challenges that using any innovative approach to learning online or utilizing technology for intervention presents, we must remain focused on continuous improvement, as shown in table 12.1 (pages 262–264).

One of our greatest challenges involved evaluating online interventions or programs to ensure fidelity of implementation so that teachers and students did not experience initiative overload. We learned to purchase online interventions with the purpose of supporting a learning goal in our school and to celebrate the learning growth that resulted from using the resource.

Another constant challenge we face involves making sure we use time wisely.

Leveraging Time

When considering time as it pertains to online interventions and programs used in blended and virtual environments, the nature of the technology implies that time for learning and additional support are more readily available. However, like the brick-and-mortar campus, when preparing to work with online interventions—whether blended or virtual—the time investment is made up front to ensure that the intervention advances learning at a higher rate. For example, to ensure that web-based interventions work properly requires a collaborative effort at the district and school levels. This leadership approach fosters autonomy and creativity (loose leadership) within a systematic framework that stipulates clear, nondiscretionary priorities and parameters (tight leadership; DuFour, 2007). Use of online tools brings new meaning to loose and tight leadership and requires a districtwide time line that speaks to the coordination of departments, such as technology, curriculum, and instruction, as well as student information services.

Table 12.1: From Concerns and Challenges to Continuous Improvement

Concerns	Challenges	Continuous Improvement
Learning	Clearly identify and prioritize learners' needs for programs or online interventions to address.	During yearly planning, when teams write academic goals, evaluate the use of online interventions and programs to ensure they align with student needs.
	Ensure that students and teachers are aware of the essential learnings that online interventions will address.	During staff meetings, share academic data and program or online intervention data as part of progress monitoring.
	Ensure that teams are addressing, monitoring, and discussing learning gaps using data from online interventions during team meetings.	Expect and monitor that teacher teams are reviewing program and intervention data during data discussion and that reports and performance are a part of team SMART goals.
	Clearly define learning times or minutes within the schedule so that online interventions are a supplement rather than the core curriculum.	Complete classroom walkthroughs during intervention time, and monitor program fidelity during class visits.
	Ensure adequate time for training, including teachers, counselors, and RTI coordinators, so staff use data and reports appropriately.	During campus improvement planning and data team meetings, identify the data points that each team will monitor.
Technology	Ensure the campus and classrooms have enough bandwidth to support the technology needs.	During campus improvement planning, include technology needs, sharing academic needs with the district team to ensure enough bandwidth is in place.
	Ensure devices purchased are compatible with online interventions.	Ensure prior to purchase that devices are compatible with all interventions or needs for campus by partnering with the technology department and keeping accurate lists of devices and ages of devices.

Concerns	Challenges	Continuous Improvement
Technology	Collaborate with the school system to ensure online interventions and services are available and accessible at the start of school with all users—teachers and students—loaded in the system properly.	Coordinate the purchase of services, training, and devices with technology by creating a time line to ensure all systems function at the point of need.
Online Program or Intervention	Provide access if the program or online intervention has a home-access component.	Partner with local businesses, such as cable companies and local libraries, to ensure families are supported with Internet access at no cost or low cost while informing parents how to access online interventions at home.
Online Program or Intervention	Clarify the use of online interventions and programs for engaging practice.	When purchasing online programs and interventions, denote which programs have a universal screener, progress monitoring, and data reports for an instructional response. Some services are good at engaging practice but do not provide data or reports in a manner that would allow a systemic instructional response.
	Purchase programs that utilize adaptive learning so that student and teacher dashboards can be used while improving the learning for students.	Complete an extensive review of programs and online interventions to ensure the analytics, reports, and dashboards are there to provide real-time feedback to students, teachers, administrators, and district stakeholders.
	Implement online interventions or programs with fidelity.	Collaborate with vendors to ensure the criteria for implementation and utilization of the programs are clear for all users; teach, monitor, and respond to criteria implementation fidelity by including reports in campus communications; celebrate teams on target; and coach others in need of assistance.

Continued ▸

Concerns	Challenges	Continuous Improvement
Online Program or Intervention	Ensure online interventions or programs provide the needed analytics and reports to all stakeholders in a systematic manner.	When requesting services of companies or vendors for online interventions, review the program analytics to ensure the system has the capability of automatically generating reports as needed with data points for all stakeholders—students, teachers, parents, principals, and superintendents. If analytics are not available, request the information necessary based on your campus time line for review of data.
	In a virtual or blended environment, ensure the program or online interventions integrate with the learning management and student management systems.	Check the compatibility of interventions with the learning management system or student management system to ensure teachers are able to integrate grades across systems to monitor the learning, provide feedback, and make data-driven instructional decisions. Ensure that there are no hidden costs with systems integrations or plug-ins.

At our Virtual School and Early College, we had to accept that technology has transformed not only the learning but also how we operate as a school system. Therefore, we made the new components, such as systems integrations, technology, and bandwidth part of the normal processes of change that we manage. In addition, we devised a time line to address the needs of the system, the schools, and the students. Areas that we considered include:

- Systems integrations
- Technology and bandwidth
- Training
- Master schedule time lines
- Uploading of student rosters and student identification numbers

Thus, we started our time line for master scheduling early enough to ensure we had all the necessary information from our students and moved the collection of the information—the registration process—online as part of our systemic transformation.

Technology and time also affect how we train personnel on the new technologies and on delivering instruction in a blended model. We found it was easier for our school to deliver the staff training and support via an online platform or a blended model as well. This leverages time, as teachers could receive training anytime, anywhere.

We also leverage time by recognizing the difference between an engaging program that provides practice and an online intervention. A good online intervention increases our efficiency; thus, we began to seek online interventions with the following characteristics.

- Universal screeners
- Adaptive learning
- Robust reporting systems or dashboards for students, teachers, and administrators
- College and career readiness behaviors addressed
- Training videos or modules built in
- Face-to-face or virtual coaching as part of the services
- Real-time progress monitoring for establishing goals, defining interventions, collecting visual data, and responding to the intervention

When we select interventions that have these characteristics, the work of educators is focused on learning, and student achievement is increased exponentially. Let's be clear, creating videos for instructional support for students and apps for practice does allow students to have access anytime and anywhere; however, to truly leverage time with interventions and ensure learning, data must fuel the decisions of your professional learning community.

Engaging programs allow for individual and class practice; however, in a PLC, it is also important for teacher efforts to be interdependent, with shared goals and accountability for reaching those goals, and in this age of technology with personalized learning, our students and parents can become an active part of the community.

Sharing Data

To achieve interdependence, we realized our teams must incorporate the reports from the program into our normal data meeting protocols, adjust our SMART goals as needed, and continue to work the plan. The data from the online interventions also give our teachers feedback for areas of instruction to improve.

In a virtual school, the processes of data sharing and planning differ from solely brick-and-mortar schools, as the students are in different places in the curriculum, which requires the teachers to set artificial time lines to plan how and when they will respond to the gaps in learning. At our school campus, we offered additional support by doing the following to ensure intervention time occurs within the school day.

- Meeting with intervention providers and campus leadership teams to discuss master schedules and campus needs to ensure each tool met the needs of the students identified as requiring Tier 2 or 3 interventions

- Collaborating with campus staff to define and clarify the use of a blended model for the delivery of effective instruction and interventions

- Coaching staff on how students, teachers, and teams should use data to maximize interventions

We often say that data fuel the team. This is true; however, if used correctly, data also fuel the learning and provide hope to the learner. This is why we expect our students to keep track of their learning outcomes and goals and expect teaching teams to keep data notebooks. Even more important, this belief is why we use online interventions, since they provide and capture the data on individual users in real time.

Accessing Technology and Interventions

One question many schools on this journey of blended learning through the utilization of online tools for RTI ask is, "What do you do if students do not have the necessary technology or Internet access?" In our school, we found the right question to ask was this: "Would technology afford students the opportunity to learn and function at high levels, and is it something they need?" This question allowed us to work on the right problem.

There are a number of ways in which mobile technology enables educational innovation and makes time for interventions. Based on Project Tomorrow's research, student access has improved across various mobile platforms (West, 2013). Eighty percent of high school students have smartphones, 45 percent have tablets, 38 percent have digital readers, and 58 percent have cell phones. These percentages are up from just a few years prior. In 2008, only 28 percent of high schoolers had smartphones (West, 2013). In 2011, only 26 percent of students in grades 6–8 had a tablet computer, compared to 52 percent in 2013 (West, 2013).

These statistics will force schools, leadership, and policies to change. In the words of Jim Shelton, deputy secretary for the U.S. Department of Education, "Students have been locked down by the concept of seat time and locked out of the technological revolution that has transformed nearly every sector of American society, except education" (as cited in Patrick & Sturgis, 2011, p. 7). This is simply not acceptable. It is tremendously apparent that technology makes determining each student's needs easy, because mastery of learning for students and quality teaching for staff are visible. The data and reporting systems allow connections to be realized at a level that traditional systems do not afford. Quality online interventions provide pre- and postassessments for progress monitoring so teachers can continually group learners as needed while providing students with their own personal playlist for learning.

The adaptability of technology allows teachers to arrange the order of instruction modules based on the learner's need and to provide teacher support and guided lessons. When thinking becomes transparent, teachers are able to see, in real time, which students are learning at a level of mastery and which are struggling on a particular skill. When schools deliver interventions in a blended model, teachers collect multiple data points as well. These data points reveal strengths in teaching that allow the teacher teams to learn from each other and place students with staff members who best understand how to deliver that instruction. This process of monitoring, revising, and extending is powerful for the teacher team and all learners. The team can extend the strength of students while addressing areas of need. This process also empowers the learner, since students have their own personal dashboards within the technology system.

Leading and Managing Personalized Online Interventions

The leadership and management of online interventions cannot be outsourced to the companies who provide them. Rather, the principal and leadership team play a critical role in leading the implementation of online interventions. We must remember that technology is only a tool; the principal is responsible for ensuring that high levels of learning are taking place for all students, and he or she must shape the process around guiding questions (see table 12.2).

Table 12.2: Guiding Questions for Ensuring Learning With Online Interventions

Fidelity of Implementation	Who creates the criteria to select and review online tools to ensure campus needs are met?
	Who determines if the online intervention meets student needs?
	Who monitors and supports teachers with intervention implementation?
	Who ensures that fidelity of implementation is understood at all levels on the campus?
Utilization of Data	Who determines which data points teacher teams will need to review to improve teaching and learning?
	Who determines the time line by which we will communicate data to all stakeholders in the professional learning community as well as what the expected instructional response will be?
	How will we make data transparent and utilize them from classroom to classroom to ensure quality learning for all staff and students?
	How do we make parents aware of their child's progress with online interventions? How do we teach parents to support their child with any portion of the intervention accessed at home?
	How do teams use the data reports in team meetings for learning?
	How are students discussing and using the data to ensure they are learning and that their needs are met?
	How are we using online interventions to work to the strength of the learner and to ensure college and career readiness skills are a part of the learning?

Professional Learning	Who determines when to schedule professional development sessions, and what points of fidelity and student achievement will we monitor and improve through professional development?
	Will on-site coaches provide implementation and coaching of the tool?
	If coaches are supporting the blended intervention, who manages their work, and how is their work used to advance learning?
	Which specific administrator is monitoring the learning we expect from these interventions and the support we provide for teachers?
Systems Integration	Have we created a time line to denote when systems are checked to ensure computers have appropriate software, icons are pushed out from the district level, and all ports are operational?
	Does the online intervention provide a system for managing teachers assigned, students placed in the system, passwords, and a backup of student information and data? If not, who will manage these processes?
	Who monitors the bandwidth of the campus to ensure devices and access are adequate for the interventions we use?
	Which team is planning to systemically ensure additional devices and bandwidth are in place as needed for classrooms and the school?

As we move from paralyzing programs to personalized learning with powerful online interventions, we must work to our strengths, grow our global PLC, and provide hope to school leaders, teachers, and students that we can and will provide high levels of learning for all—the strength of our democracy rests on our commitment and will to make this a reality for each and every student.

References and Resources

Bienkowski, M., Feng, M., & Means, B. (2012). *Enhancing teaching and learning through educational data mining and learning analytics: An issue brief.* Accessed at www.ed.gov/edblogs/technology/files/2012/03/edm-la-brief.pdf on July 7, 2014.

Christensen, C., Horn, M., & Staker, H. (2013). *Is K–12 blended learning disruptive?: An introduction of the theory of hybrids.* Accessed at www.christenseninstitute.org/publications/hybrids/ on April 21, 2014.

Conley, D. (2011). *Defining and measuring college and career readiness.* Paper presented at the Educational Policy Improvement Center, Portland, OR.

DuFour, R. (2007). In praise of top-down leadership. *The School Administrator, 64*(10), 38–42.

Fullan, M. (2004). *Systems thinkers in action: Moving beyond the standard plateau.* Accessed at www.michaelfullan.ca/media/13396063090.pdf on April 21, 2014.

Hattie, J. A. C. (2009). *Visible learning: A synthesis of over 800 meta-analyses relating to achievement.* New York: Routledge.

Jackson, Y. (2011). *The pedagogy of confidence: Inspiring high intellectual performance in urban schools.* New York: Teachers College Press.

Patrick, S., & Sturgis, C. (2011). *Cracking the code: Synchronizing policy and practice for performance based learning.* Vienna, VA: International Association for K–12 Online Learning.

Texas Education Agency. (2013). *Early college initiative.* Accessed at www.tea.state.tx.us/index3.aspx?id=4464 on July 7, 2014.

U.S. Department of Education. (2010). *Evaluation of evidence-based practices in online learning: A meta-analysis and review of online learning studies.* Accessed at www2.ed.gov/rschstat/eval/tech/evidence-based-practices/finalreport.pdf on March 31, 2014.

U.S. Department of Education. (2012). *Enhancing teaching and learning through educational data mining and learning analytics: An issue brief.* Accessed at www.ed.gov/edblogs/technology/files/2012/03/edm-la-brief.pdf on March 31, 2014.

West, D. M. (2013). *Mobile learning: Transforming education, engaging students, and improving outcomes.* Washington, DC: The Brookings Institution.

Wicks, M. (2010). *A national primer on K–12 online learning: Version 2.* Accessed at files.eric.ed.gov/fulltext/ED514892.pdf on April 21, 2014.

Epilogue

You have now taken a virtual journey of twelve unique approaches to providing all students with the time and support they need to ensure high levels of learning. This journey has included large and small schools, urban and suburban schools, schools that serve a relatively high socioeconomic community, schools that serve a majority of students living at or below the poverty level, schools from the East Coast to the West Coast, schools from the center of the United States, and schools from the northern and southern states. Undoubtedly, you have seen elements of your school in one or more of these examples. Additionally, almost every example was achieved within the school's existing resources, using current staff, and in accordance with existing federal, state, and contractual requirements.

We suspect that some educators will read the numerous examples of systematic interventions described in this anthology and claim that providing this level of support might be possible but not desirable, because such actions will result in enabling students and will not properly prepare them for the real world. These critics will instead recommend keeping our traditional approach of offering additional support but allowing students the right to fail, as this will hold students accountable for their actions and teach responsibility. We absolutely agree that responsibility is a critical life skill. As such, the real question is this, What is the best way to teach students responsibility *and* ensure high levels of learning? For educators who claim teaching responsibility is best achieved by giving students the option to fail, we challenge them to show evidence that this approach is working at their school. Do the students who decide against getting help benefit from their error in judgment and make better choices due to their failure? Are the students who choose to disregard their homework and miss deadlines becoming more responsible? Are the students tracked into below-grade-level coursework catching up and succeeding in postsecondary education and beyond? More likely, these students are missing assignment after assignment and failing class after class, semester after semester, year after year—all while showing no newly gained initiative to seek out extra help.

There is virtually no research or evidence to suggest that higher incidents of failure in school produce higher levels of responsibility, academic achievement in college, or a higher likelihood of success meeting the demands of the adult life. Considering that the United States has the second-highest collegiate dropout rate in the industrialized world (Porter, 2013), it would be exceedingly difficult to argue that our traditional sink-or-swim approach is properly preparing students for the rigors of postsecondary education. Likewise, these students are more likely to live an adult life characterized by poverty, government assistance, and incarceration (Breslow, 2012)—hardly proof that our traditional K–12 system is properly preparing our students for the current reality of the real world. Based on the overwhelming evidence, advocating for our traditional secondary approach to interventions is misguided at the least and downright unethical at the worst.

Even after embracing the need to change our traditional approaches, a school is still left with the daunting question of how to achieve these outcomes. By providing you detailed examples from real-life schools, we hope you have a clearer vision of the road that lies ahead. Your journey, however, has only begun in terms of how you use the information from these schools to impact your own. We caution you to resist two ways of thinking as you move forward with RTI at your school.

First, please recognize that the culture of every school is amazingly unique. This means that adopting a block schedule or any other idea contained in the preceding chapters requires an adaptation to your school culture. In other words, we caution against lifting ideas wholesale and superimposing them on your school. Instead, ask, "What is the thinking behind that schedule, behind that assessment or intervention practice, and how might we adapt that to fit the unique needs of our school?"

Second, we caution against the reaction, "That's a great idea, but it will never work in our building because _____." Rather than summarily dismissing great ideas too quickly, focus on what you can do rather than on what you can't. Do this by asking, "What about that idea resonates with me?" or "Even though we can't implement this idea as stated, how could we implement the thinking behind it in a way that would work on our campus?" By focusing on the process rather than simply looking at the program, you will move from the *what* to the *how* and, in doing so, will discover ways of tweaking the process that might not have been readily apparent at first.

Finally, we hope that as your journey continues, you will move forward with the realization that it can be done, it is being done, and it must be done for the sake of our students. The schools described in this book did not begin with a perfect plan or possess all the resources they perceived were required; nevertheless, they started. Surely there were skeptics, and undoubtedly there were missteps along the way, but mistakes were transformed into lessons learned, and stumbling blocks were viewed as stepping stones. The schools did not merely measure progress in test scores or credits earned but rather in the potential success of every student. Most importantly, these schools relied on their most precious resource—each other.

The key to your school's success will begin or end with your willingness to start the journey; only those willing to take a first step will discover what is possible.

As Martin Luther King Jr. states, "You don't have to see the whole staircase, just take the first step."

References and Resources

Breslow, J. M. (2012). *By the numbers: Dropping out of high school.* Accessed at www.pbs.org /wgbh/pages/frontline/education/dropout-nation/by-the-numbers-dropping-out-of -high-school on July 18, 2014.

Marable, M. (Ed.). (1999). *Let nobody turn us around: Voices on resistance, reform, and renewal—An African American anthology.* Lanham, MD: Rowman & Littlefield.

Porter, E. (2013, June 25). Dropping out of college, and paying the price. *New York Times.* Accessed at www.nytimes.com/2013/06/26/business/economy/dropping-out-of-college-and -paying-the-price.html?pagewanted=all&_r=0 on July 18, 2014.

Index

The Collaborative Administrator: Working Together as a Professional Learning Community
Austin Buffum, Cassandra Erkens, Charles Hinman, Susan B. Huff, Lillie G. Jessie, Terri L. Martin, Mike Mattos, Anthony Muhammad, Peter Noonan, Geri Parscale, Eric Twadell, Jay Westover, and Kenneth C. Williams

How do you maintain the right balance of loose and tight leadership? How do you establish profound, lasting trust with your staff? What principles strengthen principal leadership? This book answers these questions and much more in compelling chapters packed with strategies and inspiration.
BKF256

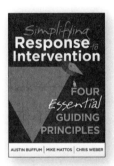

Simplifying Response to Intervention: Four Essential Guiding Principles
Austin Buffum, Mike Mattos, and Chris Weber

The sequel to *Pyramid Response to Intervention* advocates that effective RTI begins by asking the right questions to create a fundamentally effective learning environment for every student. Understand why paperwork-heavy, compliance-oriented, test-score-driven approaches fail. Then learn how to create an RTI model that works.
BKF506

Pyramid Response to Intervention: Four Essential Guiding Principles
Austin Buffum, Mike Mattos, and Chris Weber

Shift to a culture of collective responsibility, and ensure a path of opportunity and success for your students. Focusing on the four Cs vital to student achievement, this powerful four-part program will help you collect targeted information on each student's individual needs and guide you to build efficient team structures.
DVF057

Making Time at Tier 2: Creating a Supplemental Intervention Period in Secondary Schools
Mike Mattos

Discover practical strategies to build Tier 2 intervention and enrichment periods into the school day, and learn how to work in collaborative teams to create targeted interventions and overcome implementation challenges to ensure all students are successful.
DVF066

Wait! **Your professional development journey doesn't have to end with the last pages of this book.**

We realize improving student learning doesn't happen overnight. And your school or district shouldn't be left to puzzle out all the details of this process alone.

No matter where you are on the journey, we're committed to helping you get to the next stage.

Take advantage of everything from **custom workshops** to **keynote presentations** and **interactive web and video conferencing**. We can even help you develop an action plan tailored to fit your specific needs.

Let's get the conversation started.

Call 888.763.9045 today.

solution-tree.com